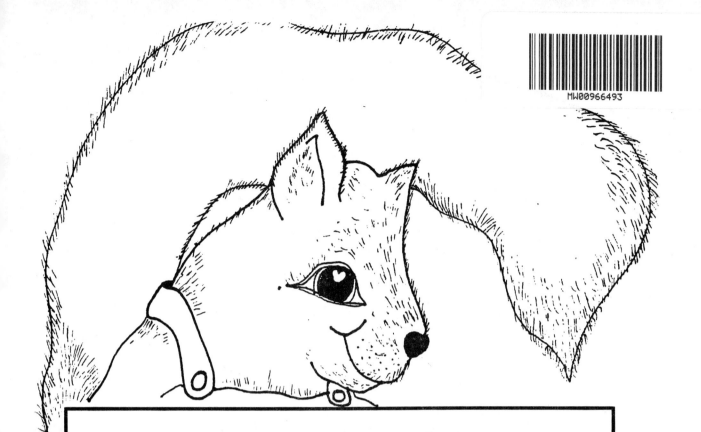

ALLIGATORS TO ZEBRAS!
Whole Language Activities for the Primary Grades

Elizabeth Crosby Stull

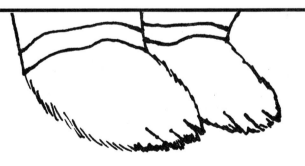

**THE CENTER FOR APPLIED
RESEARCH IN EDUCATION**
West Nyack, New York 10995

Library of Congress Cataloging-in-Publication Data
Stull, Elizabeth Crosby.
   Alligators to zebras! : whole language activities for the primary
grades / Elizabeth Crosby Stull.
     p.   cm.
   Includes bibliographical references.
   ISBN 0-87628-150-1
   1. Education, Primary—United States—Activity programs.
   2. Education, Preschool—United States—Activity programs.
   3. Language experience approach in education. 4. Animals.
   I. Title.
LB1537.S83 1991
372.21—dc20   91-32930
                                              CIP

C1501-0
ISBN 0-87628-150-1

**The Center for Applied
Research in Education**
Business Information & Publishing Division
West Nyack, NY 10995
Simon & Schuster, A Paramount Communications Company

Printed in the United States of America

This book is dedicated to my family members—Crosby, Lucas, Hackshaw, and Stull—past, present, and future.

ABOUT THE AUTHOR

Elizabeth Crosby Stull, Ph.D. (The Ohio State University), has over 20 years of experience in education as a primary teacher and teacher educator. She began her career as a teacher of grades 1, 2, and 4 in the public schools of Greece Central, Camillus, and Pittsford in upstate New York, and is currently an associate professor of education at Otterbein College in a suburb of Columbus, Ohio.

A member of the National Association for the Education of Young Children and the International Reading Association, Dr. Stull has published many articles in professional journals such as *Instructor* and *Teaching K–8* and is coauthor, with Carol Lewis Price, of *Science and Math Enrichment Activities for the Primary Grades* (The Center, 1987) and *Kindergarten Teacher's Month-by-Month Activities Program* (The Center, 1987). In addition, she has written *Children's Book Activities Kit* (The Center, 1988), *First Grade Teacher's Month-by-Month Activities Program* (The Center, 1990), and is contributing author to *The Primary Teacher's Ready-to-Use Activities Program*, a monthly program also published by The Center.

Dr. Stull has been a member of two study tours (through the Ohio State University) to Kenya, Africa, and the Galapagos Islands. Some of that animal information has been interwoven into this A—Z book to help enrich the study of animals for all children.

ABOUT THIS BOOK

ALLIGATORS TO ZEBRAS! Whole Language Activities for the Primary Grades uses the theme of animals because most children are naturally curious about animals and are attracted to them. Many children have pets to cuddle, such as dog, cat, or rabbit; and other children have pets such as goldfish, turtles, or birds. County and state fairs still award prizes to children for their pet lambs, goats, and pigs (like Wilbur in the fanciful children's story *Charlotte's Web* by E. B. White). A trip to the zoo to see the animals is an exciting and pleasureable experience for children and adults alike, especially since many zoos are in the process of making the habitats for animals more natural.

Animals always generate excitement, wonder, and many questions. There are a number of children's books that portray animals as main story characters. And educational television programs for children have, from their inception, included animals and puppets in their cast of characters. This is not by chance, it is by design. Animals appeal to children and there is much to learn from them.

The A—Z format of this book reinforces letter/sound relationships, and the whimsical animals impart factual information. This information can be skillfully woven into the reading, langauge arts, math, science, social studies, creative drama, and art curriculum using a whole language approach. A bibliography of animal books appears at the end of *Alligators to Zebras*, and numerous references to children's books are included throughout.

With this material, students are active learners, engaging in a variety of activities including the "Talk and Tell" interview section that facilitates language development via reading, writing, listening, and speaking. They are actively engaged in collecting data, graphing, making charts, making books, webbing, keeping a journal, writing letters, and locating designated areas on a map or globe. They are learning about endangered species, about animal habitats, predators and prey, animals that help us to do work, domestic animals, and much more.

There are hundreds of suggested activities in this book, and over 150 reproducible activity pages that are readily available for the busy classroom teacher. The book can be used sequentially from A—Z, or parts of it can be used to supplement units such as Sea Creatures, Birds, Engangered Species, Zoo Animals, Mammals, the study of a particular country, and so on.

Now, let's join the animals!

Elizabeth Crosby Stull

ABOUT THE
TALK-AND-TELL INTERVIEWS

Children are curious, and curiosity generates questions. Therefore, the Talk-and-Tell interviews are designed to ask and answer some questions that children might have about the A—Z animals. Hopefully, this questioning will lead to even more questions, which will send students on a search for the answers.

To help with this interview, there are two co-hosts, Tyler and Tina, who can be used as puppets to interview the animals. They can be made to look more colorful with felt pens, can be cut out, and then pasted onto a flat stick, along with the animal they are interviewing. Or a matching shape can be cut out and the puppets stapled around the edges so that a hand can be inserted from the bottom.

Tina and Tyler ask the questions and the animals answer. This can be prerecorded on a cassette tape or done live. The roles can be played by the teacher, by two teachers, by two older students, by two students in the class, by parent volunteers, and so on. The interviews can be recorded on tape so that students can listen on their own. Having the students record the interviews gives them an opportunity to develop their language skills, and to listen to the same material repeatedly in order to learn the information. Some budding talk-show hosts may even want to select appropriate music for a lead-in to the interview and for the closing.

Students can develop the personalities of Tyler and Tina (we can see that Tina likes hats!). A Talk-and-Tell Center can be set up in the room. Collect a variety of props for this area, such as a microphone, typewriter, telephones, cassette recorder and earphones, books, pencils, paper, felt-tip pens, and hats. Students can work with the interview via telephones (one asks/one answers), or cassette recorder (taking on two voices), or video recording (role playing or puppet theater).

Students can make the *Alligators to Zebra* puppets from paper plates, paper bags, socks, or a cut-out of the animals in each section, laminated and taped to a stick, and so on. This fosters language development of reading, writing, speaking, and listening.

Be sure to send a note home to parents to inform them of the animal study. Enlist their help. Some parents may have photographs, 35 mm slides, video tapes, or information books or magazines with beautiful animal pictures that they would be willing to share. Invite the local zoo director to contribute to your study of animals. Investigate the videotape offerings on animals at the local public library.

The opportunities for adding zest to the Talk-and-Tell interviews are endless.

WHOLE-LANGUAGE ACTIVITIES FOR THE A—Z ANIMALS

There are many activities that can be done to keep the study of animals fresh. Many specific ideas are listed throughout the book, and some are given below.

Art

- Paint animal murals.
- Make animal puppets from a variety of materials.
- Design animal face masks or nose masks.
- Create dioramas for animal habitats.
- Mold animals from clay.
- Make animals from papier-maché, collages, or sponge paintings.
- Design animal picture books with borders.
- Illustrate animal information charts.
- Make animal stationery for report writing.

Reading/Language Arts

- Keep a diary on one specific animal.
- Keep a journal of animal information.
- Make ABC books of different animals.
- Design animal shape books.
- Read aloud to stuffed animals.
- Write scripts for animal interaction.
- Dramatize using puppets.
- Learn the animal rhymes and record as a chorus.
- Locate and read animal poems.
- Record animal reports on tape.
- Designate a Favorite Animal Dress-Up Day with question-and-answer activities.
- Go through the alphabet and list all animals that begin with each letter.
- Perform with puppets (simulation, role-playing).

Math

- Investigate numbers relating to animals, such as size, shape, number of feet, number of teeth, weight, length, and height.
- Cook with the animal activity pages (time, temperature, measurement).
- Graph favorite animals.

- Make alphabet soup and count the letters.
- Measure body parts and compare with those of specific animals.
- Track migration routes (miles and direction).
- Graph how many animals begin with the letter A, B, C, and so on.
- Make animal puzzles.
- Make maps of how to get to the fox den, the rabbit hutch, and so on.

Science

- Examine bird nests. (IMPORTANT: Do not disturb inhabited nests.)
- Make bird nests from natural materials.
- Install an egg incubator in the classroom.
- Classify animals by a variety of categories (land dwellers, sea dwellers, those that fly, mode of travel, and so on).
- Set up a science area with real science tools (field glasses, magnifying glass, microscope).
- Categorize animals by ungulates (hoofed animals).
- Categorize animals by those with antlers or horns.
- Compile a list of predators and prey.
- Learn what is meant by a life cycle.
- Investigate endangered species and what can be done about this problem.
- Learn about animal similarities/differences/cousins.
- Examine animal footprints in the area.
- Make an animal footprint chart.

Social Studies

- Investigate how animals learn.
- Explore the care of pet animals.
- Learn about the role of the animal vet.
- Classify work animals, show animals (animals that perform feats), state animals, animal mascots, animals of presidents of the United States, and so on).
- Locate various animals' natural habitats on a map or globe.

Creative Movement

- Cross a very narrow, rickety bridge with grinning alligators swimming below.
- Be a giant, burly bear climbing a tree after honey in a beehive.
- Be a tiny cat and stalk a bird who is feeding at the bird feeder.
- Act out commands in dog obedience school, such as "sit" and "stay."
- Be a lumbering elephant bobbing along, swinging your trunk back and forth, back and forth. Slurp up some water through your trunk and throw it over your back at those pesky flies.
- Jump from lily pad to lily pad, keeping your frog feet dry, and not losing your balance and falling into the water.
- Be a goat and try to reach up for tree leaves, just like a giraffe does.
- Trot, gallop, and pull a wagon like a horse.
- Be an insect (butterfly) and break out of your chrysallis and fly away.
- Be a jaguar and swim ten laps around the swimming hole.
- Be a baby joey hopping into your mother's pouch—and missing. Try again.

- Be a hungry lion stalking a deer for a long time.
- Be a moose and bang your antlers into a tree, then go for a swim.
- Sing "Yank, yank" like a nuthatch and climb head-first down the tree.
- Be an octopus getting tangled up in seaweed.
- Slide on the ice like a penguin.
- Be a quail pecking corn in the barnyard.
- Be a rabbit and run away from a predator. Promptly sit down to cover your white cottontail and be very, very still.
- Be a scampering squirrel digging in the ground and burying nuts.
- Swim like a giant turtle. Then pull in your head and four legs for a rest.
- Be a fanciful unicorn and prance around in the woods.
- Circle in the air like a vulture, using those giant swooping wings.
- Be a whale swimming in the ocean and trying out your water spout.
- Be a sly fox with half-closed eyes surveying the land. Then decide to go after a delicious duck.
- Be a yak walking on a very narrow path over the slippery mountain tops.
- Be a zebra with fluttering eyelids. Move slowly and always change your position a little here, a little there.

These are some of the activities that are mentioned in the text that may be carried out. Also, during the Talk-and-Tell interviews, some of these activities may be explored.

ABOUT WEBBING

A web is a diagram of information. There is usually a central theme or title in the middle, and spokes that go out from the central point with a variety of headings. Under the headings, information is listed. It is an easy tool for categorizing and classifying information, and children quickly learn the format. There are a variety of webs and uses for webs, and children keep inventing more all the time. There are several included here to help get your classroom started with this process. It is an idea that has its origin in the world of business, and is more commonly known as a flowchart of information.

- ANIMALS WE STUDY—This web is used to integrate the study of animals into many curricular areas.
- ZOO ANIMALS—Work this one through with students and find out what information they know or need to learn in terms of animal names, types of housing, food, petting zoos, making a zoo, and so on.
- ANIMAL PETS—Students can use this web to organize information that is necessary for being a responsible pet owner, names of famous pets, tricks that pets can do, and so on.
- JUNGLE ANIMALS—Which animals are endangered? What are their habits? Which animals are predators? Which animals are prey? What role does color play in terms of a furry coat or feathers?
- SEA ANIMALS—How can we relate the study of sea animals to areas of the curriculum in terms of social studies (migration routes, pollution problems), science (warm-blooded and cold-blooded animals), language arts (vocabulary), math (size, weight, height), reading (storybooks about sea creatures), and art (painting, clay modeling, dioramas).
- BIRD MAPPING—This web can be set up at the window ledge that has been covered into a Bird Watch Station. It can also be used after a Bird Walk. It can be used to help focus students' attention when they do library research, since they are looking for specifics such as shapes of bird feet, types of beaks, and so on.
- MY FAVORITE ANIMAL—This is a circular web, and the students begin at the top and move clockwise around the headings. This web will help students to organize information that they need to know about their favorite animal such as body parts, habitat, food, sleep habits, weight, height, length, birth information, and so on.
- DR. BLOCTOR THE COMPARISON CROCTOR—This can be used to help students make a shape web and compare two similar animals (real or storybook) in terms of size, color, food, habitat, and so on.

Often the web can be used when students are giving oral reports, since it facilitates natural speech rather than reading of information as in a written report. The material in a web can be used to help determine what should be included in an art mural, or a diorama, or a skit. It can be useful when studying food chains, hibernation, migration, state animals, animals on coins, famous animals in history, and so on. The possibilities for this process are numerous. Students learn to organize massive amounts of information, and then break it down into smaller bits by creating new webs. This ongoing process will serve students well throughout their school life, as it promotes good study habits.

"Animals We Study" WEB

Math
- Migration — miles
- Size
- Weight
- Comparisons — graphs
- Measurement
- Amount of food eaten
- Cost of food
- Animals on money (coins, bills)

Language Arts
- Read books about animals
- Make animal ABC books
- Make Shape books
- Write animal stories
  - adventure
  - mystery
  - fantasy
- Make a talking animal cartoon
- Keep a journal of animal studies
- "Interview an animal"
- Animal Reports
- Favorite Storybook animals

Science
- Mammals
- Land Animals
- Sea Animals
- Predator/Prey
- Food Chain
- Eggs
- Hibernation

Animals

Art
- Make animal puppets
- Dioramas
- Colors
- Texture
- Shape
- Make clay animals
- Make animal mural
- Create 3-D animals
- Animals in Art Books
- Animals in Museums

Social Studies
- Work animals
  - Horse
  - Elephant
  - Yak, etc.
- Locations in U.S.A.
- Locations in the world
- Uses of animals
  - food
  - skin
  - hide
- Famous historical animals
- State Birds, Animals
- National Symbols
- Effects of pollution on animals
- Trip to the zoo

Health
- What Animals Eat
- Care of Pets
- Invite a Veterinarian to class
- Endangered species
- Create animal exercizes (hop, jump, slither, etc.)

Zoo Animals WEB

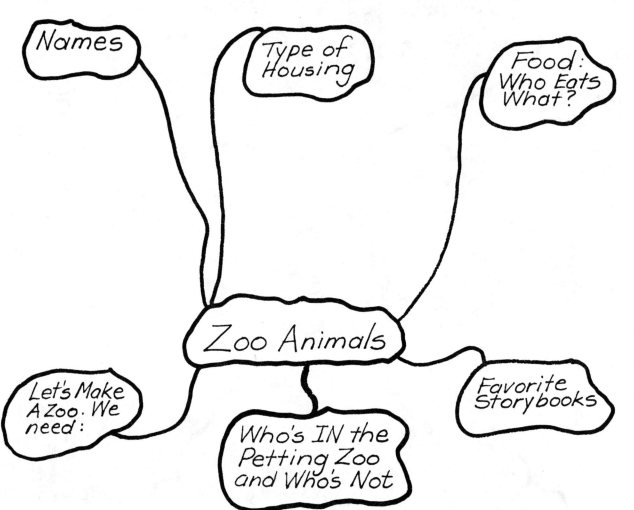

Names

Type of Housing

Food: Who Eats What?

Zoo Animals

Let's Make A Zoo. We need:

Who's IN the Petting Zoo and Who's Not

Favorite Storybooks

Animal Pets WEB

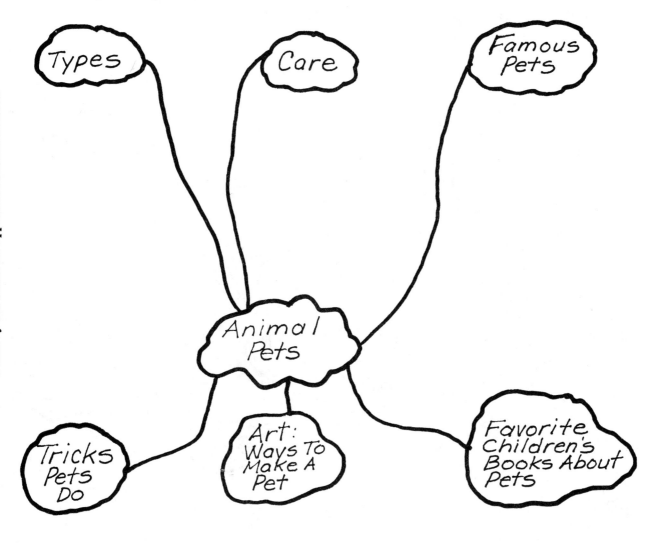

Who Are They

Endangered Species

Colors

Jungle Animals

Favorite Story Animals

Prey

Habits

Predators

Sea Animals WEB

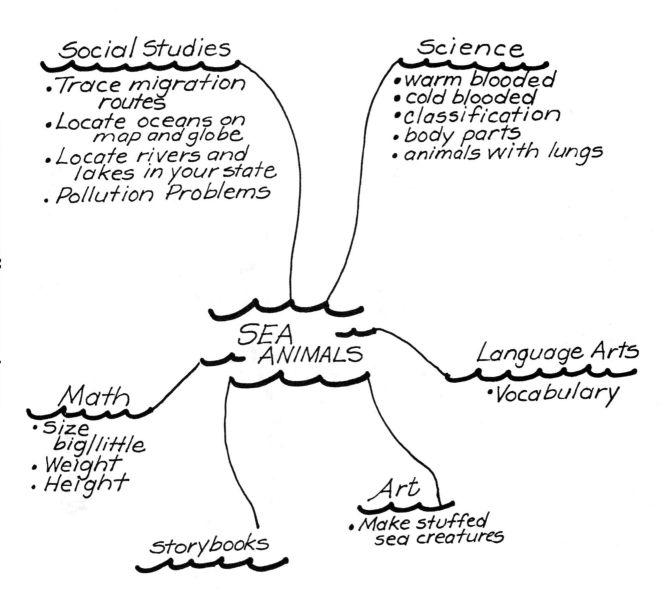

Social Studies
- Trace migration routes
- Locate oceans on map and globe
- Locate rivers and lakes in your state
- Pollution Problems

Science
- warm blooded
- cold blooded
- classification
- body parts
- animals with lungs

SEA ANIMALS

Language Arts
- Vocabulary

Math
- Size big/little
- Weight
- Height

Art
- Make stuffed sea creatures

storybooks

Bird Mapping

Types of Beaks

Body Parts

Feet Shapes

What Birds Eat

Making Birdfeeders

Who Migrates

Where?

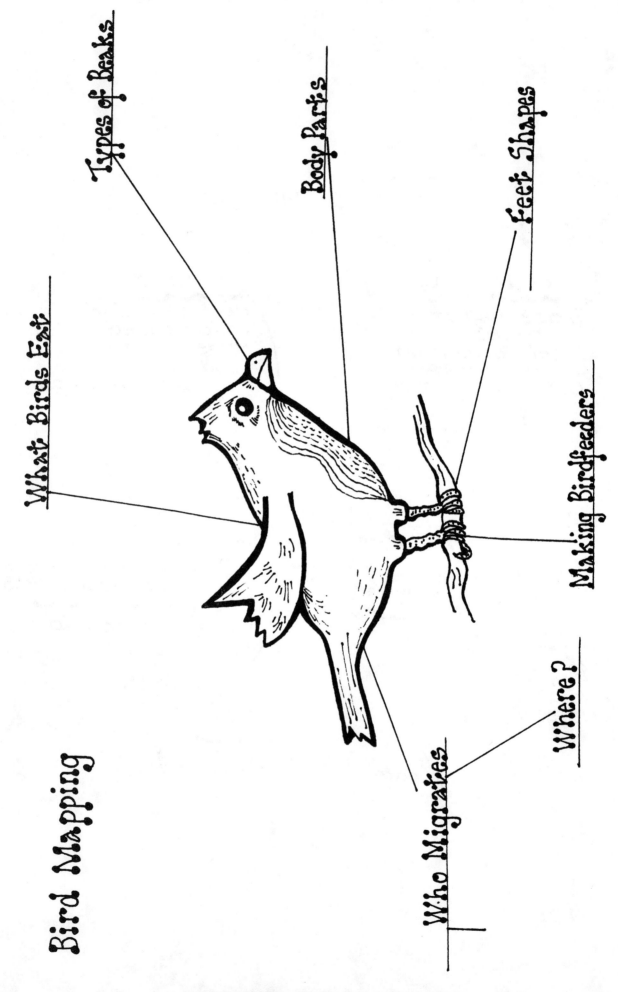

Name _____

My Favorite Animal Web

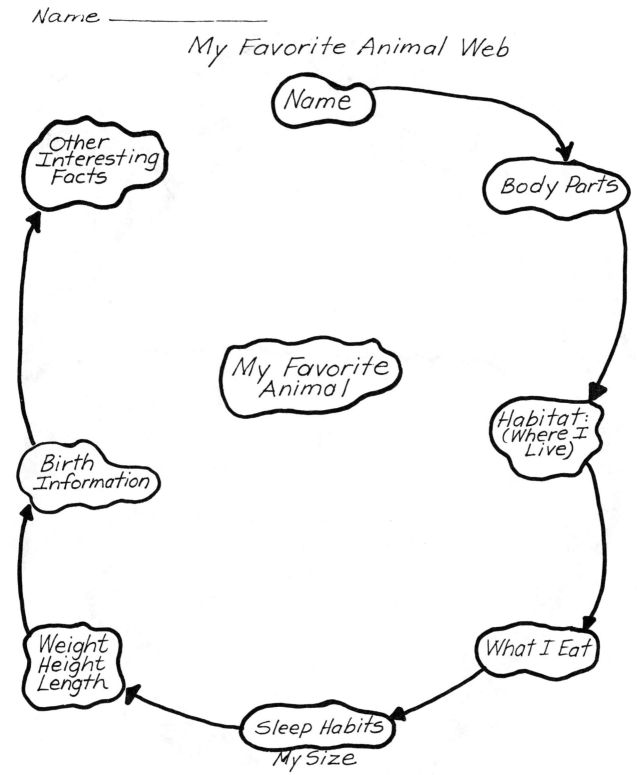

Name

Body Parts

Other
Interesting
Facts

My Favorite
Animal

Habitat:
(Where I
Live)

Birth
Information

Weight
Height
Length

What I Eat

Sleep Habits
My Size

Gently tear a large shape of your animal. Add features.
Attach this sheet to your animal too.

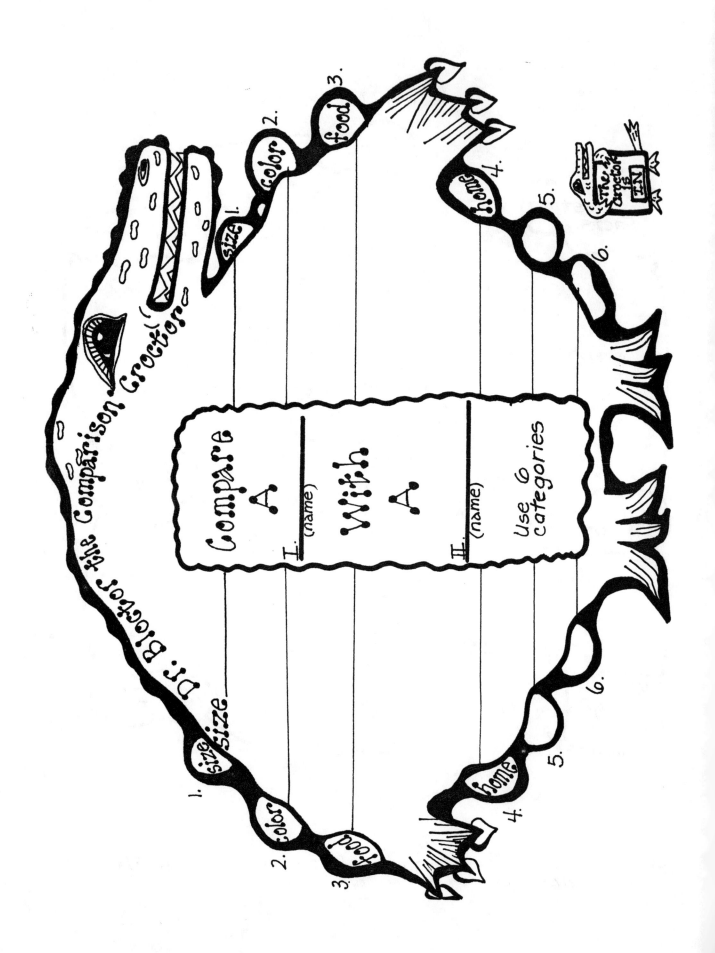

Dr. Bigg's the Comparison Croctor

Compare A
I. (name)

With A
II. (name)

Use 6 categories

size 1.
color 2.
food 3.
home 4.
5.
6.

CONTENTS

A IS FOR ASHLEY ALLIGATOR • 1

Build an "Alligator's Nest" (2) • Vocabulary Builders (2) • Help!
There's an Alligator in My Purse (2) • Yummy! I Like Seafood in My
Tummy (2) • Who Likes Seafood? (2)

We Can Work with "Three" (3) • Not Quite Three (3) • The Oval Shape
(3) • Before and After the Alligator Sat on It (3) • Alligator "Nines"
(3) • My! What Big Teeth You Have (3)

Alligator Nests (3) • What is Keratin? (3) • Let's Explore Scales (3)

Help! Our Water Is "In Trouble" (4) • Make Alligator Puppets (4) •
Beware, Alligators! (4)

Reproducible Activity Sheets

Interview Information (*draw, write, or web*)
There's an Alligator in My Bathtub (*choral reading*)
Long *A* and Short *A* Sounds (*vowel skills*)
Find Mrs. Alligator's Oval Eggs (*math*)
The Alligator Nest (*visual perception*)
From the Alligator's Mouth (*creative writing*)

B IS FOR BRANDI BEAR • 14

Reproducible Activity Sheets

C IS FOR CLANCY CAT • 28

Science 30

> The Concept of "Domestic" (30) • Classification (30) • Clancy's Cat
> Relatives (30) • Nonverbal Communication with Clancy (30) • Cat Tails
> in Nature (30)

Social Studies.. 30

> Critical and Creative Thinking About Holiday Cats (30) • Barn Cats and
> House Cats (31) • Clancy's Fancy Hats for Fancy Cats (31)

Clancy's Talk-and-Tell Picture and Rhyme.. 32

Talk and Tell: Clancy Cat... 33

Reproducible Activity Sheets

Interview Information (*draw, write, or web*)
Flip-Top Cat Book (*making a book*)
Clancy Cat's "C's" Are Alive and Well (*reading skills*)
The Bird-Watching Cat (*numbers and colors*)
Clancy's Storybook Cats Chart (*math survey and graph*)
Clancy's Cat-and-Mouse ABC Game (*letter recognition*)

D IS FOR DUKE DOG • 41

Background Information About Dogs 42

Reading/Language Arts... 42

> Duke's Pet Dog Talk (42) • Duke Likes Comic Strip Dogs (42) •
> Storybook Dogs (42) • Dogs Like to Eat (42) • Dog Expressions (42) •
> Nursery Rhyme Dogs (43)

Math.. 43

> Duke's Favorite Dog Graph (43) • Dogs and Bones Math (43) • Classify
> the Six Dog Categories (43)

Social Studies.. 43

> Working Dogs (43) • Dogs Go to School (43) • White House Dogs (43)
> • Lost and Found (44) • The Day Daisy Ran Away (44)

Science 44

> Let's Go on a Field Trip (44) • Guest Speaker (44) • Toy Stuffed
> Dogs (44)

Duke's Talk-and-Tell Picture and Rhyme... 45

Talk and Tell: Duke Dog.. 46

Reproducible Activity Sheets

E IS FOR EDDINGTON ELEPHANT • 54

Reproducible Activity Sheets

F IS FOR FRANCINE FROG • 67

Reproducible Activity Sheets

Interview Information (*draw, write, or web*)
The Measurement Frog (*measuring with a ruler*)
The Storybook Frog (*story map starter*)
Oops! Francine Spilled the Water (*science—absorption*)
Frog Photo Album (*stages of development*)
Mrs. Frog's Mud Mix (*salt dough recipe*)

G IS FOR GOLDIE GOAT • 80

Reproducible Activity Sheets

Interview Information (*draw, write, or web*)
The Long and Short of the Letter "I" (*vowels*)
The Butterfly Is an Insect (*life cycle*)
The Insect Hunter (*colors; numbers*)
Build an Insect (*recipe*)
The Insect Reunion (*review of insects*)

J IS FOR JACKSON JAGUAR • 119

Reproducible Activity Sheets

Interview Information (*draw, write, or web*)
How the Jaguar Lost His Rosettes (*creative writing*)
Special Writing Paper for Animal Stories (*creative writing*)
A Visual Story Map (*story sequence*)
Jaguar's Favorite Cat Graph (*math*)
Jaguar Jump Record (*measurement*)

K IS FOR KELLY KANGAROO • 132

Reproducible Activity Sheets

Interview Information (*draw, write, or web*)
Kangaroo Rap Tap (*creative movement; shapes*)
Help Joey Count Twenty Teeth (*math*)
Pouches, Bags, and Pockets (*containers*)
Kelly the Cutout Kangaroo (*consonant reinforcement*)

L IS FOR LOLLIPOP LION • 145

M IS FOR MIKE MacMOOSE • 157

Reproducible Activity Sheets

Interview Information (*draw, write, or web*)
Mike MacMoose Has a Tree House (*colors; numbers*)
Mike's Monster Works with Magnets (*science*)
Mike MacMoose Met a Monkey (*letter/sound recognition*)
Moose to Moose Comparisons (*comparing two books*)
M Is for Machine (*science; letter recognition*)

N IS FOR NOODLES NUTHATCH • 170

Reproducible Activity Sheets

Interview Information (*draw, write, or web*)
Noodles Nuthatch Loves Noodles (*recipe*)
Noodles Nuthatch Dot-to-Dot Puzzle (*math puzzle*)
Nest Matching (*visual discrimination*)
Bird Beaks (*science facts*)
We're Going Birdwatching (*collecting data*)

O IS FOR OLLIE OCTOPUS • 183

Reproducible Activity Sheets

Interview Information (*draw, write, or web*)
Ollie the Octopus (*vowel reinforcement*)
Ollie Octopus Loves Eight (*math streamer*)
The Many Sounds of "O" (*letter/sound relationships*)
The Shape of the Letter "O" Game (*matching*)
Ollie's Ocean Pollution Message (*environmental awareness*)

P IS FOR PERCY PENGUIN • 195

Reproducible Activity Sheets

Interview Information (*draw, write, or web*)
Endangered Birds (*endangered birds, fish, and wildlife*)
Percy Penguin's Snack Time (*letter/sound recognition*)

S IS FOR STACY SQUIRREL • 234

Sammy Spider's Surprise Party (*sounds and movement*)
Claws, Paws, and Footprints Matching Game (*visual discrimination*)
Calling All Rodents! Calling All Rodents! (*science*)

T IS FOR TRACY TURTLE • 246

Reproducible Activity Sheets

Interview Information (*draw, write, or web*)
Design a Turtle in a Shell (*body parts*)
Tracy Turtle's Mystery Shapes (*animal recognition*)
Tortilla Turtle Treat (*recipe*)
Tracy Turtle's Relatives (*science*)
Tortoise and Hare Bookmarks (*reading*)

U IS FOR UNI UNICORN • 259

Reproducible Activity Sheets

Interview Information (*draw, write, or web*)
Long and Short Sounds of the Vowel U (*vowel review*)
The Unicorn and the Umbrella (*vowel reinforcement*)
Create an Animal (*creative construction*)
Do I Look Like a Unicorn? (*creative writing*)
Uni Unicorn Has a Party (*working with concept of "one"*)

V IS FOR VALDAR VULTURE • 272

Reproducible Activity Sheets

Interview Information (*draw, write, or web*)
Nature's Garbage Can (*environmental badge*)
Countdown with a Condor (*math*)
Fabulous Feet (*science*)
The Vulture's Animal Book (*creative thinking*)
The Vulture Helps Identify Birds (*science*)

W IS FOR WALDORF WHALE • 285

X IS FOR FO-X-Y FOX • 297

Contents

Reproducible Activity Sheets

Interview Information (*draw, write, or web*)
The Fox Hunt (*letter reinforcement*)
Dial an A-B-C Animal (*animal characteristics*)
Can the Fox Trick You? (*visual discrimination*)
Fox Mask (*creative play*)
Fox and Geese Game (*animal maze*)

Y IS FOR YANCY YAK • 309

Reproducible Activity Sheets

Interview Information (*draw, write, or web*)
Yancy Yak Likes Yellow (*color; numbers*)
Yak Yak About Horns and Antlers (*science*)
Make a Yak Hat (*creative play*)
And Sometimes "Y" (*vowel sounds*)
Yancy Yak Delivers the Mail (*writing*)

Z IS FOR ZELDA ZEBRA • 321

Reproducible Activity Sheets

Interview Information (*draw, write, or web*)
The Eye of the Zebra (*visual discrimination*)
Unzip a Pocket Full of Z's (*letter reinforcement*)
Zebra Lines Writing Paper (*writing*)
Zoo Signs (*visual awareness*)
A Rebus Zoo Story (*words and pictures*)

RECOMMENDED CHILDREN'S BOOKS • 334

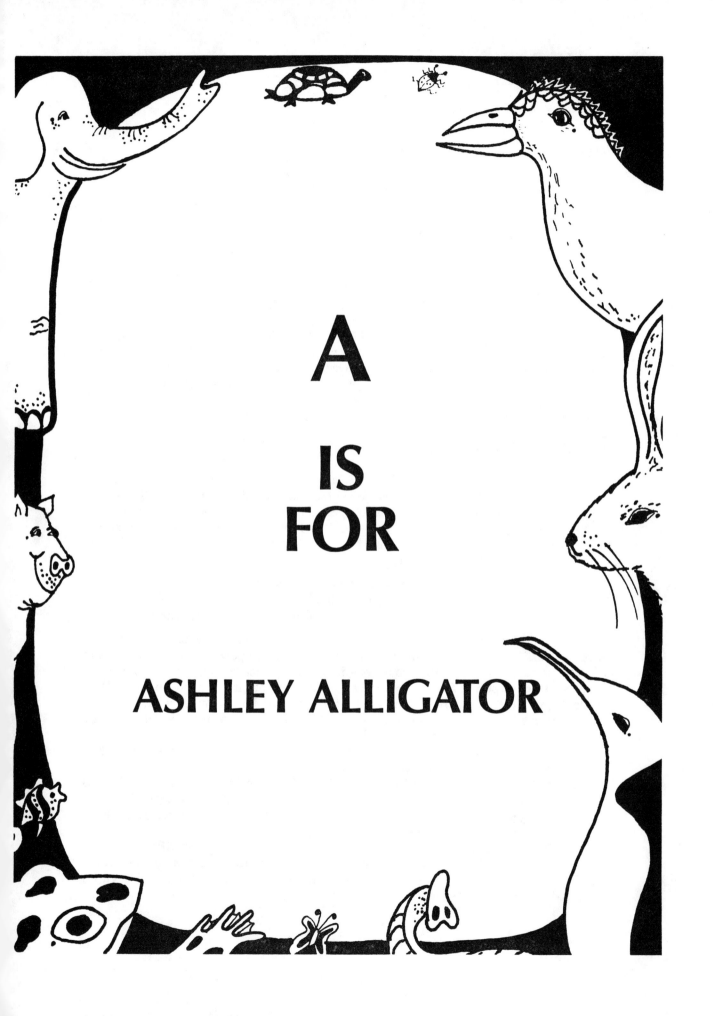

A

IS
FOR

ASHLEY ALLIGATOR

A IS FOR ASHLEY ALLIGATOR

BACKGROUND INFORMATION ABOUT ALLIGATORS: The alligator is a member of the reptile family. Its relatives are the crocodile, turtle, snake, and lizard. Alligators eat their turtle and snake relatives, and also eat shrimp, snails, and ducks that are floating on the water. It is easy to confuse an alligator with a crocodile. Just remember that the alligator is darker in color, and has a broader nose. When a crocodile closes its mouth you can see its bottom teeth, but this is not so with alligators.

READING/LANGUAGE ARTS:

1. BUILD AN ALLIGATOR'S NEST in the corner of the room from a large box covered with rough, green cloth material or green construction paper. Place leaves and sticks in the box. Glue white triangular shapes along the top and bottom for teeth. The nest can be used to hold colorful picture books and information books about alligators. If it is large enough, children can sit in the nest and read or look at the picture books.

2. VOCABULARY BUILDERS:

poacher—person who hunts alligators for their skin
extinct –when there are no more alligators
keratin –material found in alligator scales and people's fingernails

3. HELP! THERE'S AN ALLIGATOR IN MY PURSE.   Encourage students to write a creative story about an alligator that is caught by a poacher. Does it become an alligator purse? And if so, to whom does it belong—a rich person or a poor person? What's inside the purse? Bring in several old purses and put items inside of them. Have students guess who the purse belongs to by the contents. For example: ruler, chalk, felt pens, and notebook could equal teacher. What if there were athletic shoes, a jersey, shorts, and football helmet in the purse?

What if the alligator becomes a pair of shoes? Who walks in these shoes? Where does the person go? It could be a mystery story.

4. YUMMY! I LIKE SEAFOOD IN MY TUMMY.   Alligators like to eat turtles, snakes, shrimp, and snails. They also like to eat ducks who are floating on the water. Make an Alligator Snack Book in the shape of an alligator. Locate colored pictures for the book or draw them with colored felt-tip pens.

5. WHO LIKES SEAFOOD?   What kinds of seafood do people eat? Bring in labels from cans, or a list of seafood that is sold at the local seafood counter or fish market. A snack of tuna fish (dolphin-free) on crackers may just be what we would enjoy eating today. Make a Favorite Seafood Graph for the class on a large green alligator shape.

MATH:

1. WE CAN WORK WITH THREE, since alligators are hatched from three-inch eggs. Give children experience with counting and sorting three items. Place fifteen (15) crayons in a box—three red, three blue, three yellow, three green, and three orange. Mix them all together and have children pick out three of each color and group them together.

2. NOT QUITE THREE. Have a container of items that are not in groups of three, and ask children to count them and to group them so that they can tell how many more they need to make "three." (Examples: two mittens, one ruler, two pencils, and so on.)

3. THE OVAL SHAPE is the shape of alligator eggs. The oval looks like a circle that the alligator sat on and squashed. Use a piece of bulky yarn, tie the ends together, and make a circle on a flat surface. Rearrange it into the shape of an oval. Leave the material out for children to work with.

4. BEFORE AND AFTER THE ALLIGATOR SAT ON IT. Have children make the circle shape (before) and the oval shape (after). Let others guess whether it is a before or after shape.

5. ALLIGATOR "NINES." Alligators are about nine inches in length at birth. Cut pieces of string into nine inch lengths, and have students find items in the room that are nine inches long, or less than nine inches long, or more than nine inches long.

6. MY! WHAT BIG TEETH YOU HAVE. Make giant triangle-shaped teeth from white styrofoam. Bring in items for a dental health kit for an alligator. Use rope for flossing, and a scrub brush for brushing. What would an alligator use for a mouthwash? What else is in Ashley's overnight kit?

SCIENCE:

1. ALLIGATOR NESTS. Female alligators leave the water to make a nest of leaves and twigs near the shore. They lay approximately thirty (30) eggs which they cover with leaves and sand. Then they lay on top of the nest for nine months (the whole school year) to guard it. They only leave at night to go into the water, but if anyone comes close they make a hissing sound.

Students can simulate this experience as follows: Have five or six children huddle together, with a watchful alligator mother nearby. Have them slowly count to nine. Then, count slowly to nine again, but this time

> at the count of five –wiggle
> at the count of seven–begin to grunt in a faint voice
> at the count of nine –saw out of the egg with the special egg tooth in the
> > front of their mouth

Mother alligator can guide her waddling babies to the fountain for a drink, hissing all the way.

2. WHAT IS KERATIN? Have students tap their fingernails together. Their fingernails are made of keratin. This is the same material found in alligator scales.

3. LET'S EXPLORE SCALES. What other animals have scales? Be on the lookout for these mammals, fish, or birds as you examine real photographs of animals in *Ranger Rick* or *World* or *National Geographic* magazines.

And then, there are SCALES for weighing. What should this twelve-foot long "floating log" weigh? Let's find out. Then, get a real scale and weigh students individually. Make a graph of animal weights as you go through the A-Z activities.

SOCIAL STUDIES:

1. HELP! OUR WATER IS "IN TROUBLE."   Introduce and explore the concept of pollution in rivers, lakes, streams, and oceans. What can students do to help with this problem? As we go through the A-Z Book, keep track of the animals who live in the water. How many are endangered? Make a poster and, then using a paper bag, make a giant sea creature mask that fits over the head. Have a parade to warn against throwing garbage into the water!

2. MAKE ALLIGATOR PUPPETS.   Use green socks. Glue on features with felt. Students can wear the puppets when looking through picture books or when listening to stories. They can also use the puppets for creative play time and to develop oral language skills.

Another way to make alligator puppets is to use green paper plates. Fold the plate in half for the BIG alligator mouth. Cut white paper triangles for teeth and paste them around the edges. Add other features with construction paper. These alligator mouths will facilitate much talking.

3. BEWARE, ALLIGATORS!   Caution children to not get close to alligator cages at the zoo and to never reach inside any cage. Also, caution against going into the water in areas where there are alligators. Do children live in one of these areas? Find out.

**ASHLEY'S TALK-AND-TELL
PICTURE AND RHYME**

The alligator likes to eat
Lizards, turtles, juicy meat.
Here's a word of sound advice
The alligator isn't nice!

A

TALK AND TELL: ASHLEY ALLIGATOR

1. HI, ASHLEY! IS AN ALLIGATOR CALLED A "REPTILE"?

    Reptile? Yes. I'm a reptile. I'm in the same family as crocodiles, lizards, and turtles. They're my cousins.

2. ASHLEY, YOUR SKIN LOOKS BUMPY. IS YOUR SKIN WET AND SLIMY OR IS IT HARD AND CRUSTY?

    Sigh! My skin isn't nice and soft like people's skin. I have a thick, scaly, crust all over my body. My skin is made of a stiff, tough material called "keratin." It sounds just like what a rabbit likes to eat. Say "carrot" with the word "in" at the ending. CARROT IN. Now you try saying it. (Have group say keratin). Good!

3. ASHLEY, WHAT IS KERATIN?

    It's the tough material that your fingernails are made from. Animal hoofs and horns are also made of keratin. Tap your two thumbnails together and you can hear the sound of this tough stuff. Shhhh—tap and listen. Did you hear it?

4. ARE ALLIGATORS HATCHED FROM AN EGG, ASHLEY?

    Yes we are.

5. HOW MANY EGGS DOES A MOTHER ALLIGATOR LAY AT ONE TIME?

    Can you count to 30? Let's go 1,2,3 . . . 30. (Count aloud 1—30 with the group joining in. Then, hold up a see-through plastic bag with 30 large blocks or big round beads in it.) That's how many eggs a mother alligator lays at one time . . . 30.

6. ASHLEY, HOW BIG ARE ALLIGATOR EGGS?

    About 3 inches long. Do you have a ruler? Find the numeral 3. The egg is that long.

7. ASHLEY, WHAT SHAPE ARE THE EGGS?

    Just like the shape of hard-boiled eggs that you eat, only bigger. That shape is called an *oval*.

8. DOES THE MOTHER ALLIGATOR LAY HER EGGS IN THE WATER OR DOES SHE COME OUT OF THE WATER TO LAY HER EGGS?

    The grown-up mother alligator builds a nest near water. Then she lays her eggs and buries them with weeds and grass. She pats this down and lays right on top of it.

9. WHEN THE EGGS ARE SAFELY BURIED, ASHLEY, DOES THE MOTHER ALLIGATOR LEAVE THE NEST?

    Usually only long enough to get water. She guards the nest and will hiss at anything that gets too close. She can really scare you off!

10. HOW DOES THE BABY ALLIGATOR GET OUT OF THE EGG?

    Babies have an *egg tooth* on the end of their snout and use it like a saw to get out of the egg. Then the egg tooth drops off because it is no longer needed. My egg tooth helped me to hatch, or to get out of the egg, and then it goes to the alligator tooth fairy.

11. ASHLEY, HOW BIG IS AN ALLIGATOR WHEN IT IS BORN?

    Do you have a ruler? Point from the end to the 9. That makes 9 inches. That's how long an alligator is when it is born, or hatched. Now point to 3. That's how long my egg was. I was all curled up and crowded in there!

12. DOES A BABY ALLIGATOR STAY WITH ITS MOTHER AFTER IT IS HATCHED?

    Yes. She guides her babies to the water and stays with them for about one to two years. She teaches them all they will need to know. Then they're on their own.

13. TELL US, ASHLEY. WHAT DO ALLIGATORS LIKE TO EAT?

Juicy snakes, delicious shrimp, and a nice fat duck floating on the water.

14. ASHLEY, ARE YOU REALLY A BAD GUY?

Some people think so. But I do good work too. I build a 'gator hole that fills up with water and helps out a lot of other animals when the weather is dry.

15. TELL US MORE ABOUT THE 'GATOR HOLE.

It's a very deep hole that I dig by the swamp. Then, it fills up with water. Plants grow in the 'gator hole and animals go there to make their nests.

16. CAN YOU TELL US WHAT ANIMALS GO TO THE 'GATOR HOLE?

Fish and frogs find their way to the 'gator hole. Even land animals come and drink from the 'gator hole when they can't find water anywhere else. The 'gator hole helps animals survive.

17. BUT, ASHLEY, WHY DOES AN ALLIGATOR DIG IT? TO CATCH FROGS AND FISH?

I don't tell all of my secrets. What do you think?

18. HMM-M-M! HOW CAN WE TELL ASHLEY ALLIGATOR APART FROM A CROCODILE?

My side teeth don't show when my mouth is closed. When a crocodile closes its mouth, you can still see teeth from the side view. Also, our noses are different—mine is rounder than a crocodile nose. I have a nice nose, don't you think?

19. NICE NOSE? IT SURE IS LONG! YOU'VE BEEN SO COOPERATIVE, ASHLEY. SHOULD WE BE AFRAID OF YOU?

Oh . . . . Yes!

20. WHY SHOULD WE BE AFRAID OF YOU, ASHLEY?

People should never get close to alligators! Alligators get frightened and go on the attack. Come to see me at the zoo, but do not put your fingers into any cages! AND, it's not nice to throw things at me—tell your friends.

THANK YOU, ASHLEY, FOR THIS TALK-AND-TELL TIME RIGHT HERE AT THE SWAMP SITE. TODAY OUR GUEST WAS AN ALLIGATOR. TUNE IN NEXT TIME WHEN WE WILL BE INTERVIEWING A(N)

_____

INTERVIEW INFORMATION

What did you learn? Draw it, write it, or web it.

A

ASHLEY ALLIGATOR

THERE'S AN ALLIGATOR IN MY BATHTUB!

Color this make-believe alligator. Then learn the alligator chant. Say it with a partner. Say it with the class. Use your loud voice. Use your soft voice. Create your own movement to accompany the chant.

1. Alligator, Alligator, jump right in.
   Alligator, Alligator, brush your skin.

2. Alligator, Alligator, wash your nose,
   Alligator, Alligator, wash your toes.

3. Alligator, Alligator, clean the tub.
   Alligator, Alligator, rub-a-dub.

4. Alligator, Alligator, pull the plug.
   Alligator, Alligator, glug, glug, glug!

5. Alligator, Alligator, draining away,
   Alligator, Alligator, come back to play!

Name ______________________________ Date ________________________

LONG A AND SHORT A SOUNDS

Find the alligator. Put a green circle at the top of his space. Find the other items that begin with the same sound as "*a* as in alligator," and put a green circle at the top of each space. All the rest should begin with the long sound of *a*. Do they? Use your crayons to color the page.

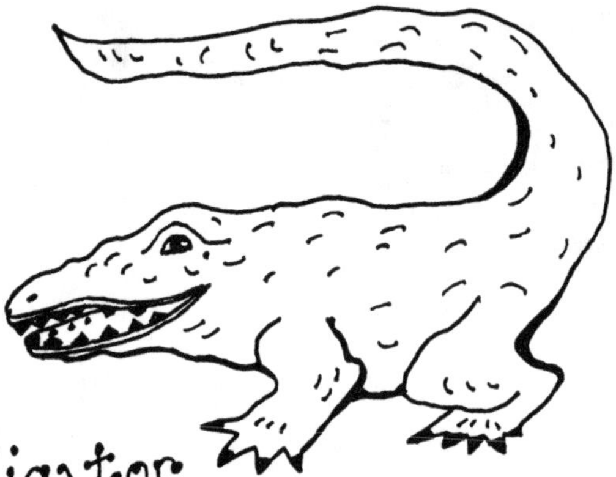

alligator

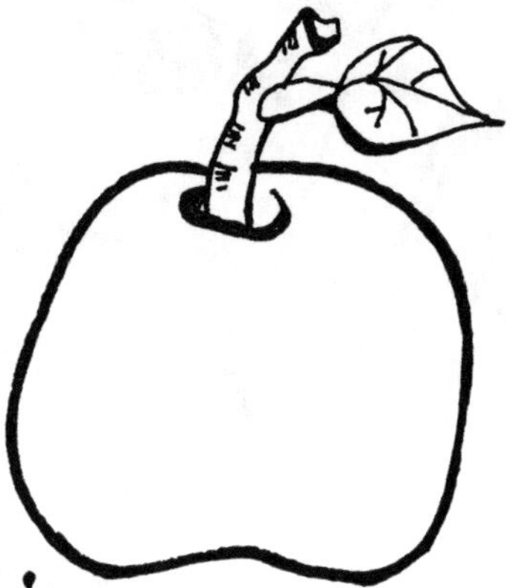

apple

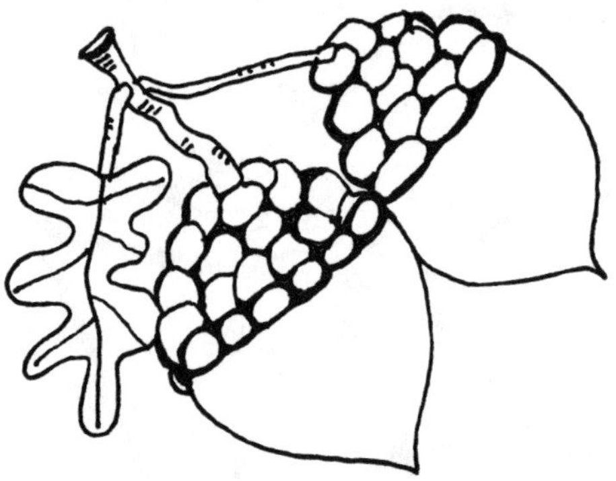

acorn

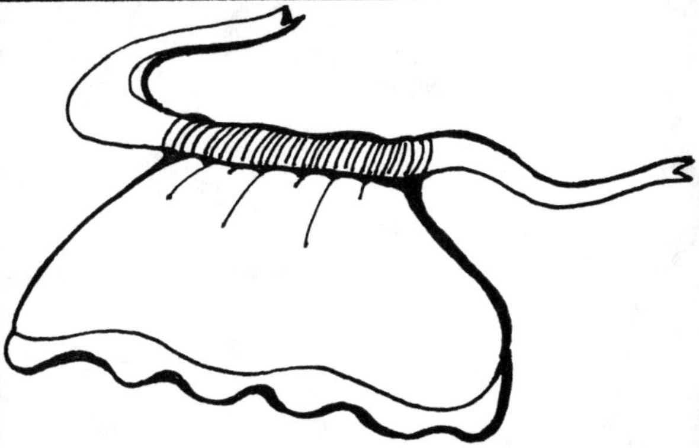

apron

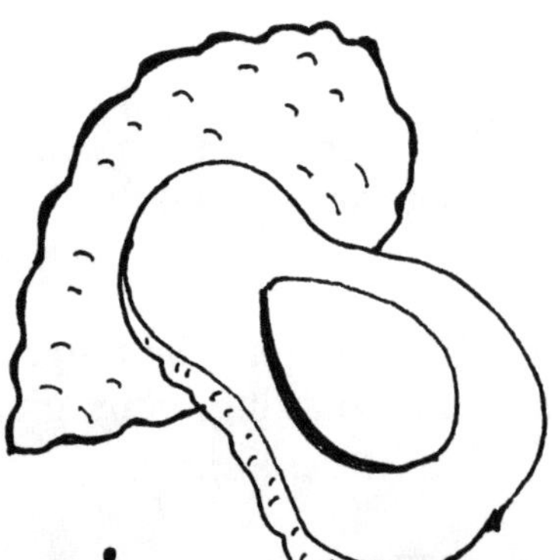

avocado

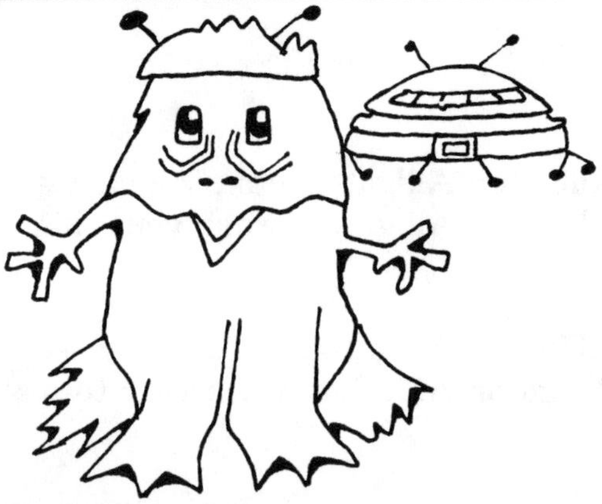

alien

Name _____

Date _____

FIND MRS. ALLIGATOR'S OVAL EGGS

An oval looks like a circle *after* an alligator sat on it. Find the oval shapes and color them red. How many are there? Color the other shapes, too. How many shapes can you name?

Name _____

Date _____

THE ALLIGATOR NEST   It's time to go back to the nest. But Mrs. Alligator has lost her way. Use your pencil to help show her the path to her egg nest. Color the area.

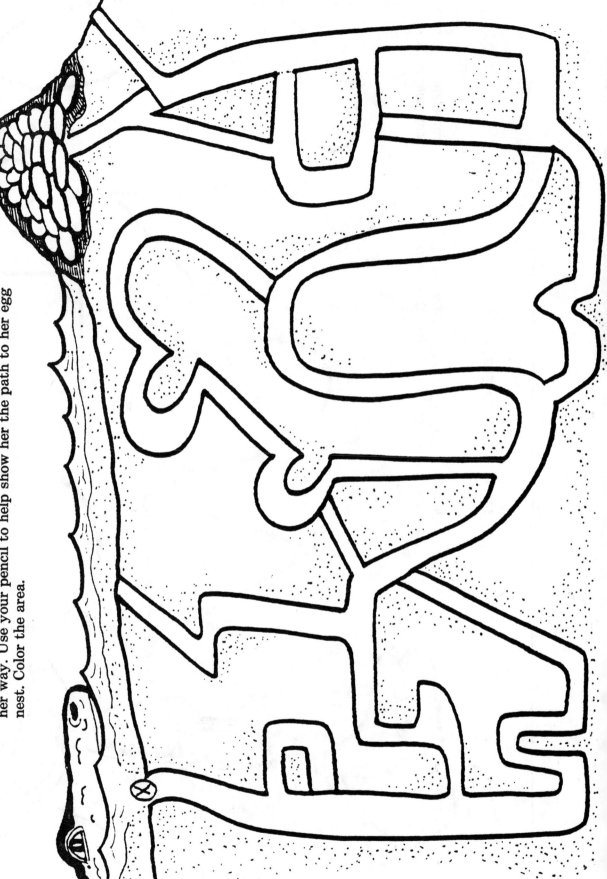

FROM THE ALLIGATOR'S MOUTH

The alligator has quite a tale to tell about one dark night when he was floating in the water. All of a sudden there was a bright light, something moving through the water, and . . . you guessed it . . . POACHERS! This alligator escaped, but let him tell you the tale in his own words. You can write the tale inside his mouth. Be careful!

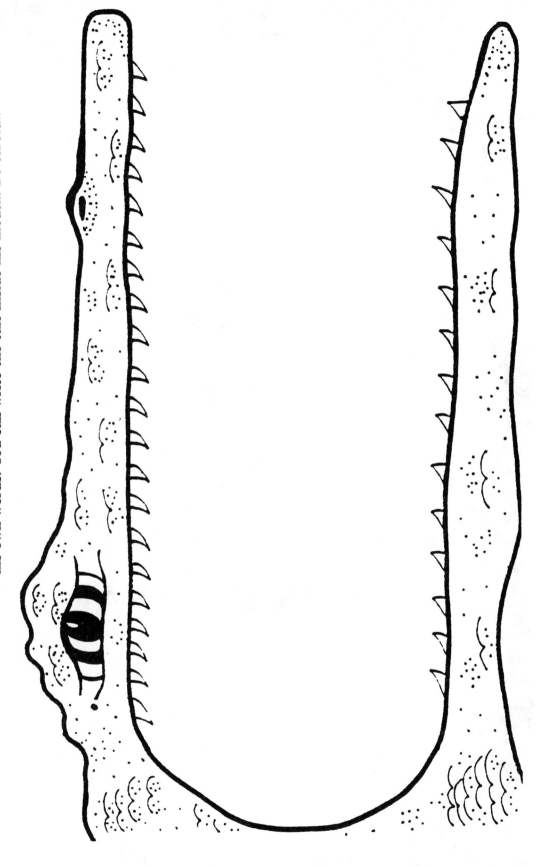

B
IS
FOR

BRANDI BEAR

B IS FOR BRANDI BEAR

BACKGROUND INFORMATION ABOUT BEARS: Bears are wild animals. They hibernate during the winter and during this time the adult females give birth to cubs—usually twins. Bears are warm-blooded mammals whose young are nursed by the mother. The female bear is an excellent teacher and the cubs stay with her from two to three years, learning all they will need to know. When the mother leaves her cubs for the final time, she sends them up into a tree and they stay there, often for days, awaiting her return. But when she doesn't return, their hunger eventually drives them down from the tree and from then on, they are on their own. Remember, the mother bear has taught them very well to fend for themselves.

READING/LANGUAGE ARTS:

1. BRANDI'S LONG WINTER NAP. Introduce the word *hibernate*. Set up a card table and place a brown shaggy rug or a tablecloth over it to simulate Brandi's cave. Have children go into the dark cave to hibernate for the winter (one minute) and then come out yawning into the springtime. Then:

> INTERVIEW THE CHILDREN USING A CASSETTE RECORDER.
> Have them identify themselves by a bear name of their choosing.
> Have them tell about what it was like inside the cave.
> Did they hear any wild animal noises? If so, what did they sound like?
> Are they hungry? (Bears eat berries and plants. Perhaps a taste of blueberry jam on a cracker would go well today with the story *Blueberries for Sal* by Robert McClosky.)

The interviews on tapes can be played repeatedly in a listening corner (or in the hibernation cave) and are excellent for language and vocabulary development. Children enjoy hearing themselves and others and are gaining practice with listening skills, as well.

2. A TASTE OF HONEY. Three "h" words such as *hibernate, hunger,* and *honey* can be introduced. Write these words on large cards so children can trace the letters. Make up sentences that use these words, and print them on large sentence strips. Students can work in pairs to read them aloud. For a treat today, we can all be hungry bears who taste honey on crackers shaped like teddy bears.

3. BRANDI SAYS SHE'D LIKE TO HAVE A TEDDY BEAR PARTY. Have students bring in their teddy bears to meet Brandi. Do they have a name? Let's list the names and tell what alphabet letter they begin and end with. Students can find bear stories at the library to read to their bears. Perhaps each bear can write a story about its school visit, or its bumpy ride to school, or how it felt meeting the other bears, or meeting new boys and girls. These bear stories could be written and illustrated and assembled into a large classroom book in the shape of a bear paw. Read from *Winnie the*

Pooh by A. A. Milne during this special Teddy Bear Party time. For "elevensies" (snack time), what do their bears suggest?

4. GOOD HEALTH BEARS.   Remember, Pooh Bear is always ready for snacks, but we need to eat good snacks. What would some good snacks be for people? Make a chart of pictures cut from magazines that show food we eat, and foods bears eat. (Bears in the wild are mainly plant eaters, but they will eat small animals. So, therefore, bears are OMNIVEROUS—they eat vegetables *and* meat.) In South America, the Indians of the Andes tie a red ribbon around the necks of animals and babies to ward off the 'evil eye' and keep them in good health. Perhaps today the bears could each be given a little red ribbon to wear for good health.

5. GOLDILOCKS AND THE THREE BEARS.   Use the activity pages for cut-outs of the main characters in the story if you plan to put on a puppet show, or a flannel board reenactment of the story. Also, divide students into small theatre groups and have them become the main characters (Goldilocks, Papa Bear, Mama Bear, Baby Bear), and also minor characters such as two students joining hands to become the doorway through which the characters enter, or trees swaying in the breeze outside in the woods, or students bending and twisting into shapes of furniture inside the house. This retelling of the story is excellent for language development and for practicing listening skills.

Note: Color the cutouts and put them together with paper fasteners so that they can move. You can also make other props for your story, such as the house, bowls, chairs, beds, trees, etc.).

MATH:

1. COMPARE YOURSELF TO BRANDI BEAR.   Cut a piece of brown kraft paper in the shape of a bear and tape it to the wall or bulletin board. It should be about 8 feet tall! Then, have children stand with their back to this friendly bear. Measure them with a yardstick, and mark and label their spot on the chart.

Have students stand back and look way up at the bear and take turns saying, "Hi Brandi Bear! My name is _____. I'm _____ feet _____ inches tall."

2. OTHER MATH CONCEPTS to develop with the Bear Height Chart are tallest, shortest, taller than, shorter than. For example, "Jacob is taller than Lorrie." "Chris is shorter than Addy." Also, "Emily is taller than Jordie but shorter than Claire."

3. TWIN BEARS.   Bears are usually born as twins. Keep track of the A-Z animals as you go along to determine how many young ones are born at one time. The range will be from one to several to hundreds (insects and the octopus).

SCIENCE:

1. BRANDI TAKES A WINTER SNOOZE.   Hibernation is the long winter sleep of many animals, including bears. Bears eat, and eat, and eat in the autumn and may gain 100 pounds. When they hibernate, they live off of the fat. They don't have to eat, drink, or eliminate during hibernation, so they give off no scent. This protects them in their caves.

Find magazine pictures of real bears in the wild so that students can see them in their natural setting. What other animals hibernate during the winter? Make a list. Make a picture chart of animals that hibernate above ground in caves and trees (bears, squirrels, rabbits) and those that hibernate below ground (chipmunks, groundhogs, frogs).

2. MY, WHAT BIG CLAWS YOU HAVE!   Bear claws are used as tools to help dig out a big cave in the side of a hill. This can lead to a discussion of tools that are helpful for people. What tools do we use in the garden? Do we use tools in the kitchen? What tools does Smokey the Bear use for fire fighting?

SOCIAL STUDIES:

1. Discuss BEARS WE KNOW, such as Smokey the Bear, Pooh Bear, Paddington Bear, and our very own special bears. Help children to realize that it is fine to snuggle and cuddle with their toy bears, but definitely NOT with real bears because they are wild animals and have very long, sharp claws. If students live in an area where there are national parks with wild bears who come up to the car, caution them to roll up the windows. Have students bring in their stuffed bears so that they can introduce them to each other. The toy bears can hibernate in the cave with their owner.

Open up one end of the hibernation cave and put a comfortable rug on the floor and many storybooks and picture books about bears that children can read to their toy bears. Books such as *Brown Bear, Brown Bear* by Bill Martin, Jr., and *The Valentine Bears* by Jan Brett can be included.

Sit in a circle and have a "TOY BEAR SHARE" experience. Ask students what stories their bears liked. What part of the story was their favorite? What word did they like best? What part was the funniest? Encourage story comparisons in a conversational language setting. (See the activity pages for bear book comparisons.)

2. BEAR FAMILY.   Although the bear prefers to live alone, there are several members in the bear family. There are black bears that are found in Yellowstone National Park, the Great Smokies, and other national parks. Locate these areas on a map of the United States. Do you live close by or far away? Another member of the family is the grizzly bear who is usually dark brown but can be light brown or gray. This bear with the humped shoulders is savage. It can be seen in the Rocky Mountains, and in Canada and Alaska. Locate these areas on a map or globe. The largest of the bears is the kodiak bear who weighs more than 1,000 pounds, and is about as heavy as a small truck. This bear kills moose, elk, and deer for food and likes to fish for salmon in the streams of Alaska. Locate Alaska on a map or globe.

Finally, the polar bear lives in the Arctic. Locate this area on the globe. The polar bear eats seal, crab, and shrimp. It also will eat seaweed. This bear is very much at home in sub-zero temperatures.

3. BEARS COME IN MANY COLORS.   Put some fresh paint in containers at the easel that will motivate the students to paint. Mix up a cinnamon color and some reddish brown, golden brown, and tan colors. Since bears are huge, encourage children to bump into the edges of the paper.

4. FUZZY SPONGE BEARS.   Use small sponges for a fuzzy effect and sponge paint the three bears, making them small, medium, and large. Later, the claws, eyes, nose, and mouth can be added with a brush.

5. POLAR BEARS IN SUMMER AND WINTER.   In summer, the polar bear has yellowish fur, and in the winter it turns pure white. Divide a page in half, and paint the same bear in the two seasons. What happens with the white bear on a white background in winter? Perhaps the snow can have a hint of blue in it so that we can identify the bear.

B is for Bear
With big, sharp claws,
That stick right out
The end of her paws.

B

TALK AND TELL: BRANDI BEAR

1. HI, BRANDI! ARE YOU A WILD ANIMAL OR A TAME ANIMAL?

    I'm a wild animal. Be careful of wild animals.

2. CAN YOU SEE ME? CAN YOU SEE THE BOYS AND GIRLS, BRANDI?

    Yes, I can see you and I can see the boys and girls. My eyes are small and I see things that are up close. I don't see too well if things are far away.

3. HOW DO YOU GET AROUND SO WELL IF YOU DON'T SEE THINGS FAR AWAY?

    I can smell them! My sense of smell is powerful!

4. BRANDI, WERE YOU HATCHED FROM AN EGG OR WERE YOU BORN LIVE?

    I'm a mammal, which means that I'm born live. Bears are usually born as twins. And, we're born in the winter.

5. HOW BIG IS A BEAR WHEN IT'S BORN, BRANDI?

    We weigh in at about one pound. That's as much as a pound bag of cookies.

6. ONE POUND IS JUST ABOUT THE SIZE OF A GROWN-UP RAT, ISN'T IT?

    That's right!

7. IF YOU'RE BORN SO LITTLE, BRANDI, HOW DO YOU GROW SO BIG AND STRONG?

    Bears drink their mother's milk. Milk is good for you. It builds strong bones and good teeth. Be sure to drink your milk.

8. BRANDI, WHERE ARE BEARS BORN?

    In a cave during the winter hibernation time.

9. WHAT DOES HIBERNATION MEAN?

    Hibernation is the long winter sleep of bears. We don't eat, drink, or go to the bathroom. (Say this slowly): Out bodies slow way down—our heart beats slowly—we breathe very slowly. YAWN! I almost put myself back to sleep just telling you about hibernation!

10. IS IT TRUE THAT THE FEMALE BEAR IS A GOOD MOTHER, BRANDI?

    Oh, yes! The mother bears takes good care of the cubs. She's like a single parent. She feeds and watches over her cubs, but she knows they need to play too. She teaches them to climb up a tree when danger is near. Also, the female bear will adopt a baby bear cub who has strayed from its natural mother and has gotten lost.

11. WHAT DO BEARS LIKE TO EAT, BRANDI?

    We eat lots of different things, but mostly plants. Also, we like berries, nuts, roots of wild flowers, and some meat and fish too.

12. WHO DO YOU THINK ARE THE MOST POPULAR BEARS, BRANDI?

    The black bear, the great big grizzly, and the polar bear, too.

13. HOW TALL IS A GROWN UP BLACK BEAR?

    About 6 ft tall. We can measure it. Put two yardsticks together the long way, end-to-end, on the wall. Look way up high to see my nose.

14. BRANDI, WE WANT TO KNOW HOW MUCH A GROWN UP GRIZZLY BEAR WEIGHS?

    They are heavy! The grizzly can weigh as much as $\frac{1}{2}$ a ton. That's 1,000 lb—as much as a small car!

15. MY, WHAT BIG CLAWS YOU HAVE, BRANDI. WHAT DO YOU DO WITH THOSE LONG 6-INCH CLAWS ON YOUR PAWS?

Hold up three fingers. (1) Bear claws help us to climb trees, (2) bear claws are used as tools to dig for food, and (3) bear claws are used to dig a cave for our winter hibernation time.

16. WHAT DO POLAR BEARS LIKE TO EAT, BRANDI?

(Use a hushed voice). They like to sneak up on a seal that is sleeping on the ice in the sun, and have it for dinner. A polar thinks a seal is delicious!

17. DO POLAR BEARS SLIP AND FALL WHEN THEY WALK OR RUN ON THE ICE?

No. Their paws have stiff bristles on the bottom—just like a big brush.

18. TELL US, BRANDI, SHOULD PEOPLE GO UP TO BEARS IN THE PARK AND TRY TO FEED THEM AND PET THEM?

Never, It's dangerous!

19. WHAT ABOUT POOH BEAR, TEDDY BEARS, AND SMOKEY THE BEAR? ARE THEY RELATED TO YOU?

They're make-believe bears who look a little bit like real bears. It's OK to cuddle a stuffed animal. But don't get close to real bears.

20. WHERE CAN I SEE YOU IF I CAN'T GET CLOSE TO YOU?

Visit me at the zoo. But, don't poke your fingers into the cage and don't go under the fence rail. Watch me from a long way off.

THANK YOU, BRANDI, FOR THIS TALK-AND-TELL RIGHT HERE AT THE NATIONAL PARK. TODAY OUR GUEST WAS A REAL BEAR. TUNE IN NEXT TIME WHEN WE WILL BE INTERVIEWING A(N)

_____

INTERVIEW
INFORMATION

What did you learn? Draw it, write it, or web it.

B

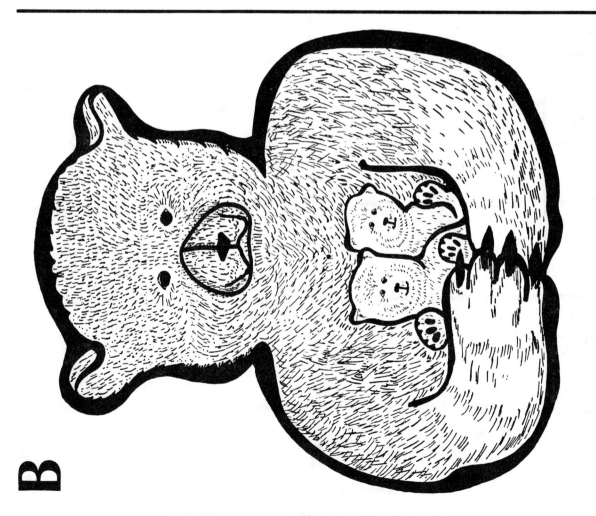

BRANDI BEAR

THE COMPARE BEAR

Read two books about bears and compare them using this chart. Read more "beary" good books to compare. Then share your bear comparisons.

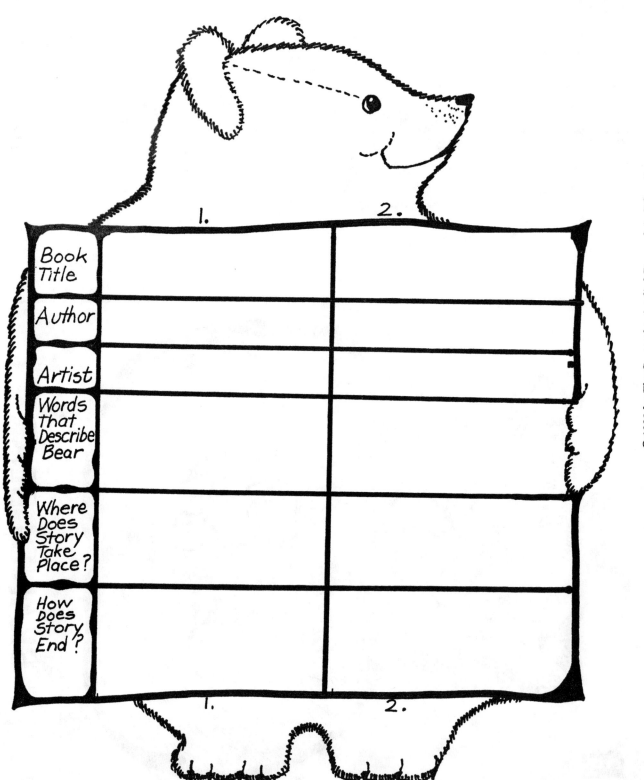

	1.	2.
Book Title		
Author		
Artist		
Words That Describe Bear		
Where Does Story Take Place?		
How Does Story End?		

Name —————————————

Date —————————————

BEAR TWIN LOOK-ALIKES

Mother bears usually give birth to two bears, or twins. Make these two bears look exactly the same. Use your crayons to make matching sweaters and short pants. Use stripes and designs with circles and squares. This is going to be fun!

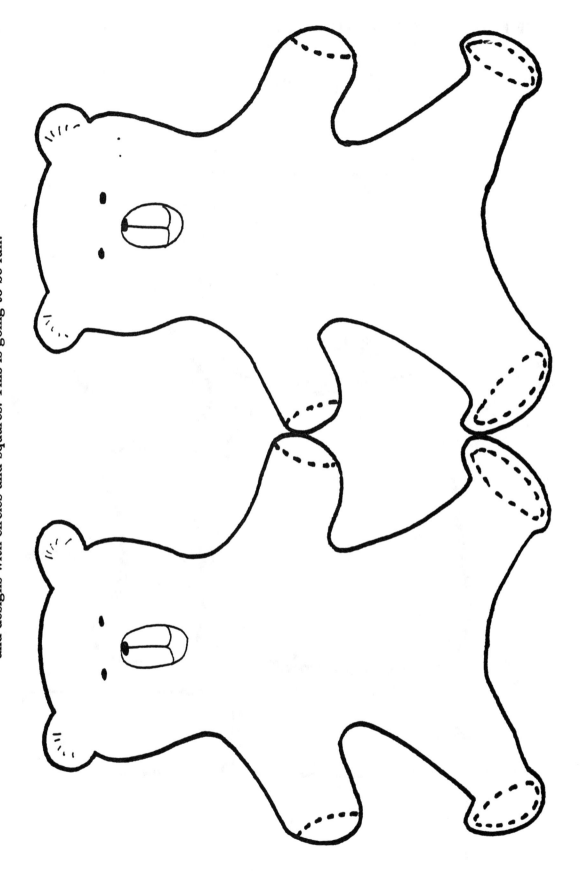

BABY BEAR

MAMA BEAR

THE THREE BEARS STORYTELLER CUTOUTS

PAPA BEAR

THE THREE BEARS STORYTELLER CUTOUTS

GOLDILOCKS

C
IS
FOR

CLANCY CAT

C IS FOR CLANCY CAT

BACKGROUND INFORMATION ABOUT CATS: Little pet cats are related to the BIG cats such as lions, tigers, leopards, and jaguars. Pet cats are tame but big cats are wild. By nature cats are nocturnal and like to be active at night when it's time for people to go to bed. But they can adjust. Many people have cats as pets because they don't require the care that dogs do, but they still need attention on *their* terms. They are independent.

READING/LANGUAGE ARTS:

1. CLANCY LIKES STORYBOOK CATS. Have children find storybooks where the cat is the main character. Share the library books. Some special favorites include *The Cat in the Hat* series by Dr. Seuss; *Hi, Cat!* by Ezra Jack Keats; *Anatole and the Cat* series by Eve Titus; and *Millions of Cats* by Wanda Gag.

Make a chart comparing the main cat character in each story. What is the name? What words describe the cat? Where does the cat live? Is the cat a house pet or does the cat act like a person (has a family, a job, and so on)? Make illustrations on the chart.

2. THE LANGUAGE OF PLAYFUL CATS. When asking questions that require a simple yes or no reply, have students answer by saying, "Mew, Mew" (yes), or "Meow!" (no).

3. MAKE A FLIP-TOP BOOK. Use a cat shape (see Activity Pages) to make a book about cats. This can be a story book cat, or it can be a cat dictionary with one item per page and a descriptive word.

MATH:

1. THIRTY TEETH. Most cats have thirty teeth. Have students count their own teeth by using their tongue rather than their fingers. Count the top teeth and then the bottom teeth. Compare numbers. How many first and second teeth do students have?

2. CALICO CATS are multicolors of brown, orange, and white. There is calico material that has brown background and orange background (even purple, tan, red, green, blue, and so on). Get some samples of the material and cut $\frac{1}{2}$ into circles and $\frac{1}{2}$ into squares. Mix all of the circles together and mix all of the squares together. Then match the calico circles and squares by color and design.

Also, cut out some cat shapes and stuff and sew some large and small calico cats. Students can make extra large ones to place in the reading corner. Perhaps a gingham dog could be made to go along with the calico cat (and it would welcome our next ABC animal).

3. THE LONG AND SHORT OF IT. Cats fall into two main groups—short hairs and long hairs. The short hairs include the common Tabby, the Burmese, Abyssinian, and Siamese. Have students locate these cats in picture books about cats. The second

group, the long hairs, have finer fur and their tail is bushy. The most common are the Angoras and the Persians.

Students can make a cat calendar for the month, using some of these beautiful cats as models.

SCIENCE:

1. THE CONCEPT OF DOMESTIC. Small cats like Clancy are *domestic* or *domesticated*, which means that they can live in harmony in the human environment. What other animals are domestic to the point where they could live in your house? Which animals could live in the classroom? Which animals live on a farm and do not harm people? List them, and illustrate them with water crayons. Read *Animals Born Alive and Well* by Ruth Heller. How many are domestic?

2. CLASSIFICATION. Cut colored pictures of a variety of cats, both wild and tame, from magazines. Classify them as wild or domestic. Also classify them by size, color, long or short hair, sleeping or not sleeping, standing up or lying down, and so on.

3. CLANCY'S CAT RELATIVES. Send students to the library for pictures of the big cats. Cut small slips of paper and put one word on them, such as tiger or lion or lion cub or jaguar and so on. The students can locate a picture or some information about the animal listed on the slip of paper that they draw from a hat that belongs to *The Cat in the Hat* by Dr. Seuss.

4. NONVERBAL COMMUNICATION WITH CLANCY. Cats communicate with their tail. When they flick it back and forth rapidly, it can mean anger. Cats flick their ears to show that they hear you. When a cat flattens its ears to its head, it usually means that it is upset. Cats wink their eyes to show pleasure.

People communicate without words, too. Have students use their body posture and face to communicate the following emotions: anger, surprise, fear, happiness, sadness, suspicion. Videotape individual students, and when it is played back, see if students can guess the emotion being conveyed.

5. CAT TAILS IN NATURE. Introduce this term to the students. Cat tails grow in marsh areas. Also, locate photographs of cat tails in information books about flowers that grow in the wild. Why would this plant be called a cat tail? Interview Clancy to find out, and Clancy might have a cat tale to tell about the cat tail.

SOCIAL STUDIES:

1. CRITICAL AND CREATIVE THINKING ABOUT HOLIDAY CATS. Witches and cats go together. *Wobble the Witch Cat* and *The Witch Who Lost Her Shadow* by Mary Calhoun are just two of the many holiday books that show the special friendship of the witch and her cat.

> Why does the witch have a cat? Why doesn't she have a dog?
> Why is the cat usually black? Why isn't it orange?
> Suppose the witch cat grew to the size of a tiger? Then what?
> What do the witch and cat do on other holidays?

This calls for some creative writing.

2. BARN CATS AND HOUSE CATS.   With different colors of plasticine, students can mold a mother cat and her litter of kittens. Use a small box and construction paper to make a diorama to house the cats. This can be a barn scene, or a closet scene, where the mother has just had her babies. This may help students to generate creative stories and creative play.

3. CLANCY'S FANCY HATS FOR FANCY CATS.   Many of the storybook cats wear hats. Go through children's books to locate cats with hats. Then, create some very, very fancy hats using cloth material glued to heavy paper. Decorate with yarn, glitter, feathers, beads, fringe, lace, and other items (parents can be asked to donate items from their sewing supplies). These fancy hats would make quite a bulletin board, especially with fancy cats to go with them. Fancy hats could be made in honor of Puss in Boots. Perhaps this calls for fancy boots, too.

C is for Cat
Holding her kitty.
Cats like to be told
You think they're pretty.

C

TALK AND TELL: CLANCY CAT

1. HI, CLANCY! HOW DO WE KNOW WHEN CATS ARE HAPPY?

I purr to show that I'm happy. It's sort of like the way you hum. Put your hand on your throat and hum right now. That's good! ALSO, I blink my eyes very slowly as I look at you. Blink your eyes slowly. That's good.

2. WHEN YOU'RE ANGRY, CLANCY, HOW DO YOU SHOW THIS?

I hiss, scream, and snarl. I also switch my tail back and forth real fast.

3. ARE YOU WILD OR TAME?

I'm a domestic cat, which means that I'm tame. But there are wild cats that live in the forest.

4. CLANCY, ARE CATS HATCHED FROM AN EGG OR BORN LIVE?

We're born live, with several brothers and sisters. This is called a litter of kittens. We can't see for three whole weeks!

5. HOW LONG DOES A MOTHER CAT SPEND WITH HER LITTER OF KIT-TENS?

We should stay together for the nursing and training time for about 8 to 10 weeks. Count that on your calendar. This makes us more contented cats.

6. HOW DO YOU SPEND MOST OF YOUR TIME, CLANCY?

Resting or snoozing. My heart and lungs are quite small, and after an active period I really need to take it easy.

7. CLANCY, WHY ARE YOU ALWAYS LICKING YOURSELF WITH YOUR TONGUE?

Cats like to be tidy. My tongue is rough and I use it as a brush. Also it makes me feel cool too, and it gives me something to do.

8. WHAT DO YOU THINK THAT AN INDOOR PET CAT SHOULD EAT, CLANCY?

Commercial dry or canned cat food is good for us. Also, some table scraps taste good. Different cats like different things to eat—just like people.

9. IS IT TRUE, CLANCY, THAT ALL CATS JUST LOVE MILK?

Some like it and some don't. You should always have fresh water in a bowl for your pet cat. I think children should drink milk and water every day.

10. IF YOU'RE AN OUTDOOR CAT, THEN WHAT DO YOU EAT?

Cats catch birds, mice, and insects that flutter by. It takes a lot of practice to catch them. First you have to be very, very quiet and then you JUMP!

11. ARE CATS BIG EATERS?

No. Cats only eat until their stomach feels full, and they then will walk away from food. Cats don't stuff themselves. A cat does not eat like a barnyard pig.

12. PEOPLE SAY YOU CAN SEE IN THE DARK. CAN YOU SEE IN THE DARK, CLANCY?

I see very well in dim light because my pupils in my eyes get very large. I'm really a nocturnal animal, which means that I'd rather sleep in the day and be on the prowl at night. But, I can change if I have to.

13. CAN YOU HEAR WELL, CLANCY?

Oh, yes! I hear things long before people do. I can hear your car motor when you're way down at the corner before you get to the house. I also hear high-pitched squeaky sounds that people don't hear—such as the voices of mice. That's why I'm such a good "mouser."

14. CLANCY, ARE CATS FRIENDLY?

Not in the way dogs are. We keep to ourselves a lot. We are what you would call independent.

15. WHAT DOES INDEPENDENT MEAN, CLANCY?

Well, it means that cats like to be alone a lot. Cats like to be petted when *they* want to be petted, not just because you feel like petting them. A cat can tell if people like them and they will stay around people when they feel like it.

16. YOUR WHISKERS ARE PRETTY LONG. ARE YOUR WHISKERS JUST FOR DECORATION?

No, they are useful! If my whiskers can fit through an opening, then I know that my whole body can squeeze through. They help me to measure just like a ruler helps you to measure.

17. DO MOST PEOPLE LIKE YOU, CLANCY?

When we're kittens, they think we're cute. When we grow up, people either like us or they don't. They seem to have very strong feelings one way or the other.

18. WHY DO YOU THINK PEOPLE HAVE A CAT FOR A PET?

Because we add beauty and grace to the home.

19. WHY DO YOU CHASE AND CATCH BIRDS? IS THAT REALLY NICE, CLANCY?

It's just our nature to do so. It's what cats do. It's called instinct.

20. CLANCY, DO YOU THINK CATS KNOW WHEN PEOPLE ARE TALKING ABOUT THEM?

Yes. So, be careful what you say. We don't like to be laughed at. We like words like pretty and beautiful, and nice, nice cat!

THANK YOU FOR THIS INTERVIEW AT YOUR PRIVATE HOME. TODAY OUR GUEST WAS A PET CAT. OUR NEXT GUEST ANIMAL WILL BE A(N)

———————————————————————————

INTERVIEW
INFORMATION

What did you learn? Draw it, write it, or web it.

C

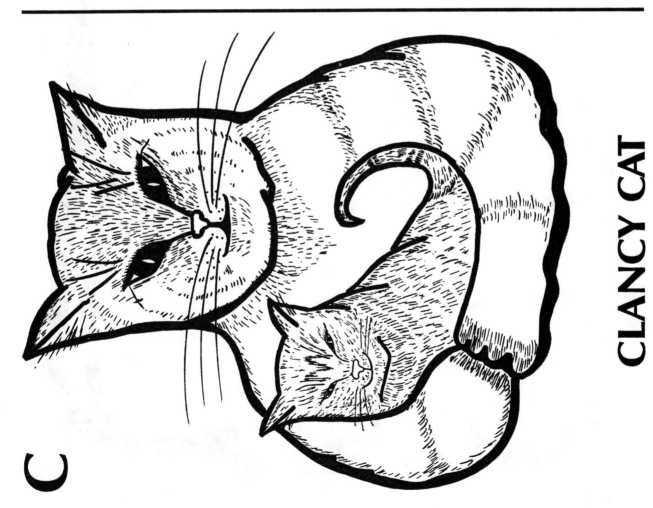

CLANCY CAT

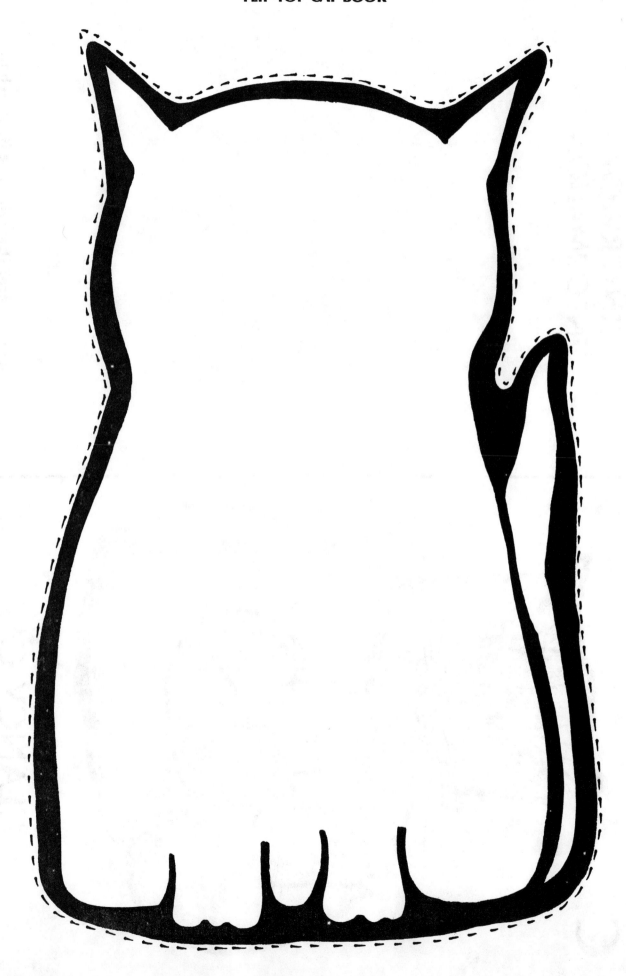

Name _____ Date _____

CLANCY CAT'S "Cs" ARE ALIVE AND WELL

Everything on this page begins with Clancy's sound, but only four are alive and well. Can you find them? Use your crayons to make them look healthy.

THE BIRD-WATCHING CAT

Cats like to watch birds. They also like to catch them. This cat is looking out of the window. How many birds does it see? Put the total in the box at the bottom of the page. Then color one bird red, two birds brown, three birds blue, and four birds yellow.

CLANCY'S STORYBOOK CATS CHART

Add two more storybook cats in the bottom squares. Then ask ten classmates to print their name in the space above their favorite cat story.

The Cat In The Hat by Dr. Seuss

CLANCY'S CAT-AND-MOUSE ABC GAME

Materials needed: one die. *Directions:* Throw the die. If, for example, you throw a three, count three spaces. Then name the letter in each space. If you miss, throw the die and go back that number of spaces. One player can play just for practice. Two or three players can play to see who gets to the mouse house first.

D
IS
FOR

DUKE DOG

D IS FOR DUKE DOG

BACKGROUND INFORMATION ABOUT DOGS: Dogs like Duke are often called man's best friend. On the average, they live to be about 12 years old. They love to please and to be petted. For this reason, many people have dogs for pets. There are over 150 different types, or breeds, of dogs in the world. Some dogs make good hunting dogs because of their keen sense of smell. Other dogs are put to work to herd cattle, pull sleds, or to guard property. There are Seeing Eye dogs who help visually-impaired people. Dogs such as Duke make loyal companions.

The American Kennel Club has divided dogs into six groups: Hounds, Toys, Sporting Dogs, Terriers, Working Dogs, and Non-Sporting Dogs. (See Math Section for more specific information.)

READING/LANGUAGE ARTS:

1. DUKE'S PET DOG TALK (Oral Language Development):
Have students tell interesting stories about their pet dogs (tricks, a funny thing they did, how they behave when . . . etc.).

Students can bring in photos of their dogs and classify them by color, size, breed, and so on.

2. DUKE LIKES COMIC STRIP DOGS.   Are there many cartoons that depict dogs? If so, how many can be found? Bring in the cartoon section of the newspaper regularly, and have children begin to read it. (Most children will be familiar with Snoopy from *Peanuts,* but there are many other pet dogs in cartoons too.) Do a "Favorite Dog Graph."

Major and minor (dog) characters. If the pet is not a major character in the cartoon (such as Marmaduke or Snoopy), how many dogs are there in the background, or minor characters?

3. STORYBOOK DOGS.   There are many fine storybooks with dogs as the main character. Read *Harry the Dirty Dog* by Gene Zion and compare the dog with another famous dog. Where do they live? Do they talk? Are they special in a family or do they live alone? How does the story begin and end?

4. DOGS LIKE TO EAT.   The next time students go to the supermarket, have them go to the pet food section and copy down the brand names of dog food, along with the flavors. Students may be surprised when they learn that in this country an entire aisle is devoted to pet food and other pet supplies, whereas in some countries pets eat table scraps. Also, have students keep track of pet food commercials on television. How many are aimed at dogs and cats?

5. DOG EXPRESSIONS.   We use the word dog in our language in colorful ways. For example, "Hot dog!" means "great!" Also, "dog days of summer" means very hot days. What other dog expressions can we find in our language?

6. NURSERY RHYME DOGS.   Remember Old Mother Hubbard who went to the cupboard to get her poor dog a bone? Remember the cow who jumped over the moon? How many dogs can we find in our favorite Mother Goose Rhymes? While we're at it, how many different kinds of animals can we find in these rhymes. Start making an ABC list of the animals and the title of the rhyme. Each student can add his or her research to a BIG BOOK of Nursery Rhyme Animals. What shape will the book be?

MATH:

1. DUKE'S FAVORITE DOG GRAPH.   Interview the students individually, and have them name their favorite type of dog. (Pictures will be helpful.) Graph the information horizontally on a long dog shape and call it Duke.)

2. DOGS AND BONES MATH.   Make construction paper cutouts of dog bone shapes. Also make cutouts of dog dishes. Place the numerals 1 through 10 on the dishes. On the dog bone shapes, write number addition and subtraction number sentences such as 3 + 4 = and 7 − 2 = and have students place them in the proper dog dish.

3. CLASSIFY THE SIX DOG CATEGORIES.   Work with the six categories of dog breeds. There are over 150 different types of dogs, so it is difficult to classify them, but The American Kennel Club has done so. These are the groups. Make a giant picture chart of the six dogs. Look for dog pictures to go with each:

HOUNDS—Hunting dogs that use their sense of smell to help catch deer, rabbits, and hares. These include the beagle, dachshund, and bloodhound.

TOYS—Small dogs that have been bred for house pets. These include the Toy Poodle, Pekingese, and Chihuahua.

SPORTING DOGS—Dogs that have been trained to hunt. They are trained to retrieve (find and bring back) game birds such as ducks and geese. Some sporting dogs are the Pointer, Golden Retriever, and Cocker Spaniel.

NON-SPORTING DOGS—Those who don't fit into any other category, such as the Bulldog and Lhasa Apso.

TERRIERS—Dogs that hunt by digging into the dirt, looking for foxes, and rabbits. Some terriers are Airedale, Fox Terrier, Miniature Schnauzer.

WORKING DOGS—Dogs who guard and protect their owners. Some herd cattle or pull sleds. Some working dogs are the Collie, Great Dane, and German Shepherd.

SCIENCE:

1. LET'S GO ON A FIELD TRIP.   A Pet Shop is an interesting place to visit, especially at a time when there are many varieties of dogs available. Check with your local pet storekeeper. Notice all of the accessories that go with pets, such as collars, toy bones, flea powder, cushions, and so on. After seeing all of these, the expression "lucky dog" and "it's a dog's life" might take on new meaning.

2. GUEST SPEAKER.   Invite a veterinarian to class to talk about pet care, with a focus upon dogs. What facilities are available in your town or neighborhood for dog care in case of injuries? Chances are that the animal doctor will have some of the following advice:

- Dogs must learn the meaning of No. Say no in a very firm voice, but don't shout at a dog.

- Dogs require daily exercise to stay healthy. Play in the yard with your dog. Walk your dog around the yard on a leash.
- Pet the dog when it responds to its name and comes to you.
- Brush a dog daily using a soft brush, and talk to the dog during this time.
- Dogs do not need regular baths, and they can catch a chill when wet.
- Feed the dog daily with commercial dog food.
- Keep fresh water in a bowl. Remember, your dog cannot ask for a drink.

3. TOY STUFFED DOGS.   Encourage students to bring stuffed animals to class. These toy dogs love to have students read stories to them, and not just stories about dogs. They are excellent listeners. They also dictate stories of their own, very quietly, in their owner's ear and sometimes in the ear of a friend . . . if they like you (and chances are they do).

SOCIAL STUDIES:

1. WORKING DOGS provide a real service in the community, serving as drug enforcers, firehouse dogs, cattle round-up dogs, Seeing Eye dogs, and so on. Many dogs like Duke go to school—obedience school. This is so they will follow directions on command.

2. DOGS GO TO SCHOOL.   Some students are amazed and/or amused by the fact that dogs go to school. Also, dogs are good students because they are so willing to please. Give out dog stickers (or use a dog-shaped stamp) for excellent workers and for those students who are trying, compliments of Duke.

3. WHITE HOUSE DOGS.   Many of the presidents of the United States have had pet dogs. Do some research to find out what type of dog they had and what their names were. One president's wife wrote a best-selling book about her White House dog. Did the presidents have other pets? Explore this topic in the library.

4. LOST AND FOUND.   Read Want Ads in the local newspaper. Are there any pets in the Lost and Found column? Create a want ad for a pet like Duke who got lost. What information would be absolutely required for the ad. Post these want ads on the bulletin board. (Perhaps some students will answer the ad in order to gain more information).

5. THE DAY DAISY RAN AWAY.   Create a story about another pet dog who ran away and got lost. What adventures happen along the way? Be sure to read aloud the *Angus the Dog* series by Marjorie Flack during story time for inspiration.

Dogs aim to please
And remember this
They like to give you
A big, wet kiss.

D

TALK AND TELL: DUKE DOG

1. HI THERE, DUKE! THERE'S A SAYING THAT A DOG IS MAN'S BEST
   FRIEND. WHAT DOES THAT MEAN?

   It means that a dog is a wonderful pet. It likes to be with you and will do anything to please you. When you're happy, your dog's happy. When you're sad, your dog's sad.

2. SHOULD PEOPLE TALK TO THEIR DOG, DUKE?

   Yes. With practice we can begin to understand what you're saying. Dogs can learn what certain words mean, such as: come, go, heel, stay, sit, good dog, and bad dog.

3. DUKE, SHOULD PEOPLE SHOUT AT THEIR DOG?

   Do you like it when people shout at you? It hurts our ears. Our ears are more sensitive than yours.

4. HOW CAN WE TELL IF A DOG IS UPSET, DUKE?

   We bark or growl or whine.

5. WHAT'S THE BEST FOOD FOR A PET DOG?

   A good commercial brand of dog food. Also, a little bit of meat and cheese tastes good. We need to have a bowl of fresh water each day, too.

6. TELL US, DUKE, HOW MANY TIMES A DAY SHOULD A PET DOG BE FED?

   Once or twice a day. Some people feed us twice because we just love to eat. Dogs are hearty eaters.

7. DO YOU LIKE TO EAT BONES?

   It's not a good idea to give me small bones because they could get stuck in my throat or hurt my insides. Very big soup bones are fun for me to gnaw on and this is good for my teeth and gums.

8. DUKE, DO YOU HAVE A DOG LICENSE?

   Yes. Most of the 50 states in our country insist that a dog be licensed.

9. THAT MEANS, THEN, THAT YOU HAVE HAD A VACCINATION?

   Yes, In order to get a license I was given a rabies shot.

10. WHY DO DOGS GET SHOTS?

    For the same reason people do. To keep disease under control and to help us stay healthy. Show me your vaccination spot. (Have children hold up an arm to show the puppet.)

11. DO DOGS ENJOY A LOT OF ATTENTION, DUKE?

    We love attention! Also, we like to be brushed daily and talked to during this special grooming time. You can call me Dukie.

12. CAT'S WASH THEMSELVES WITH THEIR TONGUE. HOW DO YOU WASH
    YOURSELF, DUKIE?

    First, please don't speak to me of cats! Cats and dogs just don't seem to get along together. And, I don't really like to hear about baths either. I know I need a bath once in awhile with a mild soap, but dogs don't enjoy being given a bath and rubbed good and dry with a towel.

13. LET'S CHANGE THE SUBJECT, DUKIE. WHAT WORK DO DOGS DO?

    Some are guide dogs for the blind, such as the German Shepherd or Golden Retriever. Some work on farms to protect sheep or guide farm animals. These dogs have a strong will to please their master. They are smart, and they pay attention.

14. HOW DO DOGS HELP THE POLICE?

Some are trained to search for hidden weapons or drugs. Our very keen sense of smell is helpful to man.

15. IS IT TRUE, DUKIE, THAT DOGS LIKE TO GO TO SCHOOL?

Sure! We're eager to learn all we can and we want to please our master. Some dogs go to training school and some go to obedience school.

16. WHAT DO YOU LEARN IN OBEDIENCE SCHOOL?

We learn to follow directions. Remember, dogs like to please their master but they have to understand what the words mean. Please train us slowly.

17. WHAT SHOULD PEOPLE REMEMBER, DUKIE, WHEN THEY ARE TRYING TO TEACH THEIR PET DOG?

Please be patient with us. We're trying! Also, dogs love to be gently scratched around the head, ears, and neck. Ummmmm-feels so good!

18. DOGS ARE BORN LIVE, AREN'T THEY, DUKIE?

That's right. Dogs are mammals. We're born in a group called a litter. We have brothers and sisters born during the same birth period. We're warm, squirmy, and hungry. Our mother licks us with her tongue—it's nice and scratchy. We stay with our mother, drinking her milk for 6 weeks or so.

19. DO YOU KNOW HOW MANY TYPES OF DOGS THERE ARE, DUKIE?

Lots! There are over 150 different types, or breeds, in the world. There's the cocker spaniel, the terrier, the Irish Setter, the Boxer, the poodle, the Great Dane . . . I could go on and on. Some dogs like to hunt and some like to be a lap dog. Pick the one that suits you, and you'll both be happy.

20. YOU CERTAINLY HAVE BEEN A GOOD FRIEND TODAY! WHAT WOULD YOU LIKE FOR A TREAT, DUKIE?

I think I'd like to have a dog biscuit, or two or three or four or five. Thanks, they're yummy!

THANKS TO YOU FOR THIS TALK AND TELL AT THE BOARDING KENNEL. A KENNEL IS A PLACE THAT WILL "BABYSIT" FOR YOUR DOG WHILE YOU'RE AWAY. TODAY OUR GUEST WAS DUKE THE DOG. THE NEXT ANIMAL GUEST WILL BE A(N)

INTERVIEW INFORMATION

D

What did you learn? Draw it, write it, or web it.

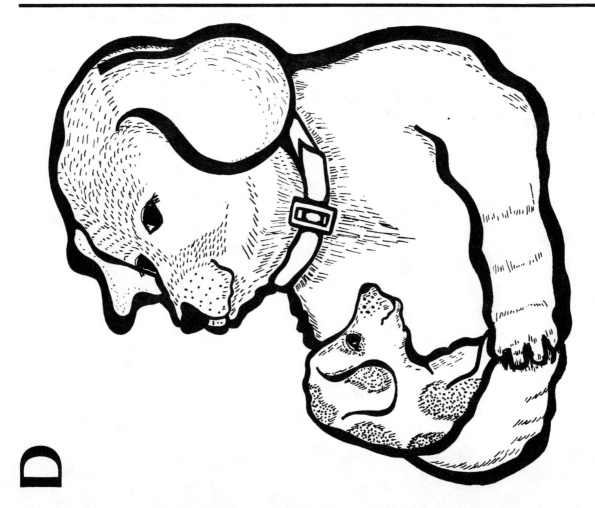

DUKE DOG

Name _____ Date _____

MAKE A DOG WEB

Who belongs in each category? Draw pictures or print the type of dog.

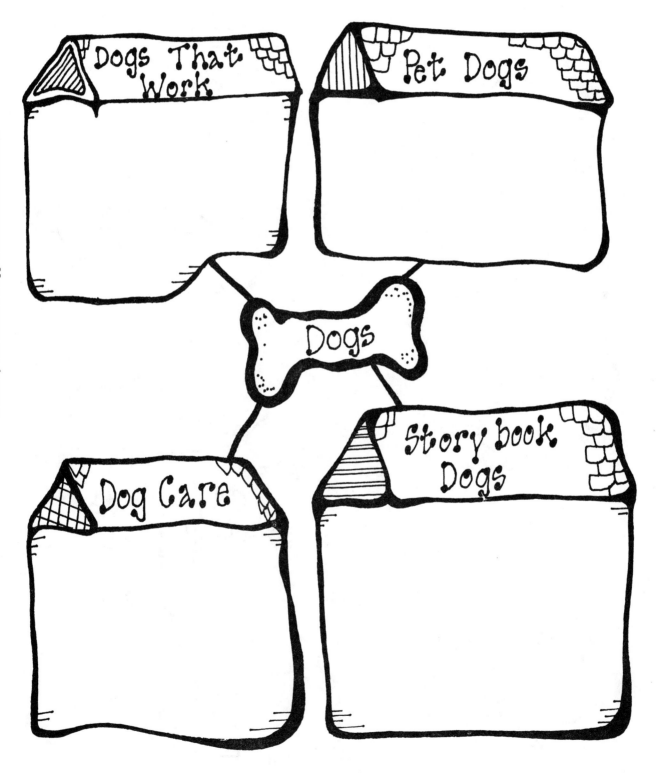

Name _____ Date _____

FOR D'S ONLY

"Anyone whose name begins with the sound of D as in Duke the Dog, please stand up!" said the teacher. These animals all stood up. Oops! Someone does not belong with Duke. Can you find the one? Color those that do belong with the D's.

Name _____ **Date** _____

FAVORITE ANIMAL GRAPH

Ask ten friends or classmates to pick their favorite animal from below. Have students write their name in the box next to their choice, starting from left to right. Which animal is the favorite? Which is the least favorite? Did any get equal votes?

								total
A								
B								
C								
D								

Name _____ Date _____

STORY TRACKING

Track your way through a good dog story. Write or draw on the paws. Share your information. Make a BIG DOG PAW BOOK to help keep track of your story tracking.

TITLE _____

AUTHOR _____

ILLUSTRATOR _____

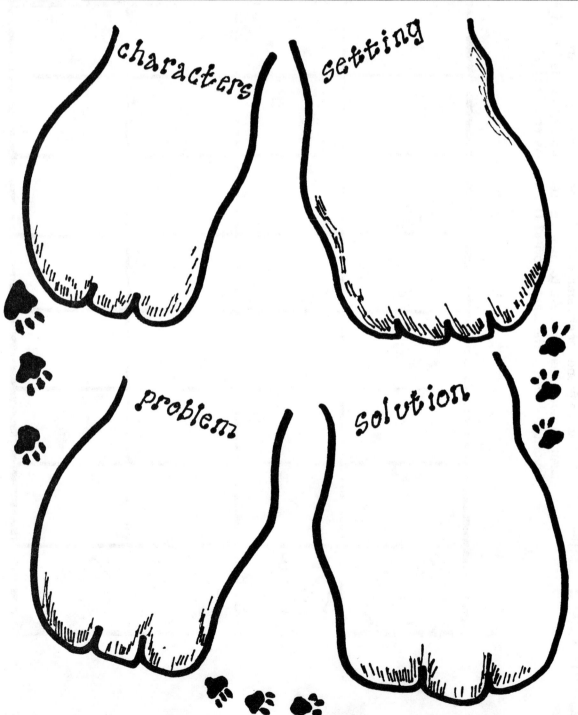

Name ______________________________ Date ________________________

DUKE THE DOG WANTS DINNER

Before Duke can have his dinner, he has to match the dog bones on the left to the dog bone answers on the right. The first one is done to get you started. Duke goes to school, too, and he says, "Don't rush! Take your time."

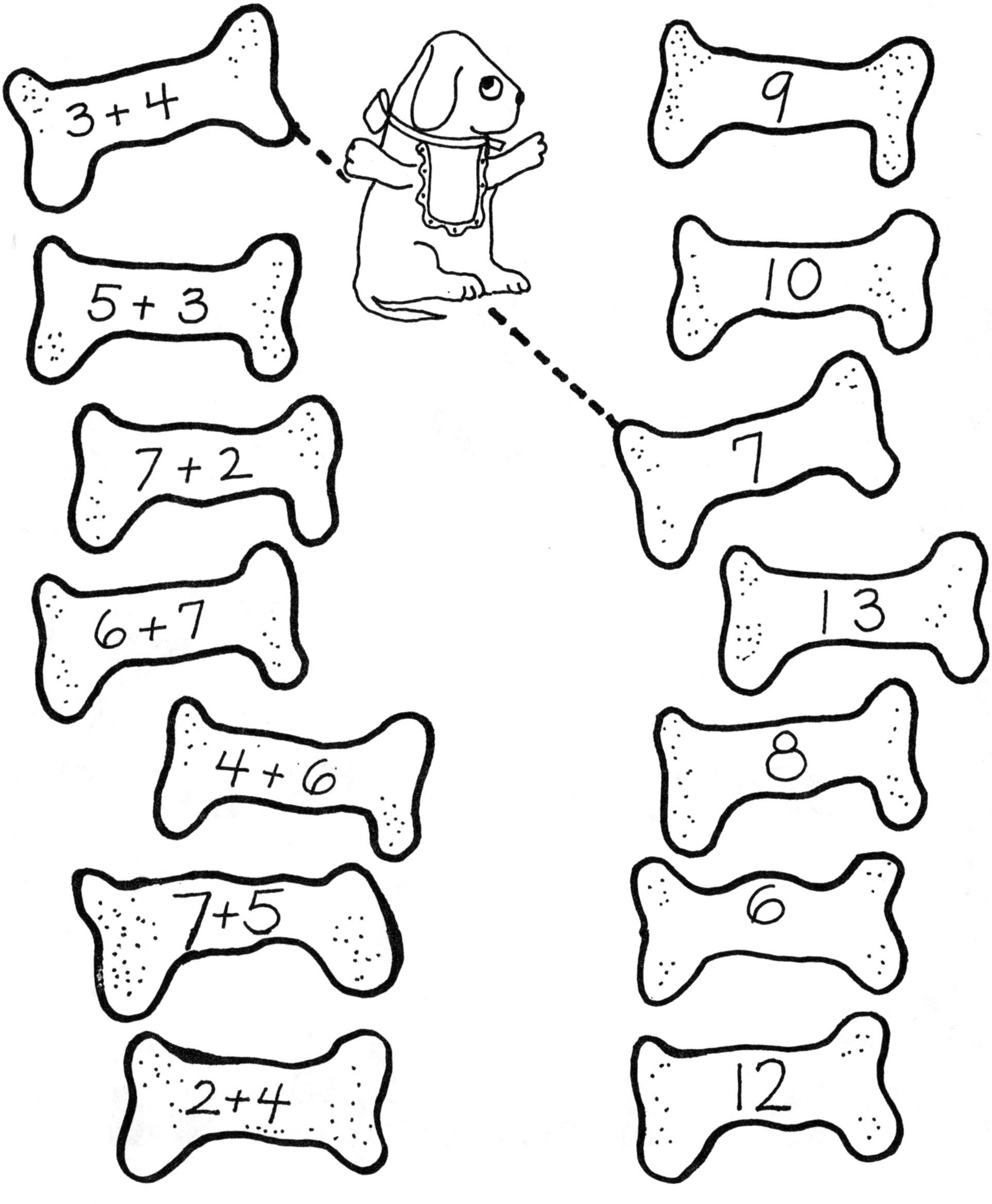
3+4
5+3
7+2
6+7
4+6
7+5
2+4
9
10
7
13
8
6
12

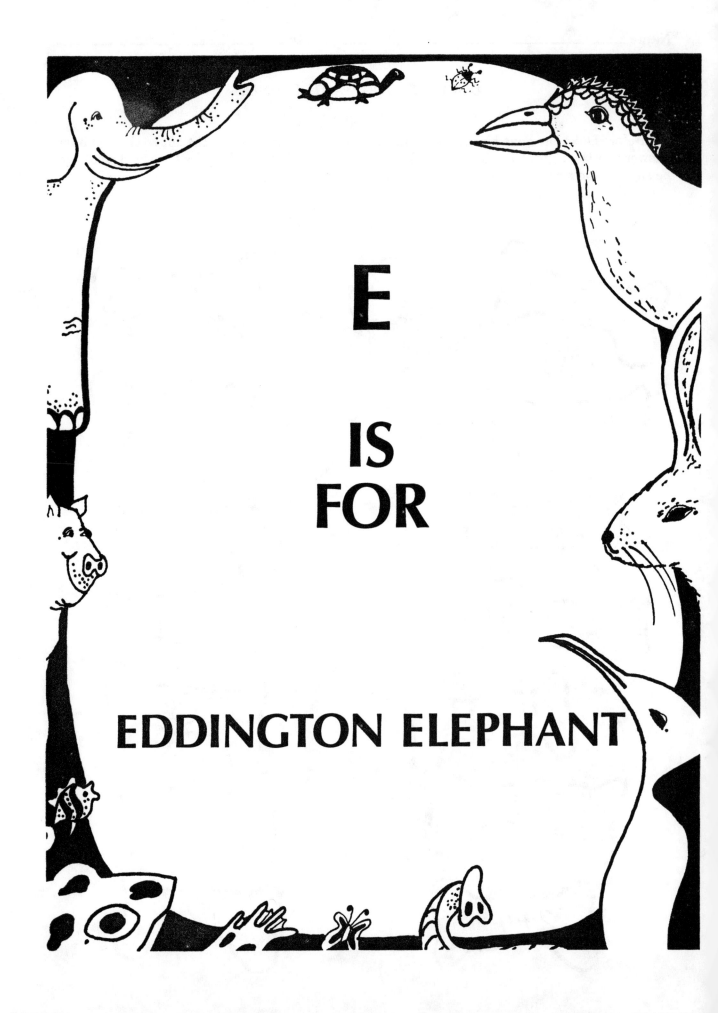

E

IS

FOR

EDDINGTON ELEPHANT

E IS FOR EDDINGTON ELEPHANT

BACKGROUND INFORMATION ABOUT ELEPHANTS: There are basically two types of elephants—the African and the Indian elephant, and they are named after the countries where they are found in the wild. How can we tell them apart? By their ears, color, and tusks. The African elephant's ears are large and flappy, whereas the Indian elephant's ears are smaller and closer to the body. Also, African elephant tusks are larger and their skin is of a darker gray color than the Indian elephant. Perhaps the most amazing and outstanding feature of the elephant is its trunk, which is really a long, fleshy upper lip. This flexible snout contains over 40,000 muscles and the animal uses it as a hand, a horn, and as a nose. Elephants can communicate through their nose by trumpeting.

READING/LANGUAGE ARTS:

1. EDDINGTON'S ENORMOUS VOCABULARY DEVELOPMENT. Somehow big doesn't really describe the elephant. Introduce words that mean large, such as tremendous, enormous, gigantic, huge. Use these words in a sentence. Write them on the chalkboard and make them take up a lot of space.

2. EXAGGERATE WITH EDDINGTON. Have students take turns finishing a make-believe, exaggerated sentence. Start with: "The tremendous, enormous, gigantic, elephant sneezed a great big sneeze and _____." Tell what happened. (Examples: the tree fell over or the moon was pushed halfway across the sky.)

3. WHAT ELSE IS GIGANTIC? There are other things in nature that are very, very big. Can we think of some? There are man-made things that are huge. Can we name some? (See the reproducible Activity Pages.)

4. "THAT GIGANTIC ELEPHANT OF A . . .". Look at really big things in our surroundings and incorporate them into our language. For example, refer to the "gigantic elephant of a school bus" or the "gigantic elephant of a swing set." What else can we find?

MATH:

1. BIG AND LITTLE EDDINGTONS. Have students help Eddington find items in the room that are either big or little.

- Sort the blocks or books in the room by big and little.
- Locate and sort items from nature that are big or little (rock/pebble).
- Give the students an item from nature (stone, twig, leaf) and have them find one that is bigger and one that is smaller.

2. HOW MUCH IS A GALLON? An elephant will walk for miles and miles to drink at least thirty gallons of water daily. Fill up a gallon container so that students

can see how much is in one gallon. Then, pour the water into quart containers to find out how many quarts are in a gallon. In celebration of a gallon, mix up a gallon of lemonade and serve it for an Eddington Gallon Treat. This would go well while listening to a good *Barbar the Elephant* story by deBrunhoff.

SCIENCE:

1. BAGGY EDDINGTON E. Elephants are known for their baggy skin. Their skin sags because they do not have a layer of fat cells underneath it. That's why elephants get cold easily when the temperature is below freezing.

For a weather chart, use a big shape in the form of Eddington E. From construction paper, make weather clothing such as boots, umbrella, scarf, hat, four mittens (maybe five—one for the snout), sun, sun blocker container, cloud shapes, and so on. Keep track of the weather for the month.

2. KISSIN' COUSINS. Ask students to identify their cousins. Do cousins always resemble one another? Elephants have a cousin called the *hyrax*. A hyrax is tiny and resembles a guinea pig. How do scientists determine relationships between animals? They study body parts, teeth, hoofs, and so on. Both the elephant and the hyrax have flattened nails on their feet, their incisor teeth grow to be large, and when the hyrax opens its mouth, tiny tusks can be seen. The leg bones in these two animals are very similar. For more information about animal cousins, read *Animals Have Cousins Too* by Geraldine Marshall Gurfreund (NY: Franklin Watts, 1990).

3. HAVING A BABY. When a female person (mom) becomes pregnant, it usually takes nine months, or one whole school year, for the baby to form and to be born. Eddington Elephant takes about 22 months, or almost two whole years. Have students figure out their age at their next birthday and add two. Where do the students predict that they will be at that time—mainly at what grade level in school? That's how old they will be when Eddington gives birth. Students will be able to see that this is a long time, indeed.

4. DOING THE ELEPHANT WALK. An elephant walks by extending its two left legs (front and back) simultaneously, and then its two right legs. It is a ride that swings from side to side. Elephants can walk for miles and miles just to get to water. Have students get down on all fours and pick up their left hand and left foot at the same time, then their right hand and right foot, and so on. What kind of music would go well with this rocking movement?

5. NO JUMPING! Elephants cannot jump. They can be trained to do many tricks in circus acts, but one thing Eddington cannot do is jump. He likes to roll over and over in the mud. The mud provides a protective coating from flies and mosquitoes. Students can roll over and back and forth. What kind of music would go well with this rolling motion?

6. THE ELEPHANT ROCK AND ROLL KING. First rock (elephant walk) and then roll (on the floor). This is how Eddington might dance. But remember, no jumping!

SOCIAL STUDIES:

1. MAP SKILLS. Help Eddington locate Africa and India on a globe or map so he can find his way home. How far are you from these places?

2. EDDINGTON IS ENDANGERED.   Poachers in Africa are making life difficult for elephants. They kill them for their ivory tusks, and sell the ivory so that jewelry, for example, can be made from it. Begin an "Endangered Species List" if you have not already done so. Read about how you can help. Write to a world leader and address the letter to the United Nations, United Nations Plaza, New York, New York 10017.

3. AN ELEPHANT IS VERY POLITE.   It has been said that an elephant will go out of its way NOT to step on a tiny animal as it makes its way across the plains of Africa. Elephants are ladies and gentlemen. Let's set up some new rules so that we can begin to act in a polite manner toward our friends.

The elephant's trunk
Can sniff and spray.
It helps to bat
The flies away.

E

TALK AND TELL: EDDINGTON ELEPHANT

1. HI EDDINGTON! IS IT TRUE THAT YOU ARE THE BIGGEST OF ALL OF THE ANIMALS THAT HAVE FOUR LEGS?

    Yes, I'm HUGE! And I'm the strongest animal, too!

2. HOW MANY KINDS OF ELEPHANTS ARE THERE?

    Two kinds—the African elephant and the Asian elephant.

3. HOW CAN WE TELL YOU APART?

    I can give you three hints. Are you listening? African elephants ears are big—twice the size of the Indian elephant. Also, the African elephant is a darker gray color and has larger tusks. Remember my hints: Look at the ears, color, and tusks.

4. THAT'S HELPFUL! MAY I ASK HOW MUCH YOU WEIGH, EDDINGTON?

    About the same as a great big truck (12,000 lb).

5. WOW! THAT'S HEAVY! AND HOW TALL ARE YOU, EDDINGTON?

    I'm 10 ft tall but some elephants are 12 ft tall. Take four yardsticks and put them end to end. That's how tall I am.

6. YOUR SKIN LOOKS LOOSE AND BAGGY. IS IT COMFORTABLE?

    Sometimes insects get inside the folds of my thick skin and make me feel itchy. The reason my skin is baggy is because I don't have a layer of fat cells underneath. That's why I get cold easily when it gets below freezing. I don't like cold weather.

7. I SUPPOSE EVERYONE ASKS YOU ABOUT YOUR BIG TRUNK?

    Yes. It has many muscles (over 40,000) and I use it as a hand and as a nose. When I'm born it just hangs there and it takes me about one year to be able to use it.

8. TELL US MORE ABOUT YOUR AMAZING TRUNK, EDDINGTON.

    It's really a long, fleshy upper lip. I can squeal and scream through it. I use it to pick up things to eat or to throw. I smell with the end of it. I'm versatile.

9. WHAT DOES VERSATILE MEAN?

    Versatile means many uses for the same thing. I use my trunk in many, many ways. I can fill it with a lot of water and then squirt it into my mouth. Your hands are versatile, because you can do many things with them.

10. IS IT FUN TO SQUIRT WATER WITH YOUR TRUNK?

    Oh, sure! It makes lots of noise. When I'm thirsty I need about 25 squirts of water before I'm happy again. Squirt, squirt, squirt. . . . I say that 25 times. Can you?

11. EDDINGTON, HOW OFTEN DO YOU DRINK WATER?

    Every day! Do you know what a quart container of milk or juice looks like? If you filled one of those up over 100 times, that's how much water I drink each day. Water is good for you. I'll walk miles and miles a day just to get that delicious water. Sometimes I walk all day.

12. DO YOU JUST GO OUT IN SEARCH OF WATER OR DO YOU KNOW WHERE YOU'RE GOING?

    Glad you asked. That's where my versatile trunk comes in. With the end of my trunk (nostrils) I can smell or sense water under the ground.

13. BUT, EDDINGTON, HOW DO YOU GET TO IT IF IT'S UNDER THE GROUND?

    I dig and dig and dig with my great big ivory tusks.

14. DO YOU HAVE TEETH?

    My tusks are really long, long teeth. My teeth weigh a lot more than you do—

they weight over 200 lb. I use them as tools to dig for water and salt. I can also use them like a club if I need to defend myself.

15. TELL ME, EDDINGTON, WHAT HAPPENS IF YOU BREAK A TUSK?

They can grow back. People like to remove my ivory tusks and make carvings on them. They use them for ornaments or decorations. But they've gone too far. Now we need to be protected from these people. They're called *poachers*.

16. I SAW A PICTURE OF SOMEONE RIDING ON AN ELEPHANT'S BACK. DO YOU LIKE THAT?

It's OK with me but people sometimes get seasick because I rock from side to side. I walk with my two left legs and then my two right legs and sway back and forth! Try doing that during play time.

17. ARE YOU BORN LIVE OR HATCHED FROM AN EGG?

I'm born live and I weigh as much as a big man! (Approximately 200 lb). When I walk, I can fit right underneath my mother for the first year.

18. DO ELEPHANTS MAKE GOOD MOTHERS?

YES! Elephants LOVE their babies! I needed my mother for food, and protection and she taught me how to drink. At first I could only make bubbles with my trunk. Elephant mothers whack their baby calf with their big trunk if the baby gets too far out of hand—usually she nudges you first as a warning. If you don't obey—WHACK!

19. EDDINGTON, IS IT TRUE THAT AN ELEPHANT NEVER FORGETS?

Well, we do seem to have a good memory. Do you?

20. SOME THINGS ARE EASY TO REMEMBER AND SOME THINGS ARE HARDER, BUT WE KEEP TRYING. TELL ME, IS THERE ANYTHING YOU CAN'T DO?

There is one thing. Elephants can't jump—not even one little bit! But you can, so have fun jumping!

THANK YOU, EDDINGTON, FOR THIS TALK-AND-TELL TIME RIGHT HERE IN AFRICA. TODAY OUR GUEST WAS A HUGE ELEPHANT. TUNE IN NEXT TIME WHEN WE WILL BE INTERVIEWING A(N) _____.
UNTIL THEN, HAPPY JUMPING!

INTERVIEW
INFORMATION

What did you learn? Draw it, write it, or web it.

E

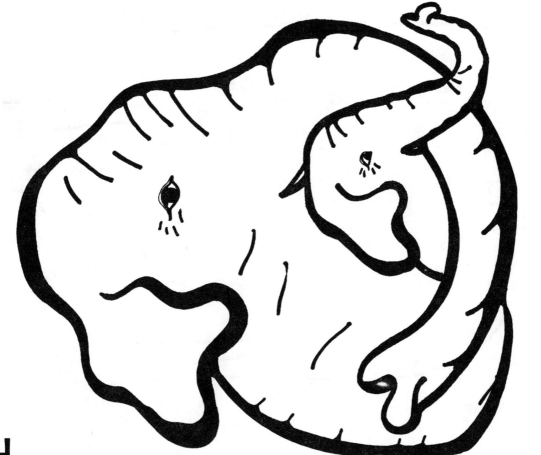

EDDINGTON ELEPHANT

Name —————————— Date ——————————

AS BIG AS AN ELEPHANT

Find items in magazines that are "as big as an elephant or as little as a mouse."
Cut them out and past them in the spaces provided below.

Little

Big

ELEPHANT PEANUT COOKIE TREAT RECIPE

This is Eddington Elephant's favorite peanut treat. Happy measuring!

INGREDIENTS:

1 cup sugar
½ cup brown sugar
2 eggs
½ cup peanut butter
1½ cups flour

2 teaspoons baking powder
1 teaspoon vanilla
1 cup salted nuts (you can count them)

THIS IS WHAT EDDINGTON ELEPHANT DOES:

1. Put the sugar, brown sugar, eggs, and peanut butter together in a bowl. Mix well.
2. Stir in the baking powder.
3. Stir in the flour.
4. Stir in the vanilla.
5. Add the nuts. (Eddington always counts them.)
6. Spread the cookie batter into a greased 9-inch square baking pan.
7. Bake for 30 minutes at 350°F. (or until dough pulls away from side of the pan).
8. Cool. Cut into small squares. Yummy!

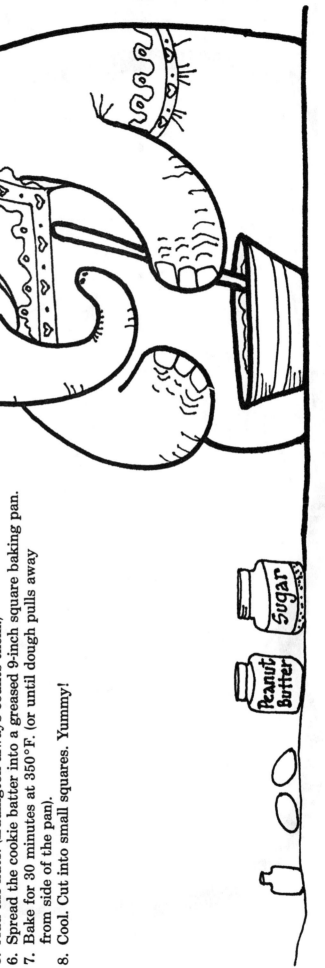

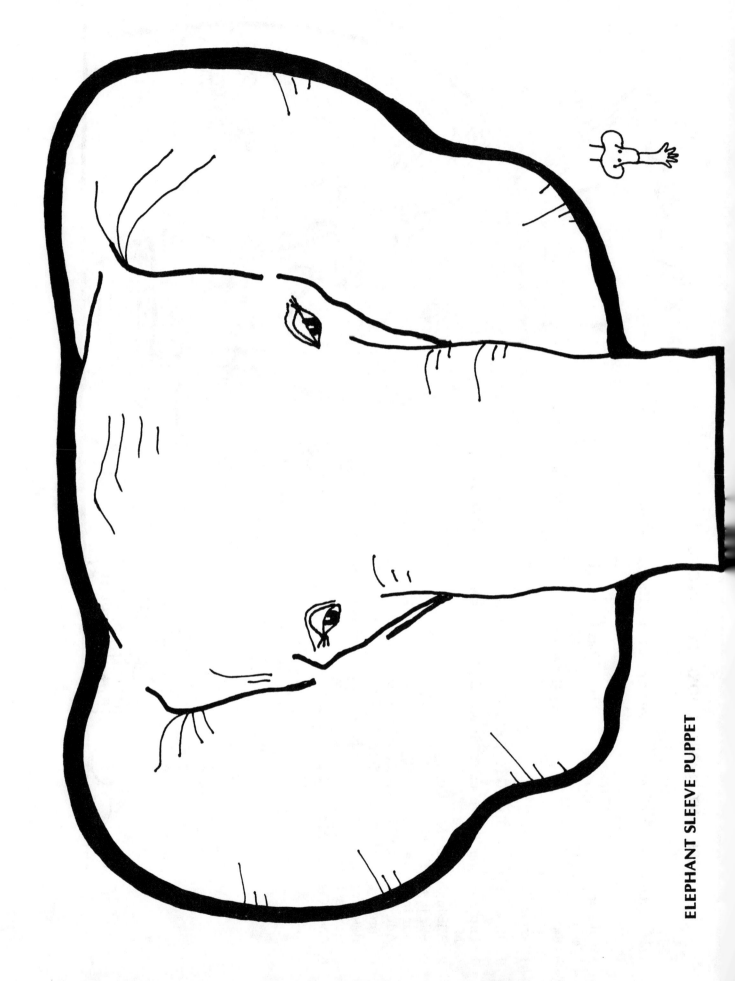

ELEPHANT SLEEVE PUPPET

Name ———————————————— Date ————————————————

AN ELEPHANT NEVER FORGETS

Make a graph on the elephant foot. Select three animals and draw one in each toenail at the bottom. Then ask at least ten people (one at a time) to name their favorite of the three. "Tell it to the elephant" by coloring the space above that toenail.

RESULTS: The favorite of the three is _____.
It got _____ votes.
What is the least favorite? How many votes did it receive?

ELEPHANTS AND OTHER GIANTS

How many giants can you find for each category? List them or draw them in the space below. Read one book for each category.

Giant Animals	Nature Giants
Storybook Giants	**Man-made Giants**

F
IS
FOR

FRANCINE FROG

F IS FOR FRANCINE FROG

BACKGROUND INFORMATION ABOUT FROGS: The adult female frog lays hundreds to thousands of eggs at one time. They look like little black dots in a mass of glue. The glue helps to protect the eggs. Within a week, the eggs begin to hatch and tadpoles emerge—a black dot with a tail. Within two months the tadpole has lungs and a pair of back legs. By $2\frac{1}{2}$ months it has front legs. Frogs belong to a class of animals called *amphibians.* Most amphibians spend the beginning of life in the water, swimming and breathing through gills just like fish. Gradually, as they grow lungs, they can breathe air and live on land.

READING/LANGUAGE ARTS:

1. FRANCINE'S VOCABULARY DEVELOPMENT:

metamorphosis–change from one stage of development to another
amphibians   –animals who begin life in water, and end up on land

Print these words on a big frog shape and learn to say them.

2. "R-R-R-IBBIT, R-R-R-IBBIT."   Male frogs make croaking sounds. Can we think of other animal sounds and also sounds that people make? Some examples are:

Animal	People
meow	ha-ha-ha
woof, woof	boo, hoo
hiss	hum-m-m
buzz-z-z	la-la-la-la

3. FRIENDSHIP.   Bring in storybooks by Arnold Lobel from the *Frog and Toad* series. What characteristics make it possible for these two to be friends? What is necessary to be a good friend? Make a FRIENDSHIP CHART of storybook friends. What will the main topics be? (Examples: Names of Storybook Friends, Comfortable Feeling Words, What the Friends Do, and so on). *Amos and Boris* by William Steig is an excellent read-aloud story about a special friendship between a mouse and a whale. *Charlotte's Web* by E. B. White has many examples of friendship. Have students write about their own special friends.

4. COMPARE FROGS AND TOADS.   Make comparison charts of real frogs and toads by finding information books about these two amphibians.

MATH:

1. MEASURING AND MOVEMENT WITH FRANCINE.   Frogs measure in length from 1 inch to 12 inches. Introduce the ruler, or reinforce the use of the ruler.

Point to the inch marks and count from one through twelve. Make a set of flashcards on Francine Frog shapes with inch lines (1 inch, 2 inches, 3 inches and so on, up to twelve inches). Mix them together and have children line them up from the smallest to longest line. Measure them with a ruler for a self-check.

2. FRANCINE THE JUMPING FROG. A frog can jump a distance of a yardstick (3 feet). Put the yardstick flat on the floor or ground, and have students line up along side of it. Measure how far each student can jump. Keep practicing.

SCIENCE:

1. FRANCINE IS NOT WATERPROOF. Boys and girls have waterproof skin, but Francine doesn't. The frog can soak in water through its skin and doesn't have to get a drink of water. People have waterproof clothing to protect their skin from weather. Some use waterproof clothing in their work.

- Let's name some waterproof clothing.
  ski jackets, gloves, hats, pants, snowsuits, parkas, boots, and so on
- Special jobs require special waterproof clothing.
  Firefighter, Astronaut, Deep sea diver

2. FRANCINE HAS EYES ON THE TOP OF HER HEAD. Frogs can peek out of the water like a submarine without too much risk of being seen. This is a protection for the frog. Begin an awareness of where animal eyes are located on their head (such as front, side, top).

3. OUR WONDERFUL EYES. Have students keep their head still and move their eyes to the left and slowly to the right, taking into account all that they can see. Then, have them cover up one eye and look with the other eye. Now, they have to move their head in order to see what they saw before, because with our two eyes we have a wide field of vision. Begin an "Eye Appreciation Awareness" and find out what we can do to keep our eyes healthy.

4. FRANCINE'S EYES HELP HER TO SWALLOW. Francine is an insect eater. She has a sticky tongue and can just reach out with it and catch insects that are flying by. When Francine swallows the insect, those bulgy eyes come in handy. As the frog swallows, the eyes blink and the eyeballs lower and help push the food down the throat into the stomach!

Create a story where an insect says to Francine Frog, "My! What big eyes you have!" and where she replies, "The better to eat you with, my dear." Let's share our stories by reading them aloud.

5. INVENT ANIMAL GLASSES. Point out that eyeglasses for people are designed so that the glasses can hook over the ears. Before that, people wore them pinched on their nose. Invent a new type of eyeglass design for people. Also, invent glasses for animals. What would they link onto? Be on the lookout for eye and ear placement on animals.

SOCIAL STUDIES:

1. WATER SAFETY TIPS FROM FRANCINE. Frogs are excellent swimmers. The frog kick is used by people to help propel them through water. Also, we use rubber flippers that resemble frog feet (webbed toes). While we are at it, let's review some water

safety tips with Francine. These can be put on a huge frog shape and called "Francine's Water Rules." Here are some starters:

Always swim with a partner.
Don't jump into a lake or river.
Ask permission to use a swimming pool.

2. FRANCINE IS A PROBLEM SOLVER.   Have children work on this problem, make a decision, and tell why they make their choice. Problem: "A frog can jump high. An elephant cannot jump. Which would you rather be, an elephant or a frog? Why?" Make a chart and record children's responses individually. Example:

I WOULD RATHER BE:

EDDINGTON ELEPHANT

1. They have a trunk. (Heidi)
2. They are big. (Jordan)
3. They have their own squirt gun. (BJ)

FRANCINE FROG

1. I like to swim. (Jacob)
2. They play in the mud. (Brad)
3. They jump high. (Stacey)

I need water, I need air.
If it doesn't rain, I don't care.

I dig in the earth, and jump right in,
And soak up water through my skin!

F

TALK AND TELL: FRANCINE FROG

1. HI THERE, FRANCINE FROG! WE HAVE A QUESTION FOR YOU. ARE YOU HATCHED FROM AN EGG OR ARE YOU BORN LIVE?

   I was hatched from an egg and I was a tadpole.
2. WHAT DOES A TADPOLE LOOK LIKE?

   It looks like a big black dot with a tail. It's always moving in the water. Then, it grows bigger and bigger and changes into a frog. A frog can breathe through its lungs. You breathe through your lungs too. I'll count to 3, and you take a DEEP breath. OK? Ready? 1-2-3. Let out the air. Good! (Try it again.)
3. THAT'S QUITE A CHANGE FROM EGG TO TADPOLE TO FROG, ISN'T IT?

   Yes. It's called *metamorphosis*. That's a big word. I'll say it again bit by bit, and you repeat it after me. OK? Ready? MET (met) UH (uh) MOR (mor) PHO (pho) SIS (sis). MET-A-MOR-PHO-SIS. (Metamorphosis.) GOOD! Now I'll tell you what MET-A-MOR-PHO-SIS means. Are you all listening? (In a hushed voiced say) It means a change in the way you look and the way you do things. I went from water to land, so I had to change.
4. FRANCINE, DID YOUR MOTHER LAY ONE EGG OR TWO?

   One egg or two? NO! Not one or two or even 10, 20, 30, 40 or 50! An adult female frog may lay from 100 to 1,000 eggs. That's a lot of eggs! Only a few of us make it from tadpoles to frogs.
5. WHY DO ONLY A FEW TADPOLES BECOME FROGS, FRANCINE?

   Well, the eggs get eaten by fish, birds, or insects. It's nature's way.
6. HOW BIG ARE YOU, FRANCINE?

   I'm 6 inches long. Look at your ruler, and cover half of it up. I'm as big as what's left. Frogs can be 1 inch long, 2 inches, 3 inches, 4 inches, all the way up to 12 inches. Can you measure all of those inches on a ruler?
7. YES WE WILL. FRANCINE, ONCE YOU GO THROUGH YOUR METAMORPHOSIS (THERE's THAT BI-I-I-G WORD AGAIN. LET ME SAY IT SLOWLY BIT BY BIT AND THEN YOU SAY IT AFTER ME. OK? READY? "MET (met) A (a) MOR (mor) PHO (pho) SIS (sis)." GOOD! ONCE YOU GO THROUGH THAT METAMORPHOSIS, FROM EGG TO TADPOLE TO FROG, DO YOU EVER GO BACK AND LIVE IN THE WATER AGAIN?

   I must stay *near* the water because I'm an amphibian.
8. THAT'S ANOTHER BIG WORD!!! FOR A LITTLE FROG, FRANCINE, YOU HAVE LOTS OF BIG WORDS! WHAT IS AN AMPHIBIAN? (am-FIB -e-an).

   An *amphibian* is an animal that begins its life in water and then grows lungs for breathing air (remember when we took a deep breath 1-2-3?). Then with lungs, we can live on land.
9. WHY DO YOU SAY YOU MUST STAY NEAR WATER, FRANCINE?

   An amphibian has to have moist skin at all times, it helps us to breathe. We don't drink water through our mouth like you do—we soak it in through our skin! That's right, we soak up water like a sponge. Your skin is waterproof but mine isn't.
10. DO YOU LIKE TO SWIM, LITTLE SPONGE?

    I'm an excellent swimmer with my strong back legs and feet. My feet are webbed just like duck feet. They make good paddles in the water.
11. TELL US, FRANCINE, WHAT DO YOU LIKE TO EAT?

    I like mosquitoes, flies, snails, and squishy worms too. They're soooo delicious and juicy!

12. UGH! CAN YOU MAKE NOISES, FRANCINE?

    I can make a sound way down in my throat. It's called croaking. Listen—
"R-r-r-r ibbit!" Now you try it. "R-r-r-r ibbit!" Good for you!

13. CAN YOU HEAR WELL?

    Quite well. I don't have ears like you do but I have special skin (membranes)
on the side of my head that picks up sound waves.

14. FRANCINE, HAS ANYONE EVER TOLD YOU THAT YOU LOOK LIKE A
    TOAD?

    Yes, we're close relatives. But frogs have smoother skin than toads. Also our
back legs are longer, so we're good at jumping high and far. I cam jump 3 feet! Three
feet is as long as a yardstick! Do you have a yardstick so that you can put it on the floor
to see how far I can jump?

15. WE CAN TRY THAT LATER. BY JUST LOOKING, THEN, WE SHOULD BE
    ABLE TO TELL FROGS FROM TOADS, RIGHT?

    Well . . . you will have difficulty because there are so many, many (more than
2,000) different kinds of frogs and toads. Get a picture book of frogs and toads and you
will see what I mean.

16. DO YOU EVER GET SCARED WHEN YOU'RE AWAY FROM WATER,
    FRANCINE?

    No. Remember, my skin is not waterproof like yours. I soak up water through
my skin. So, I can get water from rain, dew drops, and even if I just dig down into the
earth, I can soak up water from the soil.

17. THAT'S AMAZING! HOW DO YOU SPEND THE WINTER, FRANCINE?

    I hibernate.

18. WE'VE HEARD THAT WORD, FRANCINE. WHAT IS HIBERNATE?

    Remember when Brandi Bear said that bears sleep all winter? Well, bears hi-
bernate (or go into a deep sleep) for the winter and so do some frogs. Frogs dig to the
bottom of the pond where the squishy mud is nice and warm, and we sleep there through
the winter. Winter is just too cold for frogs, we'd never make it.

19. WOW! FRANCINE, ARE YOU MAGIC? YOU'VE JUST CHANGED FROM A
    PLAIN GREEN FROG TO A FROG WITH BROWN AND GREEN SPOTS. HOW
    DO YOU DO THAT?

    The amount of sunlight and moisture changes my skin color. When I change
colors, it makes it harder to catch me!

20. ONE LAST QUESTION—IS THERE ANYTHING SPECIAL THAT YOU WANT
    US TO KNOW ABOUT YOU, FRANCINE?

    Yes, Frogs only eat live things. If I'm in a cage don't throw me any dead flies
or insects—I'll ignore them. I can't see too well and I am attracted by the movement of
an insect. So remember, I like live, fresh insects that move! Thank you.

    WELL, THANK YOU FOR A FINE INTERVIEW RIGHT HERE AT THE
BEAUTIFUL POND IN THE WOODS. TODAY OUR GUEST WAS FRANCINE THE
FROG WHO CHANGED COLORS LIKE A MAGICIAN RIGHT BEFORE OUR
EYES! FROGS ARE SMALL BUT THEY USE BIG WORDS. CAN WE REMEMBER
TWO OF THEM? (METAMORPHOSIS AND AMPHIBIAN). TUNE IN NEXT TIME
WHEN WE WILL BE INTERVIEWING A(N)

INTERVIEW INFORMATION

What did you learn? Draw it, write it, or web it.

F

FRANCINE FROG

THE MEASUREMENT FROG

Use your ruler to measure these lines. Put the number of inches in each square.
Remember to put the left edge of the ruler by the first dot.
Which line is longest? Which line is shortest?

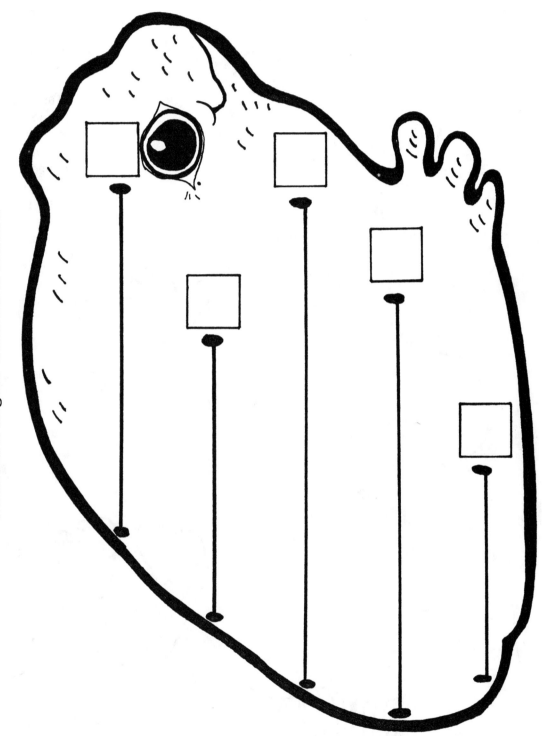

Name _____ Date _____

THE STORYBOOK FROG

The frog is in love,
He wants a kiss.
What does he promise
This little miss?

Talk, listen, think,
and then write and draw
your story map or idea
on the other side of
this sheet.
Use your crayons to
color these pictures to
show us what these two
story characters look
like.

OOPS! FRANCINE SPILLED THE WATER

Some items absorb, or soak up, liquid. Will these three items soak up Francine's water? If yes, circle them and color them. In the bottom square, draw one more thing that could be used to help Francine clean up. Francine says, "Thanks!"

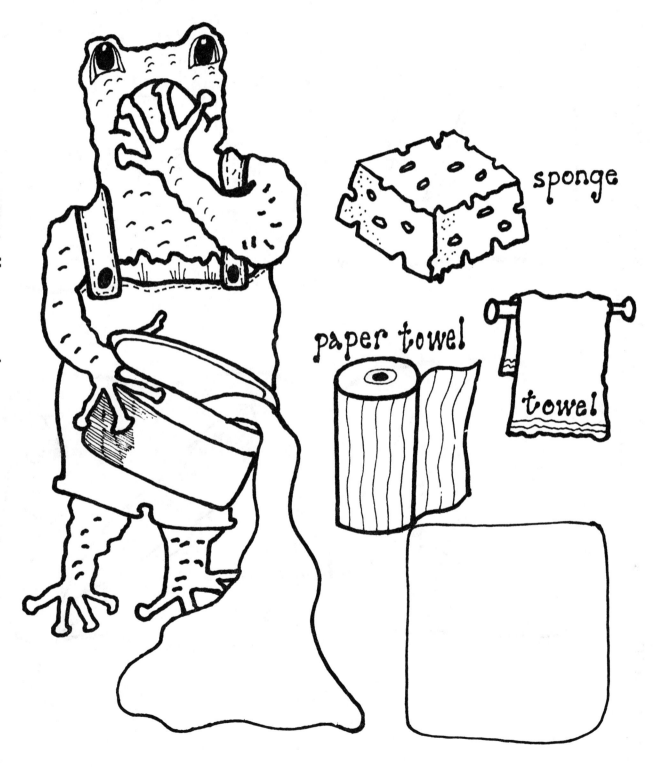

sponge

paper towel

towel

FROG PHOTO ALBUM

Cut out these photos. Paste them in a green-colored photo album. Use your crayons to change them from black-and-white to color prints. Make a nice album cover.

1. jelly-covered egg

2. tadpole

3. 8 weeks old

4. It's Me frog

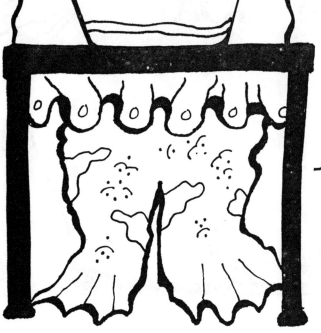

MRS. FROG'S MUD MIX

Mrs. Frog likes to make Mud Mix (salt dough) so that she can use it to form letters and words. Here is her recipe:

INGREDIENTS:

3 cups flour
2 cups salt
1 cup water
1 tsp. salad oil (if needed)

PROCEDURE:

1. Mix together the flour and salt.
2. Add the water.
3. If the mixture is too dry, add the salad oil.
4. Use the gooey mud-like mixture to roll out letters and to make words.
5. When finished, store the mud mix in a plastic bag. It will keep for two weeks.

frog

G
IS
FOR

GOLDIE GOAT

G IS FOR GOLDIE GOAT

BACKGROUND INFORMATION ABOUT GOATS: The goat was one of the first animals domesticated by man, possibly even before the dog. Goats are friendly and like people. The adult male is called a buck, the female is a doe, and the baby is a kid. They are affectionately called *nannies* and *billies*. They're social animals, and are leapers, jumpers, and climbers. Perhaps the finest contribution from the goat is the goat hair. There is cashmere, from the fluffy undercoat of the Kashmir goats of India, Angora which is used in soft blankets and sweaters, and mohair, the outer hair that is stiff and bristly and used in rugs, upholstery, artificial furs, and even wigs.

READING/LANGUAGE ARTS:

1. GOLDIE'S GOAT TALK.   Introduce the following sayings that use the word goat and try to use them today:

- Scapegoat
  –A name given to an innocent person who is blamed and punished for something he or she didn't do to please someone else. Be on the lookout for scapegoats in fairytales. We can start with Cinderella.
- "Don't play the goat"
  –An English expression meaning don't act so silly.
- "Don't let it get your goat"–Don't let someone or something annoy you.

2. GOLDIE'S A DOMESTIC ANIMAL.   Add Goldie to your list of domestic animals because she was domesticated 12 million years ago. Some say that goats were domesticated before dogs. Dogs may be man's best friend, but perhaps goats were man's *first* friend.

Have students write a dialogue between a goat and a dog about being a friend to people. Why does Goldie Goat live outdoors? Why does Duke Dog live indoors? Maybe it's because goats are gulpers—they eat everything in sight.

3. NANNY GOATS AND BILLY GOATS.   These are nicknames for goats. Discuss nicknames and have students (if they prefer) tell what their nicknames are. Usually it is an affectionate name. Are there other ABC animals that have nicknames? Can we invent some? For vocabulary development, the male goat is called a buck, the female is a doe, and the offspring are bucklings, doelings, or kids.

4. THE THREE BILLIE GOATS GRUFF.   Reenact this story using props (see the reproducible Activity Pages for finger puppets and the three-headed troll).

5. GIRAFFES AND GOATS SHARE THE LETTER G.   There are two sounds to the letter g—one is soft and belongs to the giraffe, and the other is the hard sound and belongs to the goat. Make two envelopes and put a picture of a giraffe on one and a goat on the other. Cut out many pictures of items that begin with the letter g. Then classify

them in the proper envelope. Does the item belong to the giraffe or to the goat? Keep looking for more pictures and for words too.

MATH:

    1. GOLDIE HAS FOUR STOMACHS. As with the cow, the goat has four stomach compartments. All food goes to compartment number one and is returned to the mouth as cud for more chewing. Then it goes through the other three compartments for digestion. So, Goldie has 1-2-3-4 stomachs. Some students may need work with the concept of four. Using manipulatives, have them classify items by fours.
    2. ADDING WITH STOMACH COMPARTMENTS. Work with missing addends and stomach compartments. Draw a shape on the board and divide it so that there are four sections, or stomachs. If there is hay in only one stomach, how many stomachs don't have any?

$$1 + \underline{\hspace{2cm}} = 4$$

This can be continued for the following: $2 + \underline{\hspace{2cm}} = 4$, $3 + \underline{\hspace{2cm}} = 4$
$4 + \underline{\hspace{2cm}} = 4$ and $0 + \underline{\hspace{2cm}} = 4$.

    3. GRAPHING MILK PREFERENCES. Find out how many milk drinkers there are in the classroom. Is anyone allergic to milk? Make a graph of what type of milk products students prefer, such as white milk, chocolate milk, yogurt, milkshake.

SCIENCE:

    1. HERE'S TO GOOD HEALTH! Some people are allergic to cow's milk and can drink goat's milk because it's more easily digested. It has large amounts of Vitamin A (the same vitamin found in carrots). Milk from goats is used to make butter and cheese, too. Let's explore the topic of cheese and find out how many of our favorite foods incorporate cheese. Look through cookbooks and ask grownups. The list includes some favorites such as pizza, cheeseburgers, and macaroni and cheese. Maybe we can have cheese and crackers for a healthy snack this week.
    2. GOLDIE GIVES A LESSON IN TEXTURE. Have samples of angora wool, cashmere and mohair available for the students to feel and compare. (Craft or weaving shops would have samples.) Goldie wants to know which feels the softest? What words can we list that help describe that bristly mohair?
    Goldie suggests that we examine the labels on sweaters, coats, jackets, blankets, and so on, to see if any of the words such as angora, cashmere, or mohair appear. Goldie reminds the children to examine labels at home.
    3. GET A GOLDIE. Mrs. Busby Bixby wants to have a pet goat because she likes goat's milk and goat cheese. She may also be able to cut and comb the wool and make a nice sweater. It's settled. Mrs. Busby Bixby will buy the goat! She puts a high fence around her yard to keep the goat inside. HERE'S THE PROBLEM: The goat can reach over the fence and eat the tree branches from Mrs. Busby Bixby's neighbor's favorite apple tree. The neighbor does not like goats. Oh! Oh! What should she do?
    Use the problem solving formula: (1) State the problem. (2) Brainstorm for possible solutions. (3) Try a solution. (4) Evaluate–Did it work?

SOCIAL STUDIES:

1. NANNY GOAT, THE POOR MAN'S COW.   In Europe and Asia (find these on the globe) goats are kept by many families for their milk. When some families take a vacation, the goat goes right along with them. This may be because of the rich supply of milk, or it may be that goats get into mischief when left alone. They will eat flowers, vegetation, and will strip the land. That may be why they haven't caught on as pets.

2. PET TREATMENT.   Talk about vacations and pets. Do families take pets along with them, or do they leave them in the care of others? Where do we find pet sitters? Let's discuss cost per day. Should we leave pets alone for long periods of time? Why not? Check with a local veterinarian for pamphlets to read about pet care.

3. A CLASSROOM PET.   By having a pet in the classroom, it teaches children responsibility for feeding, watering, cleaning, and general caring for an animal. Some students get over their fear of animals, birds, or fish by seeing the calm behavior of others. Who would make a good classroom pet? Go through the alphabet, and see how many letters would make an application. (For example, b-bird, b-bunny, g-gerbil, f-fish, and so on).

GOLDIE'S TALK-AND-TELL
PICTURE AND RHYME

Goats eat everything
in sight.
Close the cupboard door
at night!

G

TALK AND TELL: GOLDIE GOAT

1. HI, GOLDIE! WHEN WE TALKED TO DUKE THE DOG WE LEARNED THAT DOGS ARE CALLED MAN'S BEST FRIEND. GOATS ARE CALLED MAN'S FIRST FRIEND. WHY IS THAT?

Goats were among the very first animals to be friendly to people. That was many, many years ago! Some say we were tamed even before the dog.

2. DO GOATS MAKE GOOD PETS, GOLDIE?

You bet we do! Goats are very friendly and will follow you around. We'll snuggle up against you, and will look you right in the eye.

3. WHY DON'T MORE PEOPLE HAVE GOATS AS PETS, THEN?

They do in other countries far away. (Europe, Asia.)

4. HOW MANY KINDS OF GOATS ARE THERE, GOLDIE?

Can you count to 100? Can you count to 200? That's how many—200! We're divided into two main groups—those who make milk, and those who make wool (or hair).

5. LET'S FIND OUT ABOUT THE GOATS WHO MAKE MILK. IS IT TRUE, GOLDIE, THAT GOATS HAVE BEEN CALLED THE POOR MAN'S COW?

Yes. A goat is cheaper to buy than a cow, and needs less space to roam. Goat's milk, goat butter, and goat cheese are very good for you! Try them.

6. WHAT DO YOU LIKE TO EAT, GOLDIE?

Oh, things like grass, shrubs, and underbrush. We even strip the trees. It may be why we haven't exactly caught on as pets. We'll eat up everything in your yard.

7. DO YOU NEED A LOT OF CARE?

Not too much. We can behave so well that in some far away places (Europe) families take the family goat with them on vacation. That way, the family can have a fresh milk supply every day. We do our share to help out.

8. IS GOAT'S MILK GOOD, GOLDIE?

Delicious! It has large amounts of Vitamin A, and vitamins are good for you. Some people who are allergic to cow's milk can drink goat's milk with no problem because it's easy on your stomach. Some babies just love it!

9. AND WHAT ABOUT GOAT'S CHEESE IS IT TASTY?

Yummy! It's rich and creamy and among the best known in the whole world. Some is mild and some is strong. You should try some. How many boys and girls like cheese? Raise your hands.

10. GOLDIE, LET'S TALK ABOUT GOATS THAT MAKE WOOL OR HAIR. CAN YOU NAME ONE?

The finest cashmere is woven from the fluffy undercoat of the Kashmire goats of India. It makes a sweater feel so-o-o-o soft.

11. CAN YOU NAME ANOTHER HAIRY GOAT?

The angora goat's long, droopy hair is used to make wonderfully soft blankets and sweaters. There are more angora goats in the USA than any other type of goat.

12. GOLDIE, WHAT ELSE HAVE GOATS GIVEN TO PEOPLE?

Mohair, which is stiff, prickly hair. It's used in yarns, suits, sweaters, fabrics, and even in wigs. Goat skin is useful too for belts, shoes, and bottles.

13. GOATS ARE HELPFUL. IS YOUR SKIN TOUGH?

Yes. It's called kidskin and it is made into the most expensive of fine leathers. It makes nice gloves.

14. TELL US, GOLDIE, WERE YOU BORN LIVE OR HATCHED FROM AN EGG?

    I'm a mammal, so I was born live. Usually goats are born as twins. We're called kids and our mother is very affectionate.

15. WHAT ARE MOTHER GOATS AND FATHER GOATS CALLED?

    Adult males are bucks, young males are bucklings.

    Adult females are does, young females are doelings.

    Good friends calls us nannies and billies

16. DO NANNY GOATS AND BILLY GOATS GET ALONG WELL TOGETHER?

    Yes, we like to all be together. Goats don't like to be left alone. We like a lot of attention.

17. ARE NANNY GOATS AND BILLY GOATS CLEAN ANIMALS?

    We sure are. In a barn we like it to be clean and we do not eat off the floor. Our hay has to be put up in the loft so we can reach up for it. Never eat off the floor!

18. WE WON'T EAT OFF THE FLOOR. TELL US, GOLDIE, IN THE WILD DO YOU HAVE ANY NATURAL ENEMIES?

    Yes, we do. The wolves, leopards, and the golden eagle are all after us.

19. GOLDIE, WHERE CAN WE FIND YOU IF WE'D LIKE TO VISIT?

    Most angora goats live in the state of Texas. Can you find Texas on the map or globe? Also, you can visit me at a zoo or a farm.

20. ONE LAST QUESTION, GOLDIE. WHAT WOULD YOU LIKE PEOPLE TO KNOW ABOUT GOATS?

    We do not eat tin cans—that's a rumor! We do lick the salt from inside the can though. That's tasty! But we don't eat the cans.

    THANK YOU FOR THIS INTERVIEW HERE AT THE CHILDREN'S ZOO. TODAY OUR GUEST WAS GOLDIE, THE FRIENDLY GOAT. TUNE IN NEXT TIME WHEN WE WILL BE INTERVIEWING A(N)

————————————————————

INTERVIEW
INFORMATION

What did you learn? Draw it, write it, or web it.

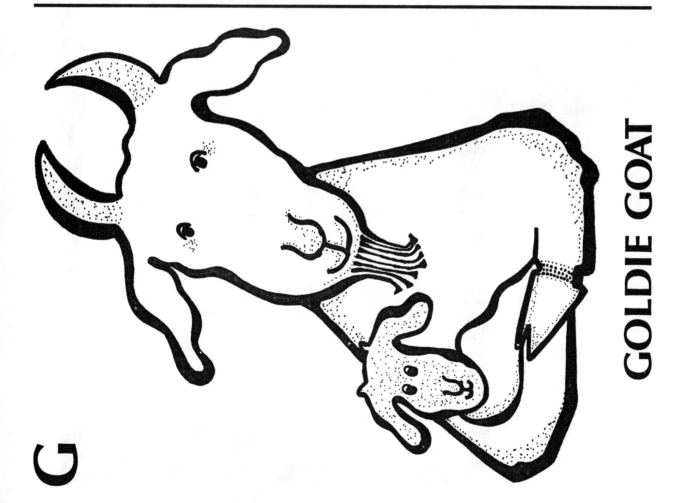

G

GOLDIE GOAT

GOLDIE THE GLAMOUR GOAT

Use this pattern to make a goat puppet. Work with a partner (and a dictionary) to see how many sentences you can put together that use Goldie Goat's sound (hard g).

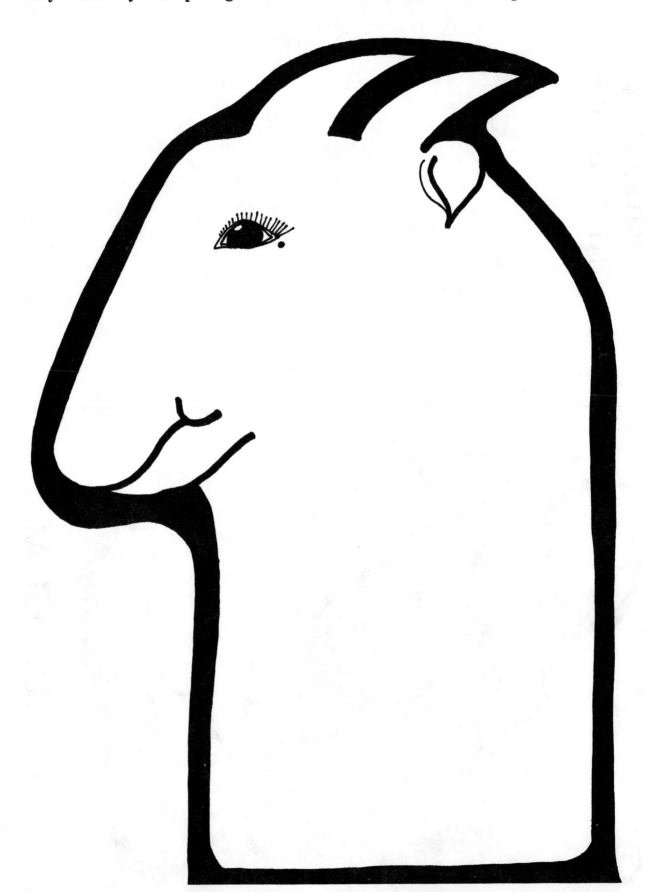

I HAVE A GIRAFFE UP MY SLEEVE

1. Practice printing the letter G.
2. Color the giraffe puppet. Cut it out.

3. Staple it to another giraffe shape.
4. Wear it on your sleeve and "look up high" for giraffe words (soft g).

THE THREE BILLY GOATS GRUFF FINGER PUPPETS (page 1 of 2)

Color the three goats and cut them out. Use them to retell the story of the Three Billy Goats Gruff.

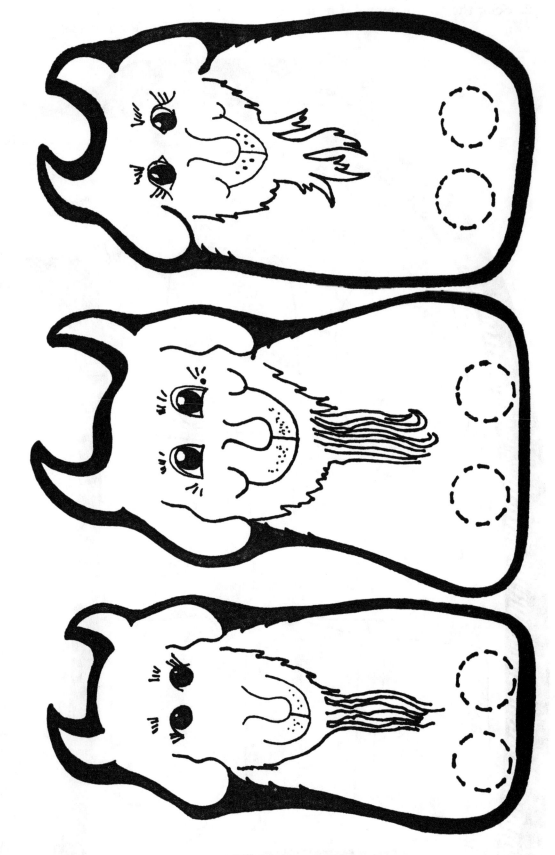

Use your crayons to make this troll scary. It has three faces! Can you find them? Then listen to the story. Retell the story. Act out the story.

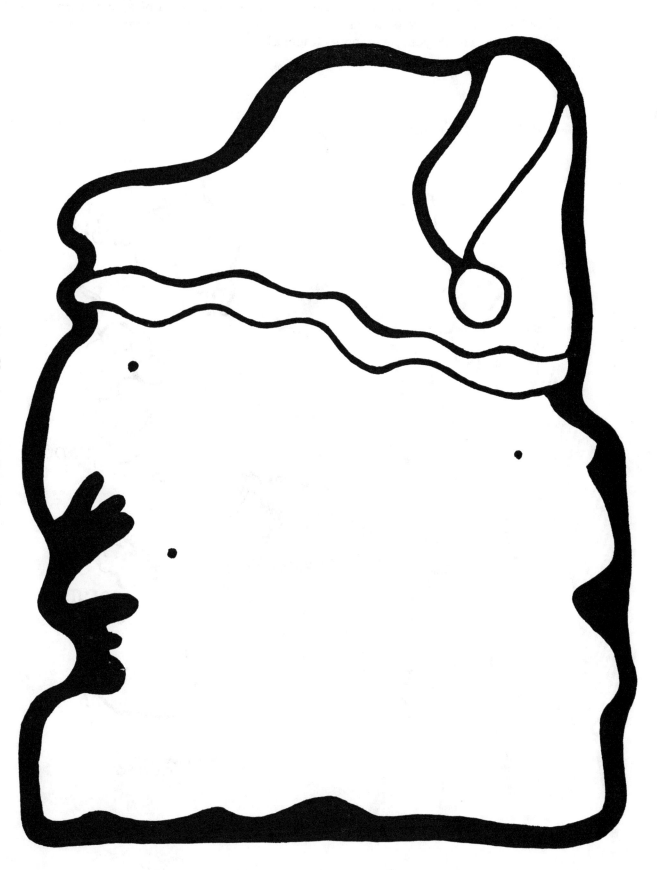

Name ——————————————— Date ———————————————

THE ADVENTURES OF GINGER GIRAFFE

Ginger Giraffe is on a hunt for items that begin with the soft sound of g, as in giraffe. If the items below have her sound, color them. If they do not, put an X on them. How many did you help Ginger find? "Thank you," whispers Ginger Giraffe. "Color me, too."

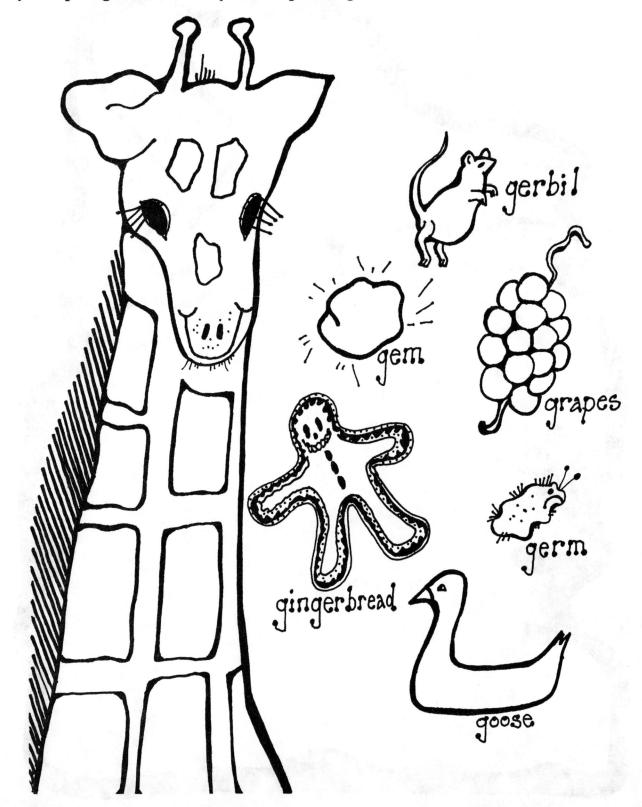

gerbil

gem

grapes

germ

gingerbread

goose

H

IS

FOR

HANDKERCHIEF HORSE

H IS FOR HANDKERCHIEF HORSE

BACKGROUND INFORMATION ABOUT HORSES: Handkerchief Horse is a mammal with hoofs. Horse hoofs are made of a horn-like material. The hoofs grow from the top down just like our fingernails, so they are continually being renewed. They can wear down, however, so special horseshoes made of molten steel are formed and nailed to the hoof. This does not hurt the horse, and in fact, is good protection and serves as a type of shock absorber.

Throughout history, horses have been extremely helpful to people. They carry and pull heavy loads on farms. They were used to pull stagecoaches and wagons when the wild west was settled and they pulled street cars, fire engines, and milk carts until they were replaced by trucks. Today, many city police officers ride on horseback. Horses like Handkerchief also provide pleasure for people, since they can be mounted and guided for riding and racing.

READING/LANGUAGE ARTS:

1. HANDKERCHIEF'S SPECIAL NAMES. The names for the markings on a horse's head are as follows:

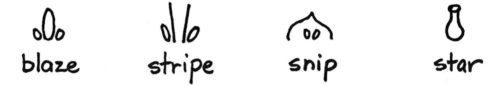

blaze   stripe   snip   star

Print these designs on horse shapes, along with the titles, and have students learn them.
2. GOOD HORSE SENSE. Have Handkerchief explain this term to students. It really means using common sense and thinking things through before acting impulsively. We use good horse sense in the classroom when it's raining and we stay indoors for recess. How else can we use good horse sense in the classroom, on the playground, going to and from school? It's time for a discussion.
3. STORYBOOK HORSES. Many books have been written about horses. Find some at the library and read them aloud to students. Also, horses play a big role in many stories even though they do not have a name. Who is pulling the pumpkin coach for Cinderella? What is the prince riding when he comes upon Snow White? Have students make a big shape book of Handkerchief Horse and include letters written from the point of view of the horse in storybooks. The horse would have quite a bit of information that was not revealed in the actual story. Let's hear it.
4. HORSE VOCABULARY. The terms are: stallion (adult male), mare (adult female), colt (young male), filly (young female). Find real pictures in information books that show sizes and markings of the various horses.

MATH:

1. SEE THE WORD "HAND" IN HANDKERCHIEF? Horses have been measured by *handspans*—the width of a man's palm (about 4 inches)—from its hoof to its wither (the highest point on its shoulder just behind the neck). How many handspans tall are we from toe to head? Let's measure. But, lead students to discover that it is much easier and more accurate to measure with a ruler or yardstick for standardization.

2. HANDKERCHIEF—WHAT A BIG HEART YOU HAVE! Horses have a large heart that pumps blood to all parts of its body. A race horse may have a 14-pound heart, an average horse has a 10-pound heart. By way of comparison, the human heart is about one pound. Work with the concept of light and heavy using a scale. Find items that weigh 1, 10, and 14 pounds.

Also, what does it mean when we say that someone is big hearted? That's right, they're generous and kind to others. How many Handkerchief hearts do we have with us today? What can we do to demonstrate it?

3. SOCKS AND STOCKINGS. Horse leg markings are known as socks and stockings.

sock   stocking

Let's help Handkerchief with counting. How many students are wearing socks? stockings? Find pictures of real horses in books and look for their leg markings.

SCIENCE:

1. HANDKERCHIEF'S LEGS PICK UP VIBRATIONS. Horse legs are amazingly sensitive and they are able to pick up vibrations through them. For example, vibrations from the ground travel up the leg bones and a horse can detect sounds coming from as far away as a mile. People can't do that, but we can feel vibrations by touching an object. Let's try. Some starters are water faucets that are on, air conditioning or register units in the room, a tuning fork, drum, or clock.

2. HANDKERCHIEF CAN SLEEP STANDING UP. CAN YOU? A horse can lock its leg joints in place which enables it to doze while standing up. To sleep more soundly, a horse must lie down. Have students try locking their knee joints to see how long they can stand still. Use the minute hand on a clock or watch to time this activity. Encourage them to build up endurance and lengthen their dozing time.

3. HORSES WEAR SHOES. Horseshoes protect the hoof of the horse. People play a game of horseshoes with horseshoes and a stake in the ground. It's time to take a good look at animal feet. How many animals have hoofs? How many have claws? Webbed feet? Paws? Classify the animals by feet. Select an animal and design special "shoes" for them. Make an ANIMAL SHOE SHOP BOOK, complete with a variety of designs. Don't forget the prices.

SOCIAL STUDIES:

1. TRANSPORTATION HORSES. Horses have played a major role throughout history by pulling covered wagons, stagecoaches, carts and wagons loaded with goods. At one time horses were used for pulling fire trucks! And horses pulled milk wagons to make door-to-door deliveries. Without horses, what animals would we have used as effectively? People even hitched horses (and mules) up to canal barges, and these teams of horses moved on land on each side of the canal, while pulling the barge loaded with goods through the water. Stress the major importance of horses in the settling of our country.

2. PONY EXPRESS. Today a letter can be delivered overnight by jet transport, or faxed instantly by machine, but at one time it was delivered by horses. The rider and horse galloped along a specific route from Point A to Point B, and then the horse was given a rest. Mail was transferred to another horse who took it from Point B to Point C, and so on. Students can simulate this relay type of mail delivery.

3. PRESIDENTIAL HORSES. George Washington is often pictured on a horse. Find pictures of other presidents on horseback. What is the major mode of transportation for our president today? How many transportation options does the current president have that George Washington did not have?

4. INVITE A POLICE HORSE TO SCHOOL. In many cities, police personnel ride horseback through parks and busy city streets as they patrol their beat. Are there police horses in your town? Often, a member of the police force will bring a horse to the school playground and describe its duties, much to the delight of children who may never have been near a horse. Students will never forget the "feel" of it, as the police representative allows them to touch the horse.

5. CREATIVE PLAY. Use a box with a rope tied to it, and put the rope around the waist of one or two students. Then, students can take turns being Handkerchief who is making deliveries of milk or mail. They can also be bringing the fire wagon to help put out the fire and save the day.

6. HORSING AROUND. Here's a puzzle for students to solve. They can get down on all fours and walk, trot, gallop, or run at top speed. These are the rules: WALK—three feet are on the ground, one is in the air; TROT—two feet are on the ground, one front hoof and the opposite hoof in back are up in the air; GALLOP—one foot is on the ground, three are in the air; TOP SPEED—all four feet can be off the ground at the same time while the horse is in midair. Good luck.

**HANDKERCHIEF'S TALK-AND-TELL
PICTURE AND RHYME**

Running, Jumping,
That's my game.
Call me Handkerchief,
That's my name!

H

TALK AND TELL: HANDKERCHIEF HORSE

1. HELLO, HANDKERCHIEF! WE HAVE A QUESTION FOR YOU. IS IT TRUE THAT YOU CAN HEAR SOUNDS SEVERAL MILES AWAY?

Yes. I can hear a storm coming long before a person can. Also, I hear through my legs. Vibrations from the ground travel up my leg bones so I can tell when things are coming even though they're still a long way down the road.

2. THAT'S FASCINATING, HANDKERCHIEF. CAN YOU SEE WELL?

Very well, thank you. My eyes are high up on my head and I can see all around except for right in front of my face.

3. HORSES ARE BORN LIVE, AREN'T THEY?

Yes, I'm a hoofed mammal. I could see and stand up right away. My legs were a little shaky, but I made it.

4. HOW LONG DO BABY HORSES (FOALS) STAY WITH THEIR MOTHER, HANDKERCHIEF?

For about 4 to 5 months. Then we're *weaned*. That means we don't drink her milk anymore. Instead we eat grass, grain, and hay. Horses also eat carrots and apples too. Carrots and apples are good for you!

5. WHAT ARE ADULTS AND BABIES CALLED?

The mother horse is a mare. The father horse is a stallion. The baby female is a filly, and the baby male is a colt. Try to learn the names.

6. YES, WE WILL WORK ON THAT. HANDKERCHIEF, CAN YOU TELL US WHAT A WEANLING IS?

That's a young horse, about 4 or 5 months old, that is in the stage of being taken off its mother's milk. During this time we get a trainer who starts to teach us things.

7. WHAT ARE SOME OF THE THINGS THAT HORSES LEARN?

We learn to be led with a halter of soft rope. We get used to having our feet handled a lot. In our second year as a yearling, we get used to having a saddle strapped to our back. A trainer is gentle but firm.

8. HANDKERCHIEF, WHY DOES YOUR TRAINER HANDLE YOUR FEET SO MUCH?

He's getting us ready for the time when we have special horseshoes made. These shoes are nailed to the bottom of our hoofs.

9. OUCH!! DOES THAT HURT YOU, HANKY?

No. Our feet are made of horn-like material. We don't feel the nails being pounded in. The shoes are good protection for the feet.

10. HOW BIG DO YOU GROW TO BE?

Horses can grow to be 6 ft tall. That's two yardsticks end to end, try it.

11. IS IT TRUE, HANDKERCHIEF, THAT PEOPLE MEASURE HORSES BY USING THEIR HANDS?

Yes. The average width of a man's hand is about 4 inches. So, they start at my hoofs and work up to my wither.

12. YOUR WITHER? WHAT IS YOUR WITHER?

My *wither* is the highest point of my shoulder—right here just behind my neck.

13. OH! WELL, TELL US SOMETHING ABOUT HOW FAR YOU CAN RUN.

I can run 4 miles without stopping. That's a long way! My spine is stiff and only my legs move. I can really travel.

14. HANDKERCHIEF, ARE THERE NAMES FOR THE MARKINGS ON THE HEAD OF A HORSE?

    Yes. If you have a piece of chalk and a chalkboard, you can draw them.

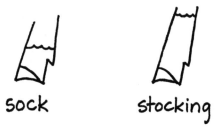

blaze   stripe   snip   star

15. THEY LOOK PRETTY! DO YOUR LEG MARKINGS HAVE NAMES TOO?

    Yes. Sock and Stocking.

sock   stocking

16. HANDKERCHIEF, YOU'RE A BIG ANIMAL. HOW MUCH DO YOU EAT IN A DAY?

    Lots and lots of hay. About 20 to 30 pounds. I chew a lot!

17. HORSES ARE VERY HELPFUL ANIMALS, AREN'T THEY?

    Yes, we are. We can pull heavy loads on farms. Long ago we used to pull stage-coaches and wagons when people moved out west. We used to pull street cars and fire trucks. Today, some police officers ride horses in the big cities.

18. WE KNOW HORSES ARE HELPFUL. ARE HORSES GENTLE, TOO?

    I'm a domestic animal, not wild. And, if I'm treated gently and trained with patience, I'm usually gentle enough for most people to ride on me. Some horses are frisky, and that means they jump around.

19. WHAT'S ONE TIP THAT YOU WOULD GIVE TO PEOPLE WHO RIDE ON YOU?

    When I run fast, or gallop, I get very hot. Lucky for me I am able to sweat. But, I need to be walked after a ride so I can cool off. A good rubdown helps, too, otherwise I could get sick.

20. WHAT ELSE SHOULD WE KNOW ABOUT YOU, HANDKERCHIEF?

    A horse is very, very sensitive. All horses get frightened by the smell of a dead animal—even a tiny dead mouse. We rear up on our hind legs and scream, "Neigh-h-h-h!" It's nature's way. Please be gentle with us, and speak quietly. No shouting! Thank you.

(In a hushed tone) . . . THANK YOU! OUR TALK AND TELL HAS BEEN CONDUCTED RIGHT HERE IN THE HORSE STABLE. TODAY OUR GUEST WAS HANDKERCHIEF THE HORSE. TUNE IN NEXT TIME WHEN WE WILL BE INTERVIEWING A(N)_____. MEANWHILE, USE YOUR GOOD HORSE SENSE AND EAT YOUR CARROTS AND APPLES.

INTERVIEW INFORMATION

What did you learn? Draw it, write it, or web it.

H

HANDKERCHIEF HORSE

Name _____ Date _____

IT MAKES GOOD HORSE SENSE

I chose this book as my "Blue Ribbon Winner."

Title: _____

Author/Illustrator _____

I chose this book because . . .

CHOCOLATE PEANUT BUTTER HORSE CHESTNUTS

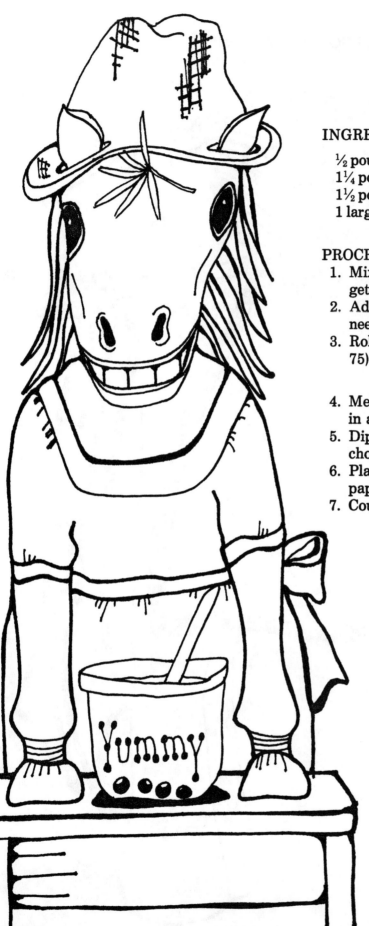

INGREDIENTS:

½ pound soft butter
1¼ pounds smooth peanut butter
1½ pounds confectioners sugar
1 large package of chocolate chips

PROCEDURE:
1. Mix the butter and peanut butter together until smooth.
2. Add the confectioners sugar. (You may need to mix this by hand.)
3. Roll the mixture into small balls (about 75).
4. Melt the chocolate chips in a double boiler.
5. Dip three-fourths of each ball into the chocolate.
6. Place the "horse chestnuts" on waxed paper to dry.
7. Count them! Eat them! Enjoy them!

Name _____   Date _____

H IS FOR HOUSE. WHO IS HOME?

Cut out the items at the bottom. Color only those that begin with the sound of h as in house and paste them in the windows. What color will you make your house?

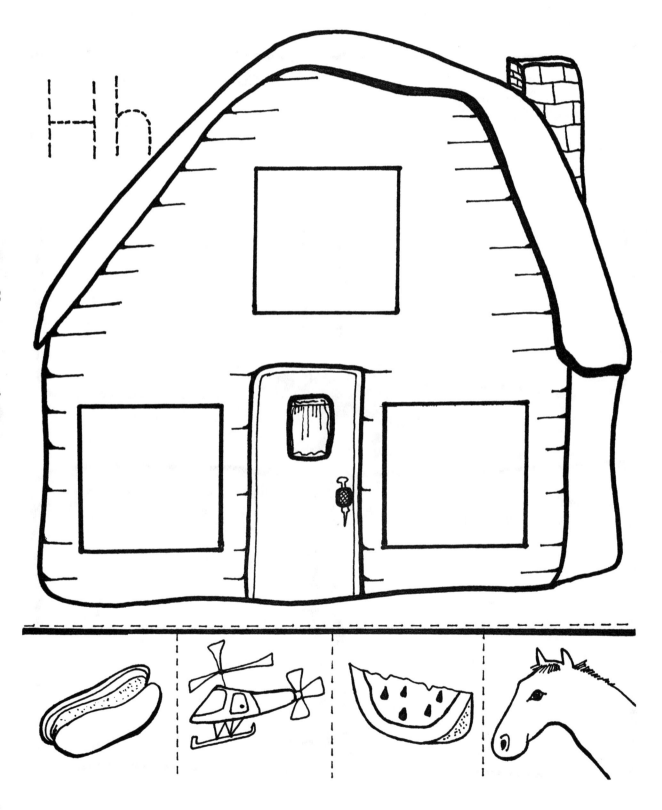

HANDKERCHIEF THE HORSE LEARNS TO CLASSIFY

Make a classification web. Write the names (or draw the pictures) of animals or birds in the spaces below. Learn the "Classification Chant."

1. There's one way to tell,
   who's got the paws.
   Classify! Classify!

2. There's one way to tell,
   who's got the claws,
   Classify! Classify!

3. There's one way to tell,
   who's got the tails.
   Classify! Classify!

4. There's one way to tell,
   who's got the scales.
   CLAS • SI • FY!! Yeah!

DIAL-A-HORSE

Handkerchief Horse operates this hot line. Animals call day and night to find out the phone number of other animals. Since Handkerchief is not home today, can you help? Locate the numeral that goes with each letter. Then add them together. That's the number!

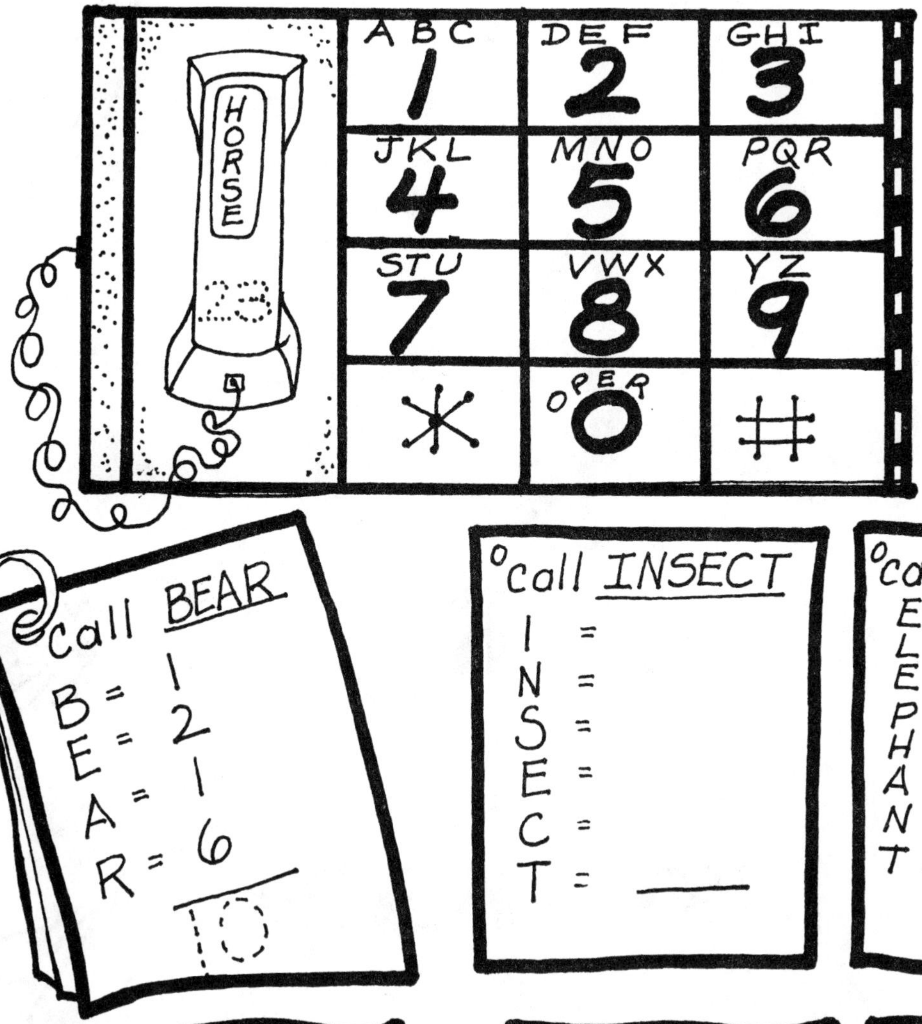

ABC 1	DEF 2	GHI 3
JKL 4	MNO 5	PQR 6
STU 7	VWX 8	YZ 9
*	OPER 0	#

°Call _BEAR_

B = 1
E = 2
A = 1
R = 6
___
10

°call _INSECT_

I =
N =
S =
E =
C =
T = ___

°call _ELEPHANT_

E =
L =
E =
P =
H =
A =
N =
T = ___

°call _GOAT_

G =
O =
A =
T = ___

°Call _____

°Call _____

I
IS
FOR

INKY INSECT

I IS FOR INKY INSECT

BACKGROUND INFORMATION ABOUT INSECTS: There are more than a million types of insects. Insect means "in sections" and insects have three sections: (1) head, with antennae or feelers, (2) thorax, with wings, and (3) tail section. All insects have six legs (that leaves out spiders, who have eight).

The eggs that insects lay are as varied as the insects. They range in shape from discs to cones to pyramids. The colors cover a wide spectrum also. The eggs are laid on plant leaves, or shrubs, or in the ground, depending upon the insect. Some insects stick their eggs into plant stems which makes the stem bulge. Insects instinctively deposit their eggs on or under the plant upon which they feed. Then, when the egg is hatched, the emerging insect has a ready source of food at hand.

READING/LANGUAGE ARTS:

1. INKY'S COLORFUL FAMILY. Inky is a ladybug and has black ink spots all over her bright red body. The bright red is a signal to others that a ladybug is not all that tasty. Very bright yellows, oranges, and so on, are sending off that visual message. Have students look through a wide variety of colorful books on insects, and classify them according to color. Make a rainbow book of insects. Page one has a red insect, page two has an orange insect, and so on.

2. INKY'S RELATIVES have interesting names to pronounce such as grasshopper, katydids, stinkbugs, butterflies, crickets, bees, moths, and so on. Many of their names are compound words. Make insect head bands and have students wear them while they hunt to find the words.

3. WE'RE READY FOR A CHANGEABLE NAME. The word to focus upon is METAMORPHOSIS. How many syllables? (5). Did we meet another animal that explained metamorphosis to us? (Francine Frog). See Activity Pages for a butterfly experience.

4. THE ABC OF INSECTS. Print the ABC's vertically on a chart, and see how many insects can be found for each letter. Have students illustrate the chart with colored felt-tip pens.

MATH:

1. INSECTS ARE ALL THREES AND SIXES. To reinforce the concept of three body parts and six legs, students can do the following:

> Cut up egg cartons and create an insect using
> three of the compartments. Have students
> count six pipecleaners and insert three on
> each side of the compartments for legs. What
> can we glue on for antennae and eyes?

2. LET'S CLASSIFY INKY'S RELATIVES.   We can work with classification of insects according to those that fly, those that we can readily find in our own backyard, those that farmers like or do not like, those that are camouflaged, and those that are colorful, to name a few.

3. MARSHMALLOW METAMORPHOSIS RECIPE.   Students can count out three marshmallows for body parts. Place them in a line on a plate. Insert six licorice legs into the second of the three body parts. Use gumdrops for eyes, and small pretzels for antennae. Children will enjoy devouring this insect as it undergoes a change (metamorphosis) from an insect to a delicious treat.

4. INSECT SHAPES.   Insect eggs are shaped like discs, cones, circles, ovals, or even pyramid shapes. Find as many as you can in information books about insects. Read *Chickens Aren't the Only Ones* by Ruth Heller, to get a good look at egg shapes and insects too.

SCIENCE:

1. EXPLORE THE CONCEPT OF CAMOUFLAGE.   Have students make construction paper insects and place them on different colored construction paper backgrounds. Which ones are easy to spot? Is the grasshopper easier to see on a green background (grass) or on a blue background?

2. GRASSHOPPER SKIN.   As the grasshopper grows bigger it outgrows its skin. The skin gets dry, bursts open, falls off, and there is new skin underneath. Then, the grasshopper gets bigger and the skin gets dry, bursts open, falls off, and there is a new skin layer underneath. This happens five times in the life of a grasshopper.

3. WHAT ABOUT OUR SKIN?   What happens when we gain weight? Our skin stretches, it does not burst and fall off. As children grow, their skin is in the process of growth too. Does our skin ever dry up and fall off? Yes, when we get a sunburn, or when the skin gets chapped in winter. We need to use protective lotions to take good care of our skin. Perhaps a hand-pump plastic container of mild skin lotion by the sink (a gift from Inky) will remind children to take care of the skin on their hands and arms, after they wash.

SOCIAL STUDIES:

1. IT'S PLAYTIME.   Play the game, "May I Come In?" For example,

> "I am a spider, may I come in?"
> "How many legs do you have?"
> "Eight."
> "No, you may not come in."
> "I am a dragonfly, may I come in?"
> "How many legs do you have?"
> "Six."
> "Yes, you may come in."

2. INSECT PICNIC PARADE.   Have each student use colorful plasticene to roll out three body parts (round or oval) and six legs (coils). Add eyes and antennae. Line all the insects in a row along the ledge to form an insect parade. At one end have a picnic

basket with a checkered cloth cover. In the basket, store snack supplies because insects love a picnic.

Here's how to make a Cheese Cricket Treat:

> Have students count out three crackers for body parts.
> Place them in a line on a plate.
> Squeeze cheese from a tube to form six legs, antennae,
>   and bulgy eyes.
> Rub wings (hands) together (that's how insects communicate).
> Enjoy the treat.

3. ENVIRONMENTAL POLLUTION.   As we spray for insect control, the environment is suffering. For an awareness of this and other pollution problems, a good resource book for students is *SAVE THE EARTH. An Action Handbook for Kids,* by Betty Miles with drawings by Nelle Davis. (New York: Alfred A. Knopf, 1991).

Flies, Mosquitos,
    Ladybugs too.
We belong to the
    Insect crew.

TALK AND TELL: INKY INSECT

1. HELLO INKY. YOUR LEGS ARE MOVING. HOW MANY LEGS DO YOU
   HAVE?

       Let's count. 1-2-3-4-5-6. Six legs. Hold up 3 fingers on each hand. OK. Now
   wiggle them.

2. HOW MANY BODY PARTS DO INSECTS HAVE?

       Let's count again. 1-2-3. Three body parts. Hold up three fingers on one hand.

3. INKY, WHAT ARE THOSE TWO LONG THINGS STICKING OUT OF YOUR
   HEAD? THEY LOOK LIKE LONG WIRES.

       They're my antennae.

4. MY TV SET HAS AN ANTENNAE. WHAT DO YOU USE YOUR ANTENNAE
   FOR?

       Most insects feel and smell with their antennae.

5. INKY, IS IT TRUE THAT INSECTS DO NOT HAVE A VOICE?

       That's true. We can make sounds by rubbing our wings or legs together. We
   can make high sounds and low sounds. Rub your hands together to see what sounds you
   make.

6. WE SOUND LIKE A BROOM SWEEPING A FLOOR. DO YOU COME FROM
   A LARGE FAMILY?

       Very, very very large! There are more than a million insects and we all look
   different.

7. IF YOU ALL LOOK SO DIFFERENT, WHAT MAKES YOU ALIKE?

       Let's count. 1-2-3-4-5-6. Six legs. And, 1-2-3. Three body parts. We all have
   how many legs (6). How many body parts? (3). Good!

8. WERE YOU BORN LIVE OR HATCHED FROM AN EGG, INKY?

       I was hatched from an egg.

9. WHAT SHAPE ARE INSECT EGGS?

       Some are round, some are egg-shaped or oval (remember the alligator sat on
   an egg and made it into an oval), and some are shaped like the cone of your ice cream
   cone. They're all different colors, too, and very pretty.

10. WHERE DO INSECTS LAY THEIR EGGS?

       Some lay them on plant leaves, some lay them on shrubs, or even under the
   ground. Some insects even stick them inside plant stems.

11. INKY, IS IT REALLY TRUE THAT THE BUTTERFLY IS AN INSECT?

       Yes. The butterfly started out in an egg, then became a caterpillar, and then
   changed into a butterfly! When insects change like that it's called metamorphosis. I
   think Francine Frog told you all about metamorphosis.

12. YES. METAMORPHOSIS IS A BIG WORD. LET'S SAY IT AGAIN, BOYS AND
    GIRLS—MET A MOR PHO SIS. GOOD. BUT WHAT DOES METAMORPHOSIS
    MEAN?

       It means changing from one form to another form. The butterfly changed from
   a caterpillar to a butterfly, just like the frog changed from a tadpole to a frog. In fairy
   tales, sometimes the frog changes into a handsome prince. Did you know that?

13. WE KNOW IT NOW. INKY, YOUR COLOR IS BEAUTIFUL RED WITH
    BLACK DOTS. YOU'RE A LADYBUG, AREN'T YOU?

       Yes I am. My red color gives a warning message, just like a traffic light. The
   red says STOP!

14. WHY DOES A LADYBUG'S RED COLOR SAY "STOP!"

It says, "Don't eat me! I don't taste good!"

15. CAN YOU TELL US ABOUT ANOTHER BRIGHT, COLORFUL INSECT THAT GIVES OFF WARNING SIGNALS TOO?

Sure. The bumblebee! It's bright yellow with black stripes. A yellow traffic light means caution or slow down. The yellow bumblebee is saying, "Be careful! Don't get too close or I will sting you!"

16. DO ALL INSECTS FLY, INKY?

No. Some beetles, moths, and crickets don't fly, but remember they have six legs and three body parts, so they belong to the insect family.

17. DID YOUR MOTHER TEACH YOU HOW TO DO THINGS, INKY?

Most insects never see their mothers. We know what to do as soon as we hatch. It's called instinct—it's nature's way.

18. YOU MEAN WHEN YOU FIRST HATCHED YOU KNEW WHAT TO DO, JUST LIKE THAT?

Yes, just like that! I knew what food was good for me and what food not to eat. I knew how to hide from danger.

19. BUT, INKY, WHERE DID YOU LIVE?

I built a nice home on my very first try. It was easy for me.

20. ONE LAST QUESTION, INKY. HOW MANY INSECTS CAN YOU NAME IN A MINUTE?

If I counted for 60 minutes (one hour), I couldn't name all of the insects in the world. But I'll name some for you. There's that ant, beetle, bumblebee, butterfly, caterpillar, cockroach, cricket, dragonfly, firefly, flea, grasshopper, grub, honeybee, hornet, inchworm, junebug, ladybug, moth, wasp, walking stick . . . I'm out of breath! Just remember, 1-2-3-4-5-6 legs and 1-2-3 body parts. Find some pictures of us in books. We're pretty!

THANK YOU FOR THIS TALK-AND-TELL TIME RIGHT HERE IN OUR OWN BACK YARD. TODAY OUR GUEST WAS INKY INSECT, THE LADYBUG. TUNE IN NEXT TIME WHEN WE WILL BE TALKING WITH A(N)

———————————————————

INTERVIEW
INFORMATION

What did you learn? Draw it, write it, or web it.

INKY INSECT

I

THE LONG AND SHORT OF THE LETTER "I"

If the item below begins with the long sound of i, circle it with red. If the item begins with the short sound of i, box it with blue. How many of each do you have? Color them.

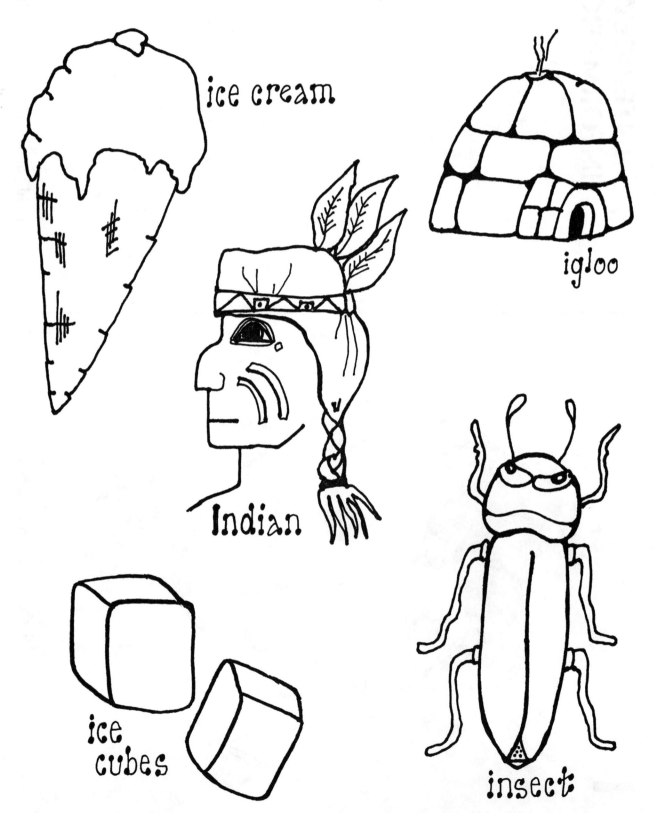

ice cream

igloo

Indian

ice cubes

insect

Name —————————————————— Date ——————————————

THE BUTTERFLY IS AN INSECT

The four stages of the life cycle of a butterfly are shown on its long body. Draw each stage in the appropriate circle. Then, use your brightest crayons to make a beautiful butterfly!

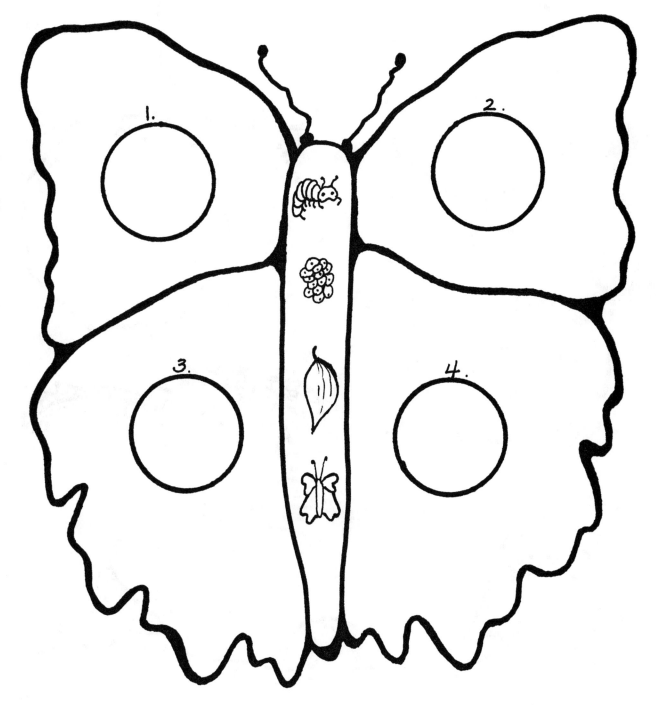

THE INSECT HUNTER

The chameleon is out hunting for insects. He can change colors quickly to match the colors of the insects, and they do not see him. In each space below, show how many insects he will catch today. Make them different colors. Give the chameleon matching colors, too.

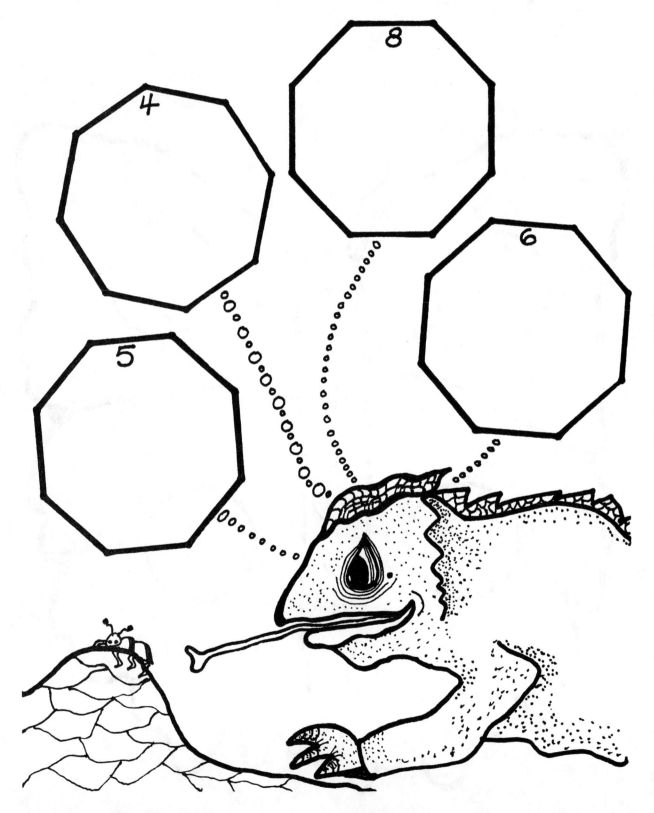

Build An Insect

2 celery sticks   (body)
6 carrot sticks   (legs)
2 licorice sticks (antennae)
2 raisins

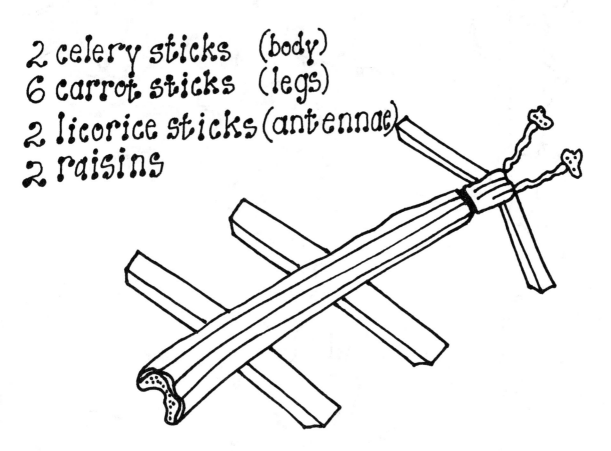

Caterpillar Train

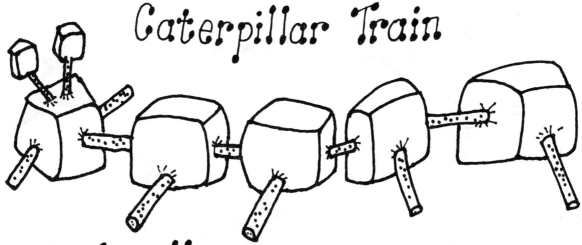

marshmallows
pretzel sticks

Name ————————————   Date ————————————

THE INSECT REUNION

These insects have gathered together because they have six legs and three body parts.
Use your crayons to make them all look different otherwise. Add your own insects to these.

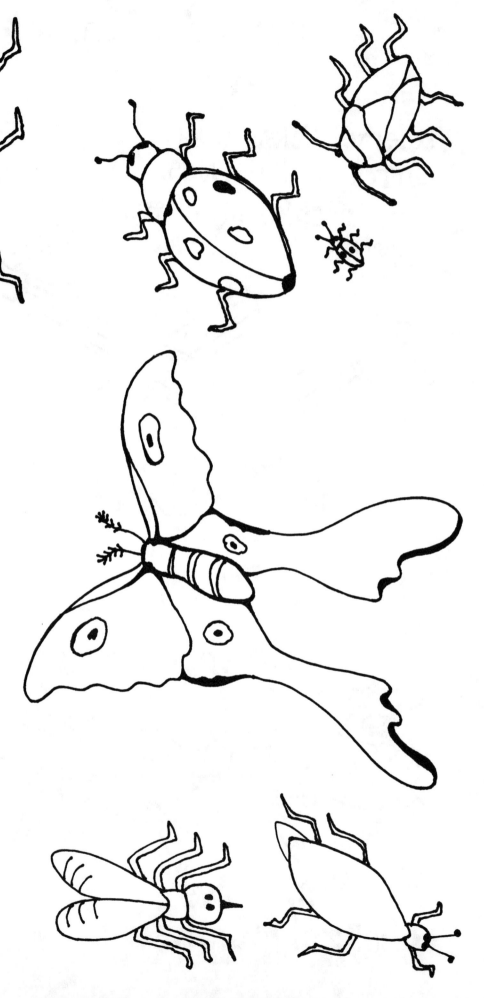

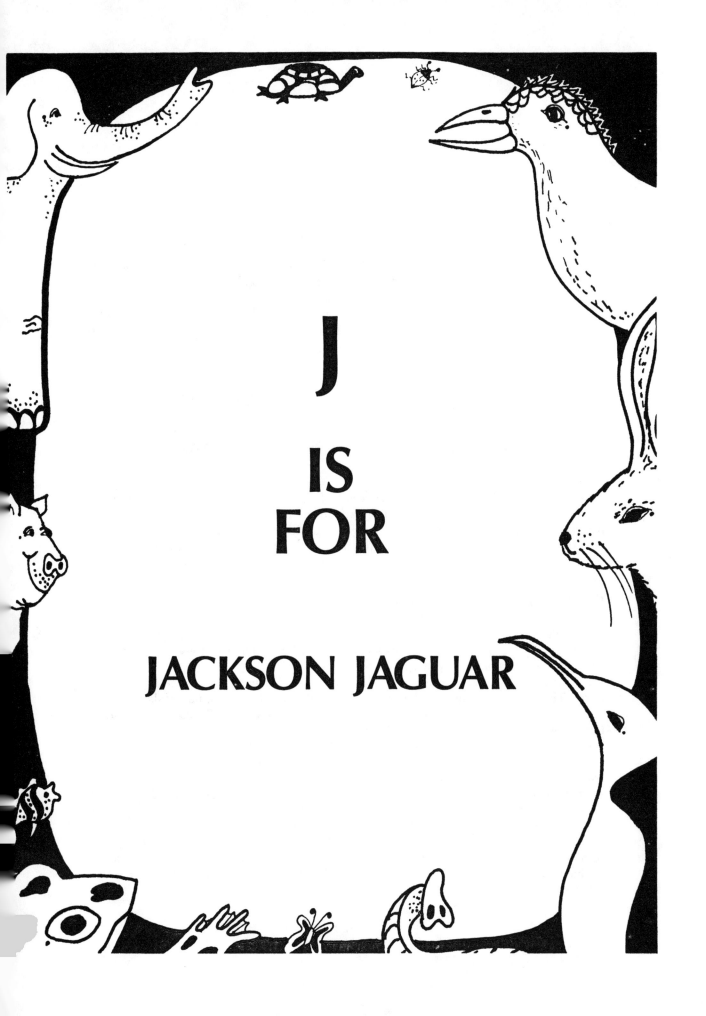

J
IS
FOR

JACKSON JAGUAR

J IS FOR JACKSON JAGUAR

BACKGROUND INFORMATION ABOUT JAGUARS: Jackson Jaguar is a member of the world's big cats, which includes the tiger, cheetah, leopard, snow leopard, and lion. The jaguar is similar in appearance to the leopard but has a stockier build. Also a leopard has spots whereas the markings on a jaguar are shaped like rosettes. They are brown, and the jaguar's yellow-orange hair shows through the middle as well as around the edges.

leopard spots

jaguar rosettes

Most jaguars live in the wild in Mexico, Central America, or South America where they are referred to as *el tigre* (the tiger). They are an endangered species, and for this reason are caught and housed in zoos so that they are protected and can reproduce.

Jaguars are excellent swimmers, enjoy the water, and seem to swim just for the fun of it. They like to dive into streams to catch alligators, crocodiles, or fish.

READING/LANGUAGE ARTS:

1. THAT'S JAGUAR WITH A J.   There are many names of boys and girls that also begin with the j sound. Students can make a list of such names. Try looking up some of them in a book of Mother Goose rhymes.

2. ABC REVIEW.   Jackson is a Big 10 member of the alphabet, since J is the tenth letter. This jaguar can help students remember all of the letters and animals that came before him: A–Ashley Alligator, B–Brandi Bear, C–Clancy Cat, D–Duke Dog, E–Eddington Elephant, F–Francine Frog, G–Goldie Goat, H–Handkerchief Horse, and I–Inky Insect. Have students practice making upper and lower case letters for these animals.

3. HOW THE JAGUAR GOT ITS ROSETTES.   Use the formula that is found in so many of the AESOP'S FABLES to help compose a story. This can be done after students listen to stories about How The Tiger Got Its Stripes, How The Bear Got Its Stumpy Tail, and so on. (See the reproducible Activity Pages.)

4. WHO IS THE PRETTIEST CAT?   Leopards have spots, tigers have stripes, jaguars have rosettes, and so on. Write a skit about the animals in which they each claim to be the prettiest. King Lion has to solve the issue and be VERY diplomatic about it. Perhaps he'll find each to be the "prettiest" in some way. This can make for a very interesting tale to reenact.

MATH:

1. THE BIG TEN.   Jaguar with a J is the tenth letter of the alphabet. This gives us an opportunity to count by tens, to write by tens, and to jump to 100 by tens with Jackson.

2. CLASSIFY THE BIG CATS.   Can students tell a tiger from a cheetah? Or a lion from a jaguar? Let's examine pictures of their fur, markings, mane, and so on, so that students can begin to distinguish one from another. Do they have a favorite big cat? Let's find out. (See activity pages for graphing.)

3. ROSETTE PEEK BOOK.   The jaguar has special markings called rosettes. Use the chalkboard to demonstrate for students the irregular, circular pattern. Find pictures of real jaguars to examine. Make a Rosette Peek Book. Every other page has an irregular circle (rosette) cut out of it so that students can try to guess what animal is on the next page. The focus is upon patterns. *Look Again* by Tana Hoban would be an excellent resource book for this activity.

4. LOOKING AT SHAPES.   Take a good look at the faces of the animals and the markings on their bodies. Use the reproducible Activity Pages to construct an animal around a particular marking pattern.

SCIENCE:

1. JACKSON'S FANGS.   Make a fang mask to show the shape of jaguar teeth. Remember that jaguars catch alligators, crocodiles, and fish and need sharp teeth for hunting. This would be a good time to remind Jackson to brush UP and DOWN at least twice a day, and to use dental floss. Make a set of teeth from styrofoam shapes and, using string, demonstrate flossing.

2. JAGUAR JUNGLE MEDICINE.   Animals roll in mud for good health, and people get shots. In the jungle, when the jaguar is wounded it instinctively rolls in the mud to cover its wounds. The molds that grow on the jungle ground are similar to the molds from which penicillin is derived. The mud, then, acts as a natural antibiotic for wild animals who are wounded and it helps to heal their sores. Remind children that this is jungle medicine talk, and is not for boys and girls—we go to the physician to get our shots. Talk about shots and how many have had shots, for what purpose, and so on. Young children are eager to talk about this subject.

3. EXTINCT MEANS ZERO.   Introduce the word *extinct*. Write or print it on the chalkboard and explain its meaning (when an animal no longer exists in the world). For example, the dinosaur is extinct. Many animals are in danger of becoming extinct, such as the jaguar, and they are referred to as *endangered species*. Students can be encouraged to locate library resources such as *Ranger Rick, National Geographic, World*, and encyclopedias in order to find other animals that are in danger of extinction. Make as "Endangered Species" chart for the classroom. Have any of our A-J animals so far been on this list? (Alligators were on the list but have been taken off; elephants are being shot by poachers who want the ivory from their tusks.)

ENDANGERED SPECIES		
Animal	Where It Lives	What's the Problem?

SOCIAL STUDIES:

1. ZOO VERSUS THE WILDS. The zoo serves as a protection for endangered species by providing food, shelter, and safety. Yet, some people think that it is unkind to keep these animals cooped up in a small space. Discuss the pros and cons of this issue.

2. A TRIP TO THE ZOO. Now is the time to begin thinking about a trip to the zoo. Many zoos have an education program for young children—perhaps there is one is your area. How many of the A-Z animals can be found in your zoo?

3. KEEPING A JOURNAL. If you are writing in a daily journal about the animals, today you might want to include the topic of "Zoo Versus the Wilds." What are the benefits of keeping an endangered animal in a zoo environment?

Write a play about two jaguars who are arguing FOR and AGAINST the zoo environment. One wants to go back to the wilds and be carefree, the other is content to be fed and housed and not be afraid. Share your journal entry with others.

4. A BIG CAT MURAL. Use an orange background and black paint. Have one group of students paint rosettes on the background, using sponges. Allow this to dry. Another group can outline (use chalk first) several giant jaguars by drawing a head shape, rectangular body, four legs and a tail. Then using black paint, put the outline around the jaguar, and add facial features. This can be a roaring success and motivates students to listen to jungle stories and to write stories about the big cats. (The same can be done for tigers and leopards. Then display these huge murals and stories in the hallway.)

5. WALLPAPER JAGUARS. What if the jaguar lost his rosettes (see the reproducible Activity Pages) and needed a pretty cover up? Find flowers, stripes, and other designs and create a fancy new jaguar. Paste this jaguar to the front of a manila folder that you can use to collect information about the big cats.

The Jaguar says
    When day is done,
If I can't swim
    I think I'll run!

J

TALK AND TELL: JACKSON JAGUAR

1. AS WE JOG ALONG, JACKSON, I'D LIKE TO ASK YOU A FEW QUESTIONS. FIRST, HOW DO YOU LIKE LIVING HERE AT THE ZOO?

    I like it because I get good food and I feel safe. I'm an endangered species, you know.

2. NO, WE DIDN'T KNOW. WHAT DO YOU MEAN BY "ENDANGERED SPECIES"?

    Well, it means that there aren't too many of us left. To make sure that we don't become extinct like the dinosaur, we are protected in a place called a zoo.

3. WELL, JACKSON, CAN YOU REMEMBER WHERE YOU LIVED WHEN YOU WERE A BABY CUB?

    Yes I can. I lived in a little den in the side of a hill. It was very dark and well-protected. I lived there with my mother and two brothers.

4. WHAT WAS IT LIKE INSIDE THE DEN, JACKSON? WHAT DID YOU DO IN THERE?

    Well, our mother licked us clean, and that felt so good! Late at night she had to leave us alone to go out to hunt for food.

5. DID YOU FOLLOW HER?

    Oh, no! We didn't dare! She gave us her warning growl as she left the den. That warning growl meant, "You stay here until I get back!" She growled at us to protect us.

6. WHEN DID SHE RETURN, JACKSON?

    Sometimes she was out all night long looking for food and did not return until it was getting light. The rabbits come out of hiding looking for food just before it gets light (dawn) and she was good at catching rabbits.

7. WHAT OTHER FOOD DID SHE BRING BACK TO YOU, JACKSON?

    Sometimes she would find a bird asleep in a tree and catch it and bring it back to us. It was delicious! Sometimes she found nothing, and we were so hungry.

8. DID YOU ALL SHARE THE FOOD?

    When the mother jaguar hunts food at night and brings it back to the cave, she doesn't eat this catch. It's for the cubs. She would go out later in the daylight to hunt for herself, so that she wouldn't starve.

9. YOU HAVE PRETTY BROWN MARKS ON YOUR GOLDEN YELLOW FUR. DO YOU HAVE RELATIVES WHO ALSO HAVE SPOTS?

    My spots are called rosettes. The leopard and the cheetah have solid spots. People who come to the zoo say that we're beautiful.

10. YOU ARE BEAUTIFUL! DO YOU HAVE OTHER RELATIVES TOO?

    I'm a member of the cat family, so I'm related to the lion, the tiger, and even to the pet kitty cats.

11. JACKSON, YOUR PAWS ARE VERY, VERY BIG. ARE THEY SOFT?

    Yes, (hushed voice) and I can move very quietly when I'm on the hunt.

12. WHAT DO JAGUARS HUNT WHEN THEY LIVE IN THE WILDS?

    We like to hunt those big deer. Wild pigs and turtles are tasty too.

13. JACKSON, CAN YOU SWIM?

    You bet! Jaguars LOVE the water and swim just for the joy of it. We're excellent swimmers!

14. DO YOU HUNT IN THE WATER?

We like to dive into streams to catch the fish. Fish are delicious! Jaguars have been known to catch alligators and crocodiles too.

15. DO YOU LIKE TO DIVE RIGHT INTO THE WATER OR DO YOU GO IN SLOWLY?

I like to dive and do belly-floppers. I get right in there.

16. WHERE DO MOST JAGUARS LIVE, JACKSON?

In the wilds of Central America and South America. People there call me el tigre (the tiger). Can you find those places on the map?

17. WE WILL DO THAT. YOU SAID IT WAS DANGEROUS LIVING IN THE WILDS, AND HERE AT THE ZOO YOU'RE SAFE. YOU EVEN HAVE A ZOO ANIMAL DOCTOR. WHAT DO JAGUARS DO IN THE WILDS WHEN THEY'RE HURT?

We roll in the mud, and it seals up our wounds. It's nature's way.

18. YOU PUT DIRTY MUD ON AN OPEN SORE? ISN'T THAT ASKING FOR TROUBLE?

It would be for people, but not for a jaguar. In the jungle, the molds that grow on the ground contain a natural antibiotic for animals. You go to the doctor and get a shot or a prescription for antibiotics—we roll in the mud. Don't YOU try it, though.

19. WE PROMISE NOT TO GET DIRT IN A SORE AND IF WE DO TO WASH IT RIGHT AWAY. WHAT ELSE HELPS TO HEAL YOUR WOUNDS?

The sun, right up there in the sky! There is nothing like good old Mr. Sunlight to help heal a wound. A little sun is good for people too.

20. WELL, HERE COMES THE ZOOKEEPER WITH YOUR SUPPER. DO YOU ENJOY BEING SERVED LIKE A KING, JACKSON?

Listen carefully, I'm purring! Hmmm-mmm-mmm. You know what that means.

YES, YOU ARE A HAPPY JAGUAR! THANK YOU FOR THIS TALK-AND-TELL TIME RIGHT HERE AT THE ZOO. TODAY OUR GUEST WAS THE GOLDEN JACKSON JAGUAR WITH BROWN MARKS CALLED ROSETTES. TUNE IN NEXT TIME WHEN WE WILL BE INTERVIEWING A(N)

—————————————————————. BOYS AND GIRLS, YOU ARE SUCH GOOD LISTENERS!! BYE FOR NOW.

INTERVIEW
INFORMATION

What did you learn? Draw it, write it, or web it.

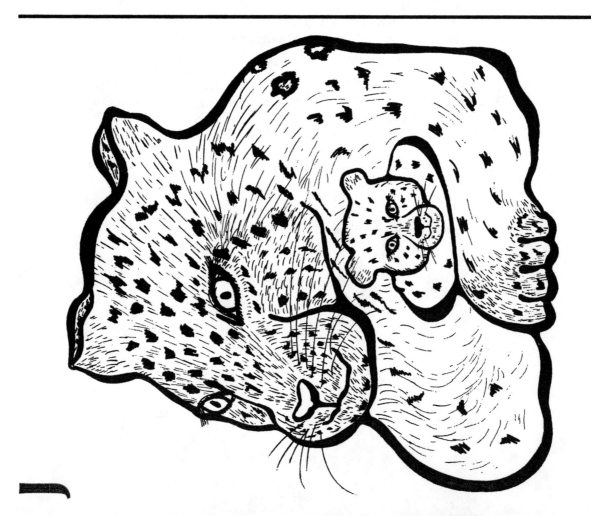

JACKSON JAGUAR

J

HOW THE JAGUAR LOST HIS ROSETTES

This jaguar needs your help. Talk, map, write, or draw your story.
How did this jaguar lose his rosettes and how can he get back his
special markings?

"The jaguar lost his rosettes.
They were as precious as pets.
He won't go outside,
If you visit, he'll hide.
He just sits at home,
    and he frets!"

SPECIAL WRITING PAPER FOR ANIMAL STORIES

(designed by Jackson Jaguar)

Name _____ Date _____

A VISUAL STORY MAP   Select a story that you like and print the title and author at the bottom of this page. Then use your crayons to show pictures of what took place in the story. Use this page as a guide to retell your story aloud.

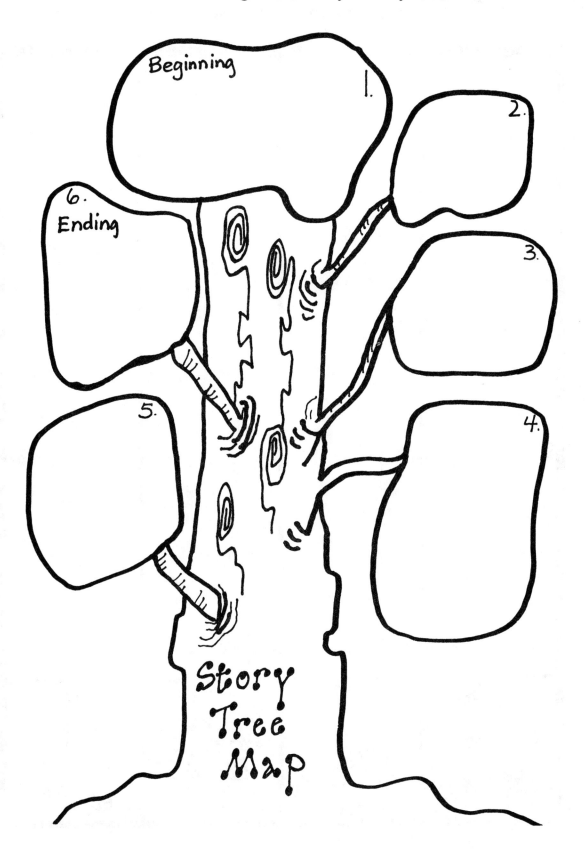

JAGUAR'S FAVORITE CAT GRAPH

Ask ten people to select their favorite cat from those pictured below. One at a time, have them draw the cat in the appropriate column, starting at the bottom. Tally the results.

tiger | lion | jaguar | pet cat

Jaguar Jump Record

_____ can jump
(name)

_____ inches in the air,

and _____ inches from here

to there.

GOAL: To jump _____ inches.

K

IS

FOR

KELLY KANGAROO

K IS FOR KELLY KANGAROO

BACKGROUND INFORMATION ABOUT KANGAROOS: A kangaroo like Kelly is called a *marsupial.* It is an animal with a pouch that is found in Australia, known as the land down under. Australia is the only continent where marsupials are found. Other marsupials include the wallaby and the wombat. There is even a marsupial mouse!

The intriguing pouch is a fleshy pocket across the lower abdomen of the female, with strong muscles that hold it firm to the body. Its elasticity enables the pouch to be stretched. The baby, or joey, is born live through the mother's birth passage, and then makes its journey instinctively to the pouch and attaches itself to the mother's teat. Because it remains firmly attached for eight months, it was believed at one time that the joeys were born inside the pouch. However, this is not the case.

READING/LANGUAGE ARTS:

1. KELLY'S VOCABULARY. We can learn some new words such as buck (male), doe (female), and joey (newly born kangaroo). When the kangaroo is old enough to go in and out of the pouch, it is called the "young at foot." Make a Kelly Kangaroo shape and cut a slit for her pouch. Put the new vocabulary words on a small kangaroo shape and have students insert them in the pouch as they say the word.

2. DO YOU HAVE A NICKNAME? The male kangaroo does. Kangaroos signal danger by making a booming sound with their huge back feet. The adult male is nicknamed Boomer. Who in our group has a nickname? How did they get this name? What special names do the children call their grandmother or grandfather or baby sister or brother? What nicknames do they have for their pets? This is a rich language development experience.

3. KANGAROO MEANS "I DON'T KNOW." There is a story that long ago when visitors went to Australia and saw a strange looking animal with a pocket, they asked what it was called. The person answering, known as an Aborigine, responded with "kangaroo." Later, it was found that the word kangaroo means "I don't know." Let's get a book of the meaning of names and find out what the names of the boys and girls mean.

4. A NONVERBAL NAME GAME. When we extend our hands with palms up, shrug our shoulders, and raise our eyebrows, it is the nonverbal equivalent of saying "I don't know." Ask students some questions after the Kangaroo interview to see if we get many kangaroo answers.

MATH:

1. LESS THAN AN INCH. When a joey is born, it is about 1 3/4" in length. Have students measure this with a ruler so they can see just how small joey is. What else is less than an inch? Measure some items to find out.

2. TWENTY TEETH, THEN NINETEEN, THEN EIGHTEEN . . . With the Kangaroo we can get a good lesson in subtraction. The kangaroo is born with 20 teeth. Because of the constant pulling and chewing of grass, the front teeth wear down, fall out, and all of the rest of the teeth shift forward. This continues throughout the life of the kangaroo. If it ends up with no teeth, it would not be able to get food.

Have 20 students stand in a semi-circle in the kangaroo's mouth pretending to be teeth. Oops! Two front ones fall out, how many are left? Count them, and shift together. Oops! Two front ones fall out, how many are left? Count them, and shift together. Keep going—but leave at least two teeth for the kangaroo so that it can continue to pull and eat long grasses.

3. HOP-TO-IT MATH.   Children will enjoy hopping like Kelly Kangaroo. Play the recording, "Waltzing Matilda", and have children jump on every third beat. Ready? Go! da da DA, da da DA . . .

4. LET'S TAKE A POCKET COUNT.   How many of us are wearing clothing with pockets today? Count the pockets in your shirt, pants, blouse, skirt, dress, and jacket. We might be amazed at the total!

SCIENCE:

1. WHAT MAKES KANGAROOS SPECIAL?   Kelly has a pouch and is called a marsupial (mar SUE pe uhl). Other marsupials are the wallaby, oppossum, and wombat. Find these interesting-sounding animals in colorful information books.

2. CLASSIFICATION OF ANIMALS.   Many of the animals that we have met are called mammals—that is, they are born live and nursed by the mother. Some of our Alphabet Animals were hatched from an egg. Let's make an A–K list and see what happens:

	Hatched	*Mammal*	*Marsupial*
A—Ashley Alligator	x		
B—Brandi Bear		x	
C—Clancy Cat		x	
D—Duke Dog		x	
E—Eddington Elephant		x	
F—Francine Frog	x		
G—Goldie Goat		x	
H—Handkerchief Horse		x	
I—Inky Insect	x		
J—Jackson Jaguar		x	
K—Kelly Kangaroo			x

Keep adding to the list as new animals are introduced.

SOCIAL STUDIES:

1. THE LAND DOWN UNDER.   Locate Australia on a map and a globe. With a piece of Velcro, fasten a little pocket there in honor of Kelly the Kangaroo. Find picture books of Australia so that we can find out about Kelly's surroundings.

2. HOW WOULD WE TRAVEL TO AUSTRALIA? Can we go by car? Is it far away? Do we perhaps need several types of transportation to get us to Kelly's home? Let's use the map and globe to help us to problem-solve this question.

3. CONTAINERS (AND POCKETS) ARE HELPFUL. How many containers can we name? There are many of them. Start with a grocery store first (cans, boxes, cartons, bags, and so on). How many do we have right in this room?

Make an ABC Chart of Containers. List all of the letters at the left, and then have students decide what goes into containers. To make a colorful chart, use a different felt-tip pen for every other letter. Also, have the students illustrate the items around the edges. Students are amazed at how many items come in containers. Read *A House Is a House for Me* by Mary Ann Hoberman. This will encourage students to come up with some creative responses because everything is a house for something else.

4. DINGOS DON'T LIKE KANGAS. The wild dogs, called *dingos,* are the natural enemies of Kangaroos. And sometimes they win, even though the Kangaroo can run up to 25 mi/h and can hop 4 feet at one time. Also, the eagles that swoop down with their big claws can do much damage to the kangaroos and weaken and kill them for their food.

5. THE FOOD CHAIN IN NATURE. Nature's way means that nature sees to it that all of the animals have something to eat. Sometimes this means being eaten by a bigger animal, who is then eaten by a yet bigger animal. Perhaps this is a good time to begin with food chain information for those children who are ready.

A kanga has a
Pouch for a lap
And that's where joey
Takes a nap.

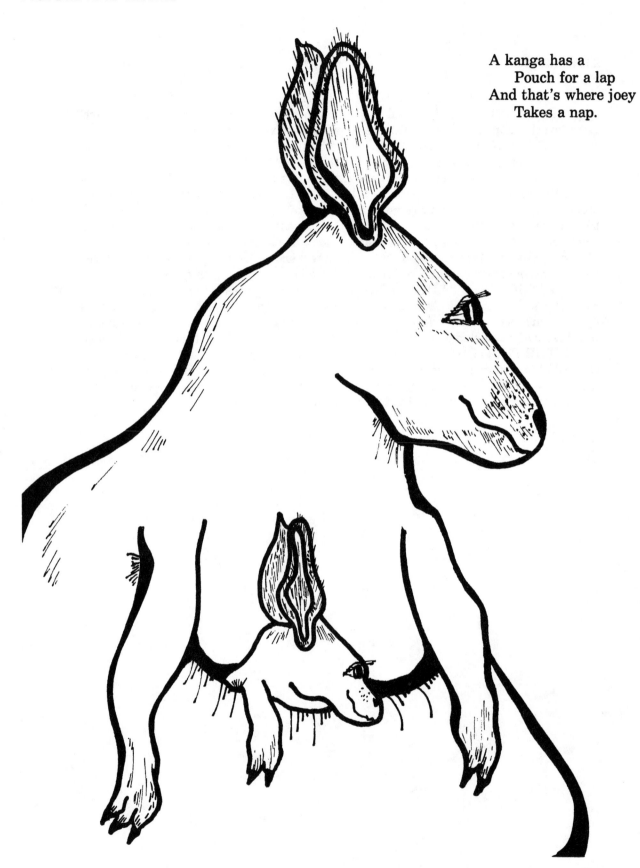

K

TALK AND TELL: KELLY KANGAROO

1. HI THERE, KELLY KANGAROO. WE HAVE A QUESTION FOR YOU. WERE YOU BORN IN A POUCH?

No, I wasn't born in the pouch. I was born live and crawled into the pouch and began to nurse right away.

2. HOW LONG DID YOU STAY IN YOUR MOTHER'S POUCH, KELLY?

For about one whole school year (about 8 months). Then I got too big and had to get out.

3. WHAT DID YOU DO WHEN YOU GOT OUT OF THE POUCH?

I tried to get back inside, but I was too big. My mother's pouch just couldn't stretch any more to hold me.

4. KELLY, TELL US. WHAT IS IT LIKE INSIDE OF THE POUCH?

It's warm, furry, and soft. The pouch shuts tight at the top just like a handbag. It's a safe feeling in there.

5. SOUNDS LIKE IT IS SAFE. WHAT IS A BABY KANGAROO CALLED, KELLY?

A baby kangaroo is called a joey. The mother is a doe, and the papa is a buck.

6. DOES ANY OTHER ANIMAL HAVE ONE OF THE THOSE POUCHES?

Yes. The wallaby has a pouch—that's a smaller-sized kangaroo. And the opossum has a pouch, and so does the wombat.

7. THOSE ARE DIFFERENT SOUNDING NAMES—WALLABY AND WOMBAT—WHERE DO YOU COME FROM?

We're from Australia. Maybe you can find it on the map or globe.

8. YES, WE WILL LOOK FOR IT. KELLY, IS THERE A SPECIAL NAME FOR ANIMALS WITH POUCHES?

We're called marsupials (mar SUE pea uhls). Can you say it? Mar SUE pea uhl. Good!

9. KELLY, HOW LONG DOES IT TAKE BEFORE A BABY KANGAROO, A JOEY, IS TRULY ON ITS OWN?

About a year and a half. That's a long time. During that time we are called the young at foot. Sometimes the mother has a joey in the pouch *and* a young at foot. She keeps busy.

10. IS THE KANGAROO A GOOD MOTHER, KELLY?

She's the best! She strokes the joey's back, and nuzzles the joey, and she makes clucking sounds to call us back when she senses danger.

11. IS SHE GENTLE?

As gentle as a breeze, and usually very patient. A young joey learns by imitating his mother. We watch her and then do exactly as she does. She's a good teacher.

12. KANGAROOS LIKE TO HOP, DON'T THEY, KELLY?

We sure do! We can hop three feet at one time. Put a yardstick down on the ground to see how far that is from end to end. We can move along at about 25 miles per hour—I could keep up with your school bus by hopping along.

13. THAT WOULD BE FUN TO LOOK OUT THE WINDOW AND SEE YOU HOPPING RIGHT ALONG ON YOUR BIG FEET. HOW BIG DO YOUR FEET GROW?

Do you have a ruler? My feet are about 12 inches long. They're just right for hopping.

14. DO YOU USE YOUR FEET FOR ANYTHING ELSE BESIDES HOPPING?

Yes we do. The adults signal danger with a hard booming sound of their big feet. The adult male is even nicknamed Boomer.

15. WHAT DO YOU LIKE TO EAT, KELLY?

Kangaroos like juicy grass. We chew our cud just like a cow.

16. DOES ALL OF THAT CHEWING WEAR DOWN YOUR TEETH?

Yes it does. The front teeth wear out first and fall out and then the rest of the teeth all move forward.

17. DO YOU HAVE BABY TEETH AND SECOND TEETH?

No. When our front teeth fall out, the rest just move forward in our mouth. We have about 20 teeth to start with and they fall out and move, fall out and move, fall out and move all of our life. We end up with very few teeth.

18. DO YOU LIVE IN PEACE OR ARE THERE ANIMALS THAT ARE OUT TO GET YOU?

The wild barking dogs called *dingos* go after us. And those giant eagles swoop down at us with their big claws, too!

19. YOUR GREY-BROWN COAT IS NICE AND CLEAN. DO YOU HAVE TO WORK HARD TO KEEP IT CLEAN, KELLY?

Yes, Kangaroos lick themselves clean just like the family kitty cat. We have four claws on our paws and we use them as rakes. We rake, or comb, our claws through our coat to keep it nice and clean.

20. THANK YOU FOR TALKING WITH US, KELLY KANGAROO. WE LIKED LEARNING ALL ABOUT YOUR POUCH. IT MAKES YOU SPECIAL. AND NOW WE KNOW THAT YOU ARE A MARSUPIAL.

Well, since you are interested, I can tell you one more thing about marsupials. (Whisper: There's even a marsupial MOUSE in Australia!) Bye, now. Come and see me at the zoo!

BYE-BYE, KELLY. THANK YOU FOR THIS TALK-AND-TELL TIME RIGHT HERE AT THE ZOO. TODAY OUR GUEST WAS KELLY KANGAROO WHO HAS A GREAT BIG POUCH! TUNE IN NEXT TIME WHEN WE WILL BE INTER-VIEW A(N)

_____. TAKE GOOD CARE OF YOUR SECOND TEETH SO THAT THEY DON'T FALL OUT!

INTERVIEW
INFORMATION

What did you learn? Draw it, write it, or web it.

K

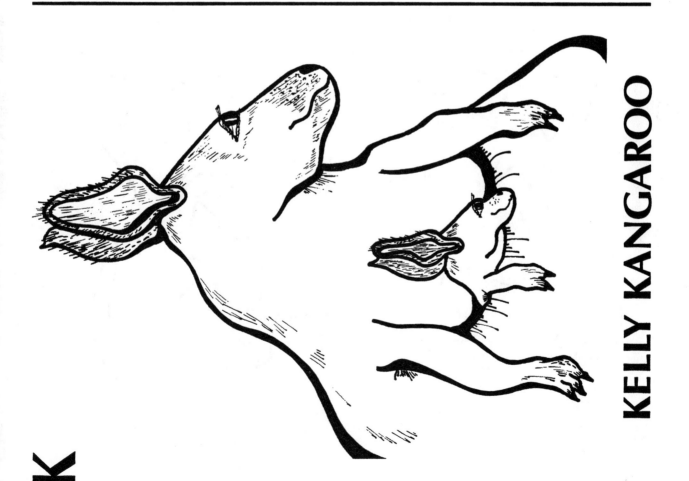

KELLY KANGAROO

Put your right toe in front
Put your right toe in back
Put your feet back together
Make your hands—clap, clap!

Put your left toe in front
Put your left toe in back
Put your feet back together
Make your hands—clap, clap!

Hop ahead—1, 2, 3
To the left—1, 2, 3
Hop back—1, 2, 3
To the right—1, 2, 3
THAT'S A SQUARE—clap, clap!

A square I can jump
And a circle, too
Just call out a shape
I can jump it for you!
_____ clap, clap!
(call out)

Name _____

Date _____

HELP JOEY COUNT TWENTY TEETH

The kangaroo is a marsupial, an animal with a pouch. The baby, or joey, is born with twenty teeth. Because of constant pulling and chewing of grass, the front teeth wear down and the rest shift forward. This continues during the animal's lifetime.

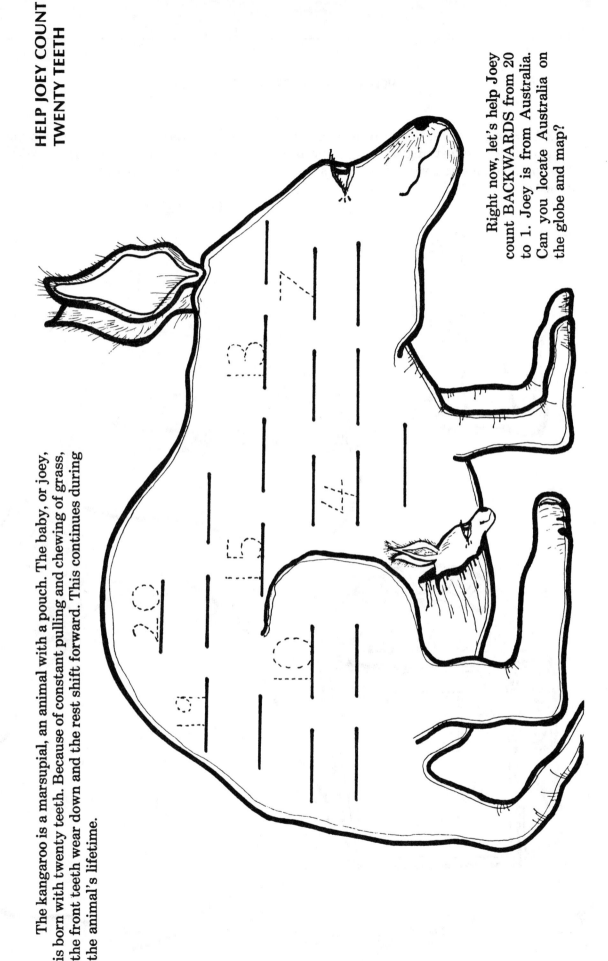

Right now, let's help Joey count BACKWARDS from 20 to 1. Joey is from Australia. Can you locate Australia on the globe and map?

Name _____ Date _____

POUCHES, BAGS, AND POCKETS

Kelly Kangaroo wants you to use this as a riddle page. Select one of the items and say, "I'm thinking of something that _____ and it is _____." Call upon someone to guess what it is. If that person guesses correctly, then it's his or her turn. If he or she does not guess, then give another clue.

Do you have a pocket?

1. First, color Kelly Kangaroo. Then carefully cut her out on the thick black line.
2. Cut the slit for Kelly's pouch.
3. Paste the top and bottom pieces together so that they match.
4. Find magazine pictures that begin with Kelly's sound and place them into her pouch.

Variation: You might play this game with a classmate. One student can be Kelly and can either accept or reject the items offered to her for her pouch.

KELLY THE CUTOUT KANGAROO (page 2 of 2)

L

IS

FOR

LOLLIPOP LION

L IS FOR LOLLIPOP LION

BACKGROUND INFORMATION ABOUT LIONS: The lion, or King of the Beasts, is the second largest cat in the world. The largest is the tiger. The lion is a predator— actively stalking and seeking other wild animals to eat. Predators often play an important role in the balance of nature by catching and eating the weak, sick, or old animals. Even though the lion is a *predator,* it is also *prey,* as other wild animals seek out the lion cubs.

READING/LANGUAGE ARTS:

1. LOLLIPOP'S LANGUAGE LESSON.   Introduce the word *ferocious* by writing it on the chalkboard. Have children say it and learn to use it. It refers to anything that can be overpowering—even things in nature such as hurricanes, rain, wind, heat, and so on.

2. IT IS WITH GREAT PRIDE THAT WE PRESENT LOLLIPOP.   That's one way to use the word pride. Also, pride is the name given to the group of lions that live together—they live in a pride.

3. SANDPAPER TONGUES.   All of the big cats, and even your little kitty who is related to Lollipop, have rough tongues. Have several samples of different grades of sandpaper available during the interview so that children can feel the tongue of the lion. Elicit descriptive words about this rough texture (itchy, pinchy, tough, bumpy, and so on).

MATH:

1. LION NUMBERS.   As many as 8–10 lionesses might stay together in a pride because females tend to stay together. There could be a grandmother, mother, and daughter in the pride. Have students make shoebox jungle dioramas, and place from 8–10 cutouts of lions in the scene.

2. THERE IS ONLY ROOM FOR ONE KING.   The males roam singly or sometimes in small groups over large areas until they can take over a pride and become the king. After examining many colorful pictures in information books, paint a picture at the easel of one magnificent male lion.

3. THE CONCEPT OF FIRST AND LAST.   The female lions go on the hunt and kill the prey, while the lion waits. Is it because the king is lazy? Is it because the King wants to be served? No, it's because the King has bad teeth. The male lion's teeth are not as strong as the female's teeth, so she is the one who goes for the kill. This is a very strenuous activity, so when she is finished she is not about to start eating—she needs rest first. That's when the King of Beasts goes in and starts tearing apart the kill. The female rests and is usually the last one to eat.

4. THE CONCEPT OF HALF.   With the alphabet letter l, we are almost one half way through the alphabet. How many of the animal rhymes have children learned? Are

they saying them every day? How many of the animal pictures from this book can they identify? How much information have they learned from the interviews? Perhaps this is a good interview question for them to ask, and then they can present this material to Mike MacMoose who is coming up next.

SCIENCE:

1. PREDATOR/PREY.   Introduce these two words to the students. The predator is an animal on the hunt. The prey is the animal that is being hunted. Lions sleep by day and go on the hunt at night. We say that they are nocturnal animals. Some people like to work at night, or stay up late and we refer to them as nightowls. How many nightowls do we have in the group? How many morning glories?

2. CLASSIFICATION OF ANIMALS A-L.   How many of our animals are predators? How many are prey? Let's try to classify them. Remember—sometimes a predator is also a prey. For example, hyenas and leopards are always hunting for lion cubs. Therefore, the lion can be either, depending upon the situation.

3. WHO LIVES IN A GROUP?   Lions do, and they're referred to as prides. Elephants live in herds, fish live in schools, sheep live in flocks. Check through the A-L animals so far to see what their group is called. People live in small groups. What are they called? (Family).

SOCIAL STUDIES:

1. LOLLIPOP CAN GET AGGRESSIVE.   Watch out! The hungrier the lion, the more aggressive it becomes. Lions can feast one day on a zebra and a giraffe and then not eat for four or five days. Then they have to go on the hunt again because they get hungry. Do people get cranky, or change their behavior when they are hungry? Does a baby cry, a dog whine, a cat meow when it's time to eat?

2. LIONESSES ARE GOOD BABYSITTERS.   The adult female has a litter of from one to five cubs. One mother will babysit for the cubs while another mother is on the hunt in an effort to protect the cubs from other predators. When the female returns, she gives a low roar and the cubs run to greet her and there is much nuzzling, licking, and physical contact. Set up the play corner. Who wants to babysit with Lollipop? She needs to work on her math facts, too.

3. PRACTICE TABLE MANNERS.   Eating is a social activity. In the interview the lion admits to not having any table manners. Let's review table manners for people. Today when students have a snack, they can pretend to teach some manners to Lollipop. Do this in an enjoyable way, and watch the manners improve, too!

4. WEAR A CROWN.   Make paper crowns and sprinkle them with gold glitter. Today we are wearing the crowns in celebration of the King of the Beasts.

5. LION FACES.   Have students study the faces of lions in books and then paint the face of the lion at the easel this week. Also, lion faces can be constructed using a circular paper plate for the face, loopy yarn for the mane, and construction paper details for facial features.

6. MAKE A ROYAL ROBE.   Bring in a large piece of purple cotton cloth. Have students decorate it with yellow paint. Allow it to dry. The good citizen who is King for a Day can be draped in the glamorous robe for story time. This would also be good for creative play, along with the crowns and faces.

**LOLLIPOP'S TALK-AND-TELL
PICTURE AND RHYME**

Lion is called
The king of beasts
And he dines first
At animal feasts.

L

TALK AND TELL: LOLLIPOP LION

1. GREETINGS, LOLLIPOP LION! WHERE IS YOUR HOME?

    Can you find Africa on a map or globe? I live on a reserve in Africa.
2. WHAT IS A RESERVE?

    It's like a fenced-in natural park for wild animals. People are not allowed to hunt there.
3. LOLLIPOP, ARE YOU WILD OR TAME?

    I'm a wild animal who hunts other animals. We call that a predator. I'm a meat eater, and I can be ferocious!
4. IN STORYBOOKS THEY CALL YOU KING OF THE BEASTS. ARE YOU THE KING?

    Yes, but even animal Kings work very hard. I don't always catch every animal that I run after even though I can run faster than a city bus (30 mi/h).
5. WHAT IS YOUR FAVORITE FOOD WHEN YOU GO HUNTING, LOLLIPOP?

    I'm not too fussy. I like zebras, baby elephants, baby rhinos, baby buffalo, and baby giraffes. They're called my prey.
6. WHY DO YOU PREY UPON YOUNG, WEAK BABY ANIMALS THAT CAN'T PUT UP A FIGHT? IS THAT FAIR?

    In the animal world, which is different from the way people live, lions help to stop disease from spreading by killing the weak and sick. It's nature's way.
7. THEN YOU'RE NOT SUCH A BAD GUY! ARE YOU A MEMBER OF THE CAT FAMILY?

    Yes. I'm second largest of all of the wild cats in the world. The tiger is a little bigger.
8. HOW BIG ARE YOU?

    I am 8 ft long. Can you measure that with your rulers? Put 8 together, end to end.
9. YOU'RE BORN LIVE, AREN'T YOU?

    Yes, I'm a mammal. A female lioness has from one to five babies. It's called a litter. At birth I'm called a cub, and I'm helpless.
10. IS A MOTHER LION KIND TO HER BABY CUBS?

    Very. She plays with us and teaches us to obey her lead—it's for our own safety. When several lionesses have cubs they often put their young together and take turns caring for them, sort of like day care. We're one big happy family.
11. DO YOU STAY TOGETHER FOR LONG, LOLLIPOP?

    Some female lions stay together their whole lifetime. Often, a grandmother, a mother, and a baby live together with their families. Most males move on, and don't stay together in the pride.
12. WHAT IS A PRIDE?

    It's another word for group. You know that elephants live in herds, and sheep live in flocks, well, lions live in prides.
13. DOES THE MALE LION PROTECT THE PRIDE?

    That's his main job. His roar can be heard for miles and it means, "Stay away! This is my place!"
14. DOES THE MALE LION HUNT FOR FOOD?

    He can, but usually the female lioness does the hunting because her teeth are better. She has to surprise the prey and then lunge and attack with her teeth and claws.

She hunts alone if she sees a small animal, or she hunts with other lions if the prey is a very large animal.

15. HOW DO LIONESSES HUNT IN A GROUP?

They silently and slowly surround a large animal, such as a giraffe. Then one lioness jumps right at the large animal and two or three lionesses run in to help.

16. DO YOU ALL EAT THE ANIMAL RIGHT THERE ON THE SPOT?

When a large animal is killed, the whole pride shares the meal. The female has to take a rest first because she's tired from the hunt. The male lion eats first. We're messy eaters and we fight over the food.

17. WHY DO YOU FIGHT OVER FOOD, LOLLIPOP?

We're hungry and we tend to stuff ourselves with food. We have never learned table manners like people, and we never know when we will eat again. We may not have another meal for a week. We can't just go to the store and buy food like people do.

18. OTHER THAN FIGHTING OVER FOOD, HOW WELL DOES THE PRIDE GET ALONG?

Great! We greet each other by rubbing heads. We rest together with our bodies draped over each other and we moan because we're happy. We like to be near each other.

19. LITTLE KITTY CATS HAVE A ROUGH TONGUE. DO YOU HAVE A ROUGH TONGUE, LIKE SANDPAPER?

Yes. We clean ourselves with it and we clean each other too. We sit around and lick each other's faces and neck for as long as three whole minutes!! This feels so good to furry lions. Don't you try it, though! It's germy.

20. IF WE CAN'T TRAVEL TO AFRICA, WHERE CAN WE SEE YOU?

In a zoo or even in a circus. But beware—my hunter instinct is always there! I'm ferocious! That's a big word, FER O SHUS. Say it. Good! Open your mouth very wide, show your teeth and say it, FER O SHUS!

THANK YOU FOR THIS TALK-AND-TELL TIME RIGHT HERE AT THE WILDLIFE CENTER. TODAY OUR GUEST WAS A WILD LION NAMED LOLLIPOP. TUNE IN NEXT TIME WHEN WE WILL BE INTERVIEWING A(N)

―――――――――――――――――――――

REMEMBER, DON'T EVER GET CLOSE TO A LION BECAUSE THEY'RE FEROCIOUS!

INTERVIEW INFORMATION

What did you learn? Draw it, write it, or web it.

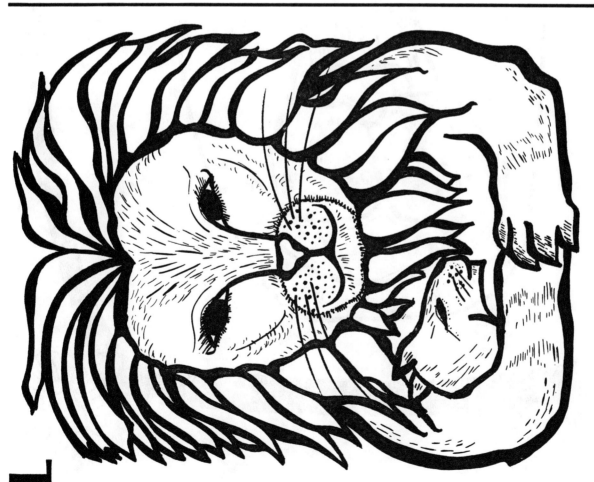

L

LOLLIPOP LION

THE LION PUPPET PET

Cut out the puppet shape on the dark line. Paste strips of gold, tan, and brown around the puppet for a beautiful mane. Attach the face to a sturdy cardboard strip and use the puppet for story telling.

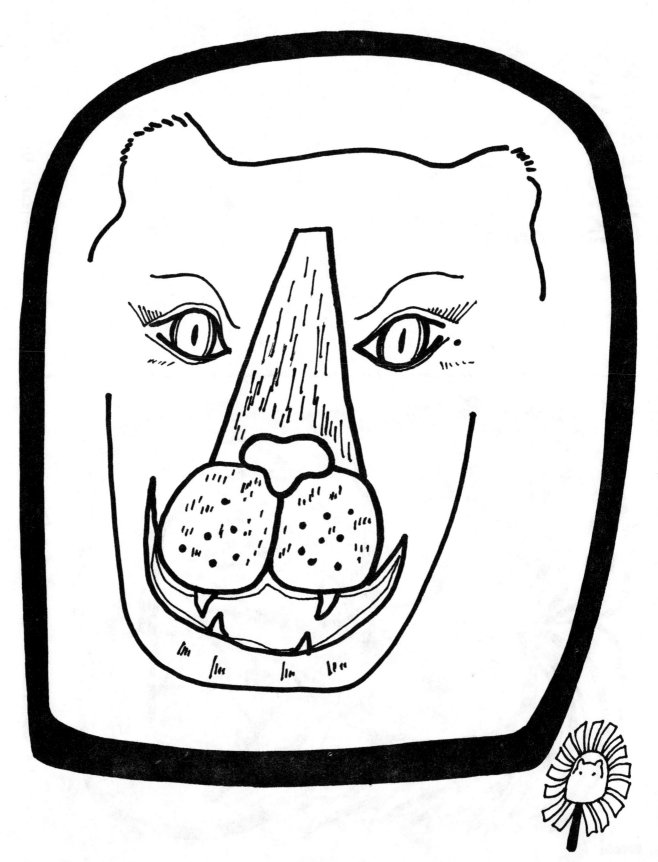

LOLLIPOP LION'S COLLECTION OF "L" ITEMS

Lollipop Lion has found three items that belong with the sound of l as in lion. Can you locate them below? Circle them and color them with bright crayons. Make up a sentence about each item.

LOLLIPOP LION'S TRIP TO THE ZOO

For one player: Name an animal or bird that begins with each letter from A through L so that the lion can get back to the zoo in time for dinner. How might two people play this game? Any ideas? Make up your own rules.

LION'S ROAR AWARD

You did something very special to earn this!

To-

For-

LOLLIPOP LION'S PICTURE BOOK PLAN

You need 7 sheets of 9″ × 12″ colored paper. Cut out the 6 designs here. Paste each design of animal skin, hide, or fur right in the middle of a blank sheet of paper. Then, draw an animal around the shape, using the pattern as a starting point. Make 6 different ones, and then make a cover page for your book. Good luck! Be sure to share your books. They should all be different.

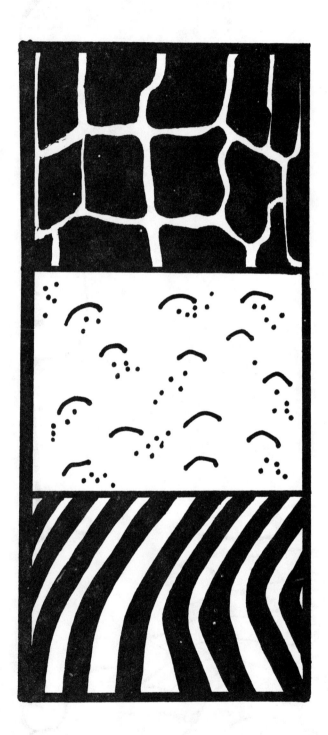

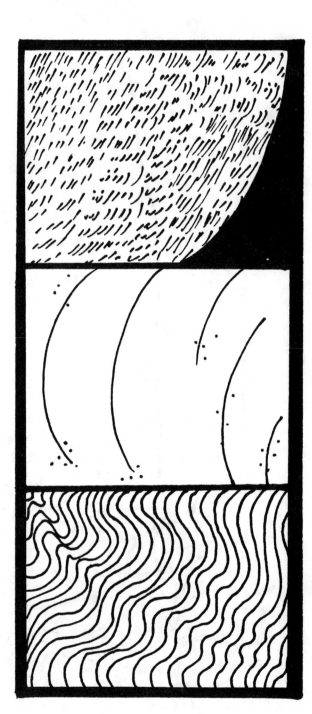

© 1992 by The Center for Applied Research in Education

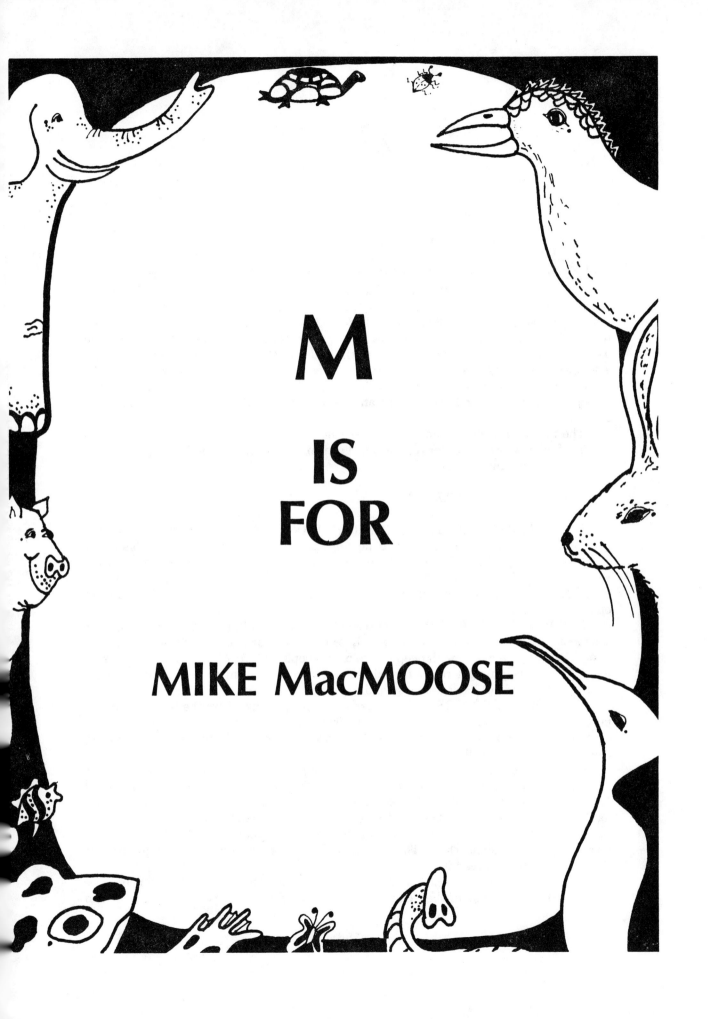

M
IS
FOR

MIKE MacMOOSE

M IS FOR MIKE MacMOOSE

BACKGROUND INFORMATION ABOUT MOOSE: Moose is from the Algonquin Indian name *musse* or *twig eater*. It is a large, hoofed mammal, and a member of the deer family. The moose is herbivorous, eating only plants. It can do much damage to forests since it destroys trees by pulling off the bark and branches. The magnificent antlers are usually found on the males. The antlers first appear as swellings, then knobs, and then as bone covered with soft skin. When the skin peels off, the polished bone is underneath. The antlers serve as a cooling devise for the moose since blood does flow through the antler skin and is cooled by the breeze. This majestic headgear seems to be a symbol of strength used in mating. In the winter, antlers loosen and fall off, and grow again in the spring.

The moose is a solitary animal. Its excellent swimming skill enables the moose to quickly find new territories for roaming and grazing. Its natural enemies in the wild are the grizzly bears and wolves.

READING/LANGUAGE ARTS:

1. ONE MOOSE, TWO MOOSE, THREE MOOSE. Regardless of the number, the word moose remains constant. There is no singular or plural form of moose. This is not the case for many other animals, is it? For many we must add an s or es at the end when we mean more than one (plural). Have students list the singular and plural name forms of the animals that we have met so far (alligator/alligators, bear/bears, cat/cats, and so on).

2. SOLITARY MEANS ONE. Introduce the word *solitary* and the concept that the moose is a solitary animal, or one who lives alone. The moose must do everything for itself. Contrast the moose with people. Are most people solitary? No. What do adults do for us just to help us get ready for school? How can we begin to be a little bit more solitary (independent) like the moose and begin to help ourselves?

3. STORYBOOK MOOSE. There are many storybooks where the Moose is an important character. The *Morris and Boris* stories by Bernard Wiseman offer a number of escapades for the two main characters. Compare these books in terms of the setting, conflict, and problem-solving.

4. PUPPET SHOW. Write and produce a puppet show dramatizing a book about a moose. Or, interview the moose puppet and ask the same 20 questions that are asked in the interview section. Then, think of one more. Keep interviewing the animals, and have them interview each other too, for some talk-and-tell experiences.

5. BOOK REVIEWS. On a TV talk show, have the animals do a one-minute commercial for a book about them. They can show the book, and tell just enough about it that we can't wait to read it.

6. JOURNAL TIME. Students can write in their journal from the point of view of the moose in a season of their choice. Gather the writers together. Each student can

tell what he has written, and then read it. Then ask students if they have any other suggestions for the story.

MATH:

1. MIKE MacMOOSE EXPLORES SEASONS. The moose antlers make Mike aware of the seasons of the year. Antlers grow in spring and fall off during early winter. What other seasonal changes in nature do we find that make us aware of the passage of time? Make a strip picture depicting a moose in the four different seasons.

2. CHECK THE DISTANCE. Moose cannot see well for a great distance. Use animal flash cards or a chart of ABC letters, and measure to see how far away students can be and still easily identify the animal or letters. Measure to the nearest foot.

3. MIKE MacMOOSE MAKES HALF. With the letter M we are halfway through the alphabet animals. M is the thirteenth (13) letter of the alphabet and there are 26 letters. Review or teach the concept of half—two equal parts of a whole.

4. MOOSE ANIMAL REVIEW. Make a large envelope and include the picture and rhyme that goes with each of the animals that we have worked with so far (A–M). How many can we identify? How many rhymes do we know? Make up songs or chants or movements to accompany the animal rhymes.

Have students reach into the envelope and remove a picture. What two facts can they tell about that animal? If they need help, perhaps they can call upon a friend for assistance.

SCIENCE:

1. YOUR NOSE BRINGS NEWS. Moose have a very keen sense of smell. Arrange to have plastic containers with holes poked through the lid. Place aromatic items inside and see if students can identify the items, using only their sense of smell. (Some items: cottonball soaked with oil of cloves, cottonball soaked with perfume, orange slices, buttered popcorn, and so on.)

2. A CROWN OF BONES. Make moose crowns from oaktag and have children wear them during creative play. Who else wears crowns? (King, Queen, Prince, Princess, Contest Winners, Student-for-the Day, and so on). Students can make a variety of crowns from oaktag, or decorate old hats to use during playtime.

3. ANTLERS, SCALES, PAWS, AND TAILS. Which of our A–M animals have crowns of horns or antlers? Who has scales? Which ones have paws, hoofs, or webbed feet? And let's examine the great variety in their tails! What an opportunity for more classification experiences.

SOCIAL STUDIES:

1. MOOSE THREAD. In the early days of our country, moose hide was used for clothing, shoes, and snowshoes. Stiff moose hair was used for thread, and antlers were made into a variety of tools. Try to imagine what type of tools could be made from moose antlers. (Examples: rakes, shovels, combs, and so on).

2. ANIMAL HIDES. Check through the ABC animals so far to see what we use or used at one time. For example, alligator was used to make belts, purses, wallets, and

shoes. This may lead to a discussion of endangered species and why we no longer need to kill animals for their hide, hair, or tusks. Today we have man-made (synthetic) materials.

3. THUMBNAIL SKETCHES.   Place large construction paper thumbnails on the bulletin board. Students can select one to write a sketchy outline of one of the animals that we have addressed thus far.

4. MOOSE TALK.   Set up a radio talk show studio with chair, desk, microphone, and other props and have two or three animals talk about their environment, or about a particular issue in which the students show a great deal of interest.

Moose swims the lakes
    With head held high.
He likes to keep
    His antlers dry.

M

TALK AND TELL: MIKE MacMOOSE

1. HI MIKE MacMOOSE! WHERE DID YOU GET THE NAME MOOSE?

    The Algonquin Indians named the moose. It means twig eaters. Twigs grow on trees, and antlers grow on my head.

2. I LIKE YOUR BIG ANTLERS! ARE YOU RELATED TO SANTA'S REIN-DEER?

    Well, yes. A moose is the largest deer in the world and the largest of all animals with antlers, or horns.

3. CAN YOU TELL US ABOUT YOUR ANTLERS, MIKE?

    It feels like wearing a crown of bones on top of my head. It's good protection—other animals stay away!

4. DO THOSE ANTLERS HURT? WHY DO YOU BANG YOUR HEAD AGAINST THE TREES IN THE AUTUMN?

    First, they don't hurt. Second, I bang against trees to help knock off my antlers. Antlers grow back again every Spring and they fall off in Winter. It makes Winter so much easier without carrying around the antlers.

5. ARE YOU A MAMMAL, MIKE MacMOOSE?

    Yes, I'm born live.

6. DID YOU GET GOOD CARE WHEN YOU WERE A BABY?

    Excellent! A huge mother moose with her calf is not bothered by any animals. When someone does come too close, the female moose rears up on her hind legs, just like a horse, and strikes out with her hoofs.

7. WHAT ARE MALES AND FEMALES CALLED, MIKE?

    The male is a bull, the female is a cow, and the babies are called calves.

8. DO YOU LIVE IN PACKS, HERDS, OR GROUPS?

    No. A moose is a solitary animal. Solitary means that moose live alone. We're loners.

9. MIKE, DO YOU HAVE ANY NATURAL ENEMIES IN THE WILDS?

    Sigh—yes! Buffalo and wolves, and of course, those grizzly bears!

10. HOW DO YOU MANAGE TO GET ALONG ALL ALONE IN THE WILDS?

    The mother moose has a strong instinct to teach her calf everything she knows about survival.

11. CAN YOU TELL US WHAT SHE TEACHES YOU, MIKE?

    She teaches the baby calf how to backtrack, how to circle and come up behind the enemy, and how to freeze or be absolutely, perfectly still, (slow voice) without even moving your eyes. Try it!

12. DO YOU LIKE TO FIGHT?

    No. I would rather run. A moose is fast and can outrun a horse.

13. DO YOU HEAR WELL?

    Very well! My sense of smell is excellent too. My eyesight is not too good, though.

14. MIKE, WE HEARD THAT YOU'RE AN EXCELLENT SWIMMER. IS THAT CORRECT?

    Yes it is, thank you. A healthy moose can swim for over five miles without stopping. Also, it sure does give our skin some relief from those pesky ticks. They bite!

15. YOU'RE SOOOO BIG. HOW MUCH DOES A MOOSE WEIGH?

    About as much as a small truck.

16. THAT'S HEAVY!! WHAT IS YOUR FAVORITE FOOD, MIKE?

I like leaves, twigs, and tree branches. I think tree bark is tasty too.

17. WHAT? AREN'T ALL OF THOSE POINTY, PRICKLY THINGS BAD FOR YOUR STOMACH?

It would be for your stomach, but not for mine. My stomach has four sections. Sections 1 and 2 digest the food, then return it to my mouth where I can rechew it. It's called chewing my cud, just like the cows do.

18. DO YOU LIKE COWS, MIKE?

I never go near them. I will graze with horses, sometimes.

19. HOW MUCH DO YOU EAT IN A DAY?

Moose are big eaters. We eat about 50 pounds of food every day. That's more than you can lift! (As much as five 10-lb bags of potatoes).

20. IT'S VERY LOVELY HERE AND WE HAVE TO LEAVE NOW. ARE YOU SURE THAT YOU DON'T MIND IF WE LEAVE YOU ALL ALONE?

Not at all. Moose have lived like this for ages and ages. But, thanks for the visit.

THANK YOU FOR THIS TALK AND TELL RIGHT HERE IN ALASKA. TODAY OUR GUEST WAS THE GREAT BIG MIKE MacMOOSE. TUNE IN NEXT TIME WHEN WE WILL BE INTERVIEWING A(N)

_____. THIS IS STATION "ABCD-EFG-HIJK-L-M Is for Moose."

M

INTERVIEW INFORMATION

What did you learn? Draw it, write it, or web it.

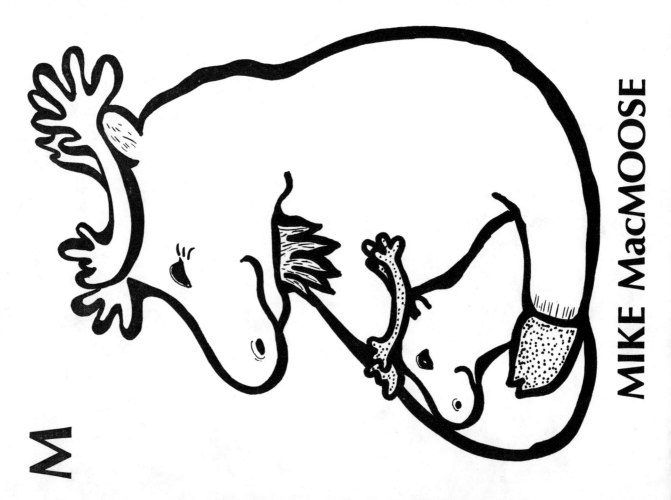

MIKE MacMOOSE

MIKE MacMOOSE HAS A TREE HOUSE

Mike MacMoose met three migrating birds—one is red, one is blue, and one is brown. They asked if they could each make a nest in his tree house of antlers. Mike has agreed. Use your crayons to show each of the birds in its new home.

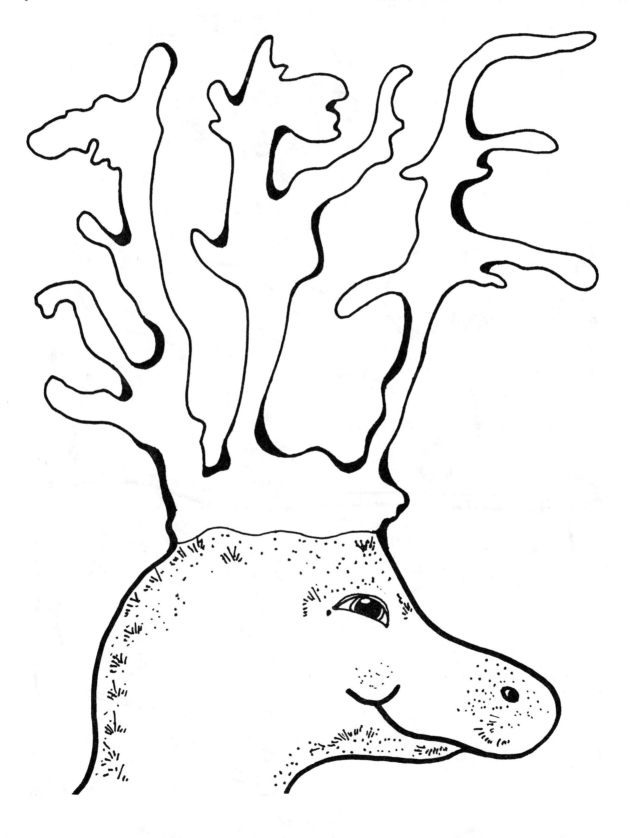

MIKE'S MONSTER WORKS WITH MAGNETS

This monster is excited about magnets. He is holding a horseshoe magnet. Color the items that will be attracted by the magnet. Put an X on those that will be repelled. Then get a real magnet and try out these same items.

Name _____ Date _____

MIKE MacMOOSE MET A MONKEY

One day, Mike MacMoose met a monkey who said, "I am going to try to trick you!" "Good," laughed Mike. "I love surprises."

Then the monkey said, "Color everything on this page that begins with the sound of M as in monkey." Mike got his crayons and began to work.

Get your crayons and help Mike. Should you color the monkey? Maybe that's the trick!

MOOSE TO MOOSE COMPARISONS

Read two books about moose and compare them using this chart. Share your comparisons.

Book Title		
Author		
Artist		
What is Moose named?		
What type of story is it?		
What part did YOU like best?		

Name _____   Date _____

M IS FOR MACHINE

The great big letter M on this page is divided into parts. There is a picture in each of the parts. Here is your job: Color only those items that are MACHINES, even if their sound does not begin with the letter M.

Let's talk about machines.
What are 3 characteristics that
they have, and do not have?

MACHINES DO . . . . . .
        have moving parts
        what else?

MACHINES DO NOT . . . . . .
        breathe
        what else?

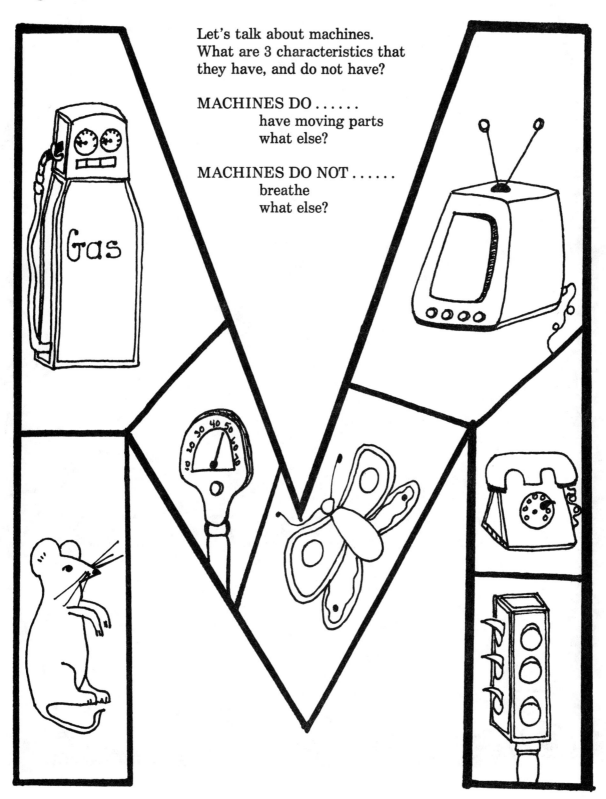

N

IS
FOR

NOODLES NUTHATCH

N IS FOR NOODLES NUTHATCH

BACKGROUND INFORMATION ABOUT NUTHATCHES: The nuthatch is a small, nut-eating bird. It does not migrate in winter because it has a very strong beak that enables it to crack nuts and find food. It can be sustained on hard seeds found in woods and forests because it can get at the food inside the seed. This bird is related to creepers and titmice, characterized by the sharp beak and short tail. Like all birds, the nuthatch has *hallow bones*. Hallow bones enable birds to fly, since solid bones would add to their weight and could make the lift-off and flight difficult, if not impossible.

READING/LANGUAGE ARTS:

1. NICKNAMES FOR NOODLES. The nuthatch has a nickname. It is called the upside down bird because it creeps from the top of the tree trunk to the bottom going head first. Actually, it gets its name from a combination of nut and hatchet because it can crack nuts with its very strong beak. Many birds fly to the ground but the nuthatch prefers to creep down the tree trunk to the ground. We talked about nicknames with Kelly Kangaroo. This time, let's give nicknames to the Alphabet Animals that we have met so far. We can make up names from things they do or from physical characteristics.

2. BIRD SHAPE BOOKS. Children are naturally interested in birds. Make a bird shape book about Noodles. Children can draw illustrations to go with the text, and be sure to show the nuthatch creeping down the tree head first.

3. ARTISTS AT WORK. Put fresh bright colors at the easel and have students paint a large bird. Make a sentence strip to put at the bottom of the picture. Later, turn this into a giant picture book of birds.

4. BIRD PICTURE BOOKS. Have an assortment of colorful bird books in the room so that students can examine them. Be sure to look at beaks, claws, crest, length of tail, length of legs, and so on. Have all students do an in-depth study of just one bird. Then, have each student take a different bird to make a comparison. Share the information on charts, graphs, logs, or other written form, and also give oral reports using visuals.

5. BIRD BOOKMARK. Make a big bird bookmark to use with animal books. The tail feather can be extended out of the top of the pages, in honor of Noodles. This bird "tool" can help us find our place in the book.

MATH:

1. UPSIDE DOWN WITH NOODLES. Teach the concept of right side up and upside down by using books, rulers, and items in the room. Play the Upside Down Game. Noodles Nuthatch can be the lookout person. Have a student leave the room or go into the coat area for just a second. Then place something upside down in the room (wastebasket, box of crayons, large book). Sh! Quiet! Noodles can call the student back into the

room. The class can make Noddles' sound of "Yank, yank, yank" when the student is getting close to the upside down item.

2. THREE PLUS ONE.   Noodles has four toes, three in front and one in back. This enables Noodles to encircle tree limbs and perch with stability. It also enables the bird to dig in and maintain its balance when climbing down the tree trunk.

Look through bird books with a focus upon feet. How may 3 + 1 can we find? How many 2 + 2? (Woodpecker).

SCIENCE:

1. CAN YOU COME OUT TO PLAY? It is interesting to note that at one time scientists thought that birds didn't play, but now some bird behavior is considered to be play. Crows were thought to have some form of play, and that may be because they are more intelligent than many of their other fine-feathered friends. But birds have been observed "playing" in water, playing with wind currents, and so on. Discuss the games that children play and the joy that they get from play. Maybe they can teach Noodles a game.

2. TRA-LA-LA-LA-LA.   The nuthatch has a song that sounds like "Yank, yank, yank," which it sings in order to send out territorial messages. That is one purpose of a bird's communication. Those who study birds (ornithologists) have discovered that birds send out many messages such as distress calls, alarm calls, calls to gather together, attack calls, mating calls, and so on. Some birds, such as the crow, has over 50 types of calls. Obtain a recording of bird calls at your local library and have students learn some of them. Perhaps signal calls can be set up in the classroom by Noodles, such as a special call for lining up, a different call for clean-up time, a different call for lowering our voices, and so on.

3. SET UP A FEEDING STATION.   This is an excellent activity for young students particularly during the winter in northern climates. Secure a large styrofoam ball, coat it generously with peanut butter, and have students roll it in bird seed. Place it inside of a used potato or onion net bag and hang it in a nearby tree so that children can observe the bird activity. A large soup bone or a piece of suet in a net bag also works well and does not have to be replenished frequently.

4. SET UP A BIRDWATCHING AREA.   Designate an area by the window as an area for birdwatching. Bring in field glasses and a bird book for easy identification. Bird-watcher hats may inspire students to spend some time making and recording observations as they peer out of the window. Teach the students to use binoculars.

5. NUTHATCH REVIEW.   Tape only the interview questions, and let the students answer them.

SOCIAL STUDIES:

1. FRIENDSHIP.   The nuthatch and the chickadee get along together in nature. Discuss the concept of friendship and the qualities that we seek in a good friend. With the students, make a chart that begins with "A Good Friend Is. . . ." and have students supply the words or phrase. Then read it. Then do it.

2. SOCIAL ANIMALS.   What animals are social animals? That is, they live with people or live together in herds, caves, nests? Which ones are solitary animals? Scientists believe that animals that live in groups have higher intelligence than those that live

alone, because living in groups requires paying attention to more signals. A very interesting resource book for our A-Z Animals study is *Fish Facts and Bird Brains* by Helen Roney Sattler with illustrations by Giulio Maestro.

3. TREES ARE HOMES FOR BIRDS, AND AN IMPORTANT NATURAL RESOURCE.   Be a paper saver. Paper is made from trees that have been cut down. But paper can be recycled and used again and again. Have students become aware of environmental opportunities to recycle all kinds of paper and begin in the classroom. Find out where the nearest recycling center is in your city or town. Have students begin to set up a plan for recycling at home.

4. BIRD PHOTO MONTAGE.   Cut colored pictures of birds from old calendars and magazines and make a large photo montage of overlapping bird pictures. (Similar to a collage). What a bright, colorful addition to your room this will be!

This upside-down bird
Is turned around.
He walks down tree trunks
To reach the ground.

N

TALK AND TELL: NOODLES NUTHATCH

1. HI THERE LITTLE BIRD! DO YOU HAVE A NICKNAME?
    Yes. I'm called the upside-down bird.
2. THE UPSIDE-DOWN BIRD? WHY ARE YOU CALLED THE UPSIDE-DOWN BIRD?
    I like to creep down tree trunks head first. It's a habit.
3. WHAT COLOR ARE YOUR HEAD FEATHERS, NOODLES?
    My head feathers are black. It looks like I'm wearing a hat.
4. AND WHAT COLORS ARE YOUR OTHER FEATHERS?
    I have white breast feathers and the rest of my feathers are a pretty blue color.
5. NOODLES, WHERE DO THE NUTHATCHES LIVE?
    In forests or orchards—we like lots and lots of trees.
6. WHERE DO YOU LIKE TO BUILD YOUR NEST?
    In an old tree trunk or in an old woodpecker hole if I can find one.
7. HOW MANY EGGS DOES A NUTHATCH LAY AT ONE TIME, NOODLES?
    Hold up one hand. Spread your fingers. Count 1-2-3-4-5. FIVE. That's how many eggs a nuthatch lays at one time. The eggs have red and purple specks on them. They're pretty!
8. THEY SOUND PRETTY. IS A MOTHER NUTHATCH KIND TO A BABY NUT-HATCH?
    Both my mother and father are kind. They mate for life, so they go through many seasons together.
9. NOODLES, WHAT DO YOU LIKE TO EAT?
    I love insect eggs! Yummy! And I like seeds, acorns, fruit, and suet that I find at the feeding station.
10. WHAT IS A FEEDING STATION?
    It's a place set up by people who feed the birds all winter. We really appreciate those big bird feeders. Your class can make one and set it outside; it's easy.
11. THAT'S A GOOD WINTER IDEA! DO YOU HAVE MANY OTHER BIRD FRIENDS?
    Yes, the nuthatch and the chickadee get along very well together. We're good friends.
12. DO BIRDS PLAY ANY SPECIAL GAMES THAT YOU CAN TEACH US?
    Sigh! Birds don't play much! Even when we're babies, we don't play. Birds are busy trying to find food. Maybe the crows play just a little, but other birds, rarely play!
14. IMAGINE THAT! BOYS AND GIRLS LOVE TO PLAY! WELL, DOES THE NUTHATCH MIGRATE, OR FLY SOUTH FOR THE WINTER?
    We don't go too far. With such a tough beak, we can crush hard seeds, so we can find food all winter and don't need to move away.
15. DO YOU EVER SHED YOUR FEATHERS, NOODLES?
    All birds shed their feathers or molt every year. But we try to do it little by little; just a few feathers at a time and not all at once. If too many fall out at one time, we stay out of sight. We hide until they grow back in.
16. WHY DO YOU STAY OUT OF SIGHT? DON'T YOU WANT TO BE SEEN WITH-OUT YOUR PRETTY FEATHERS?

Well, birds need feathers to protect themselves. Without feathers we are awkward and can't protect ourselves. So, we hide a lot during this time.

17. THAT MAKES SENSE. WE'VE BEEN LOOKING AT YOUR FEET. HOW MANY TOES DO YOU HAVE?

1-2-3-4, Four toes. Three in front and one in back. They help me to grab hold of tree branches and not fall off.

18. IS IT TRUE THAT YOUR BONES ARE HOLLOW, LIKE BIG MACARONI WITH A HOLE IN THE MIDDLE?

That's right. All birds have hollow bones rather than solid bones like people have. We fly better without that extra weight.

19. NOT EVERYONE HAS HEARD ABOUT THE NUTHATCH, NOODLES, SO WE'RE GLAD TO MEET YOU. WHO DO YOU THINK IS THE BEST-KNOWN BIRD IN NORTH AMERICA?

That's easy. The robin. Everybody knows the robin.

20. HOW MANY KINDS OF NUTHATCHES ARE THERE?

There are three, white-breasted, red-breasted, and brown-breasted.

21. NOODLES, IT'S TIME TO SAY GOOD-BYE. THANK YOU FOR THE CHAT. DO YOU HAVE A SPECIAL SONG FOR US?

Yes. This is my song. Listen carefully. Ready? "Yank! Yank! Yank!" I hope you like it.

WE HAVE BEEN CHATTING WITH A NUTHATCH RIGHT HERE IN THE PRETTY WOODS. TODAY OUR GUEST WAS A FRIENDLY BIRD NAMED NOODLES WHO TOLD US THAT HE SINGS BUT HE DOESN'T GET MUCH PLAYTIME. THOSE BIRDS WORK TOO HARD! TUNE IN NEXT TIME WHEN WE WILL MEET A(N)

_____. BYE BOYS AND GIRLS, "YANK, YANK, YANK."

INTERVIEW INFORMATION

What did you learn? Draw it, write it, or web it.

N

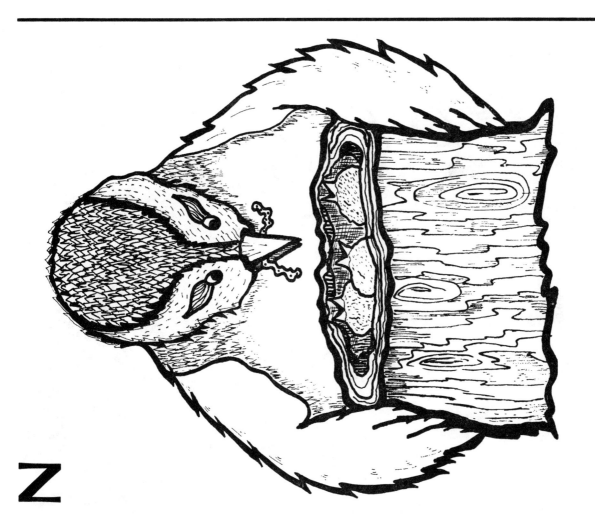

NOODLES NUTHATCH

NOODLES NUTHATCH LOVES NOODLES

What does Noodles like for supper? You guessed it! Spaghetti noodles with sauce.

Here is her favorite recipe for you.

YOU NEED:

1 pound spaghetti
6 quarts water
2 quarts spaghetti sauce
salt and pepper

WHAT TO DO:

1. Simmer the spaghetti sauce in a pot.
2. Bring the 6 quarts of water to a boil.
3. Gently add the spaghetti noodles. Stir to separate them.
4. Boil for about 10 minutes or until tender, stirring occasionally.
5. Drain the spaghetti.

THEN: Mix $\frac{3}{4}$ of the sauce with the spaghetti. Serve the spaghetti on a dish or in a cup. Add sauce to the top.

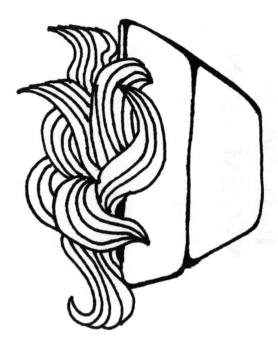

Name ———————————— Date ————————————

NOODLES NUTHATCH DOT-TO-DOT PUZZLE

Noodles Nuthatch has a puzzle for you. Use your pencil to connect the dots. What surprise does this nuthatch, the upside-down bird, have in store for you?

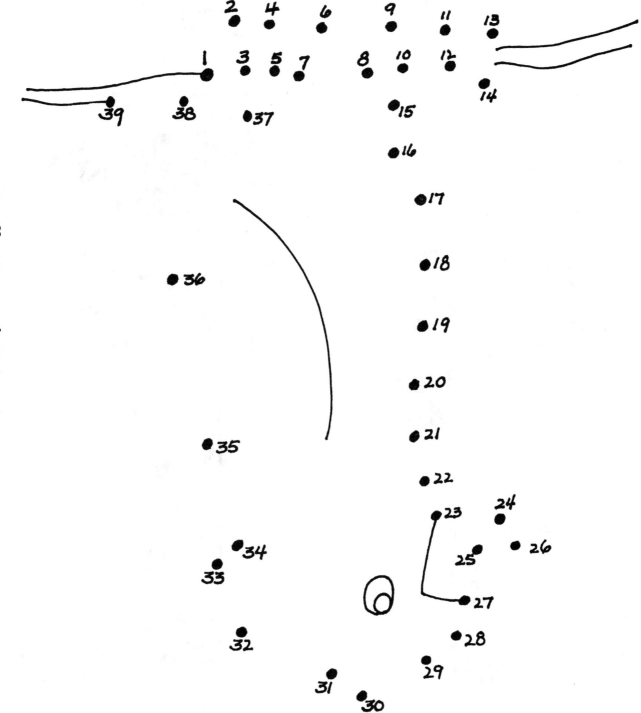

NEST MATCHING

Match the nests on the left to the identical nests on the right. Color them. How can we find out who lives in some of them? Let's get some bird books from the library.

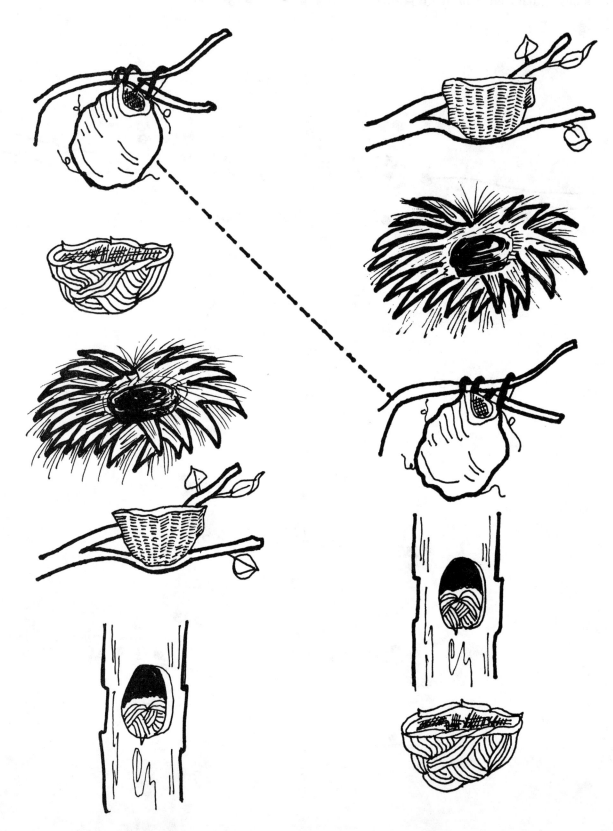

Name _____ Date _____

BIRD BEAKS

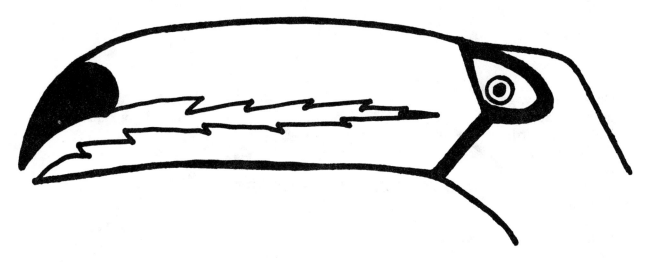

Beaks and bills come in different shapes and sizes. You
can tell by the beak the type of food that the bird eats.
Draw one bird in each of the squares below and identify it.

Fish Catcher	Fruit Eater
Meat Eater	Seed Eater

Name _____ Date _____

WE'RE GOING BIRDWATCHING

On a nice day, go outdoors and start looking for birds. Birds are easy to see, and during the day, they are busy looking for food.

Look, listen, and then record your information.

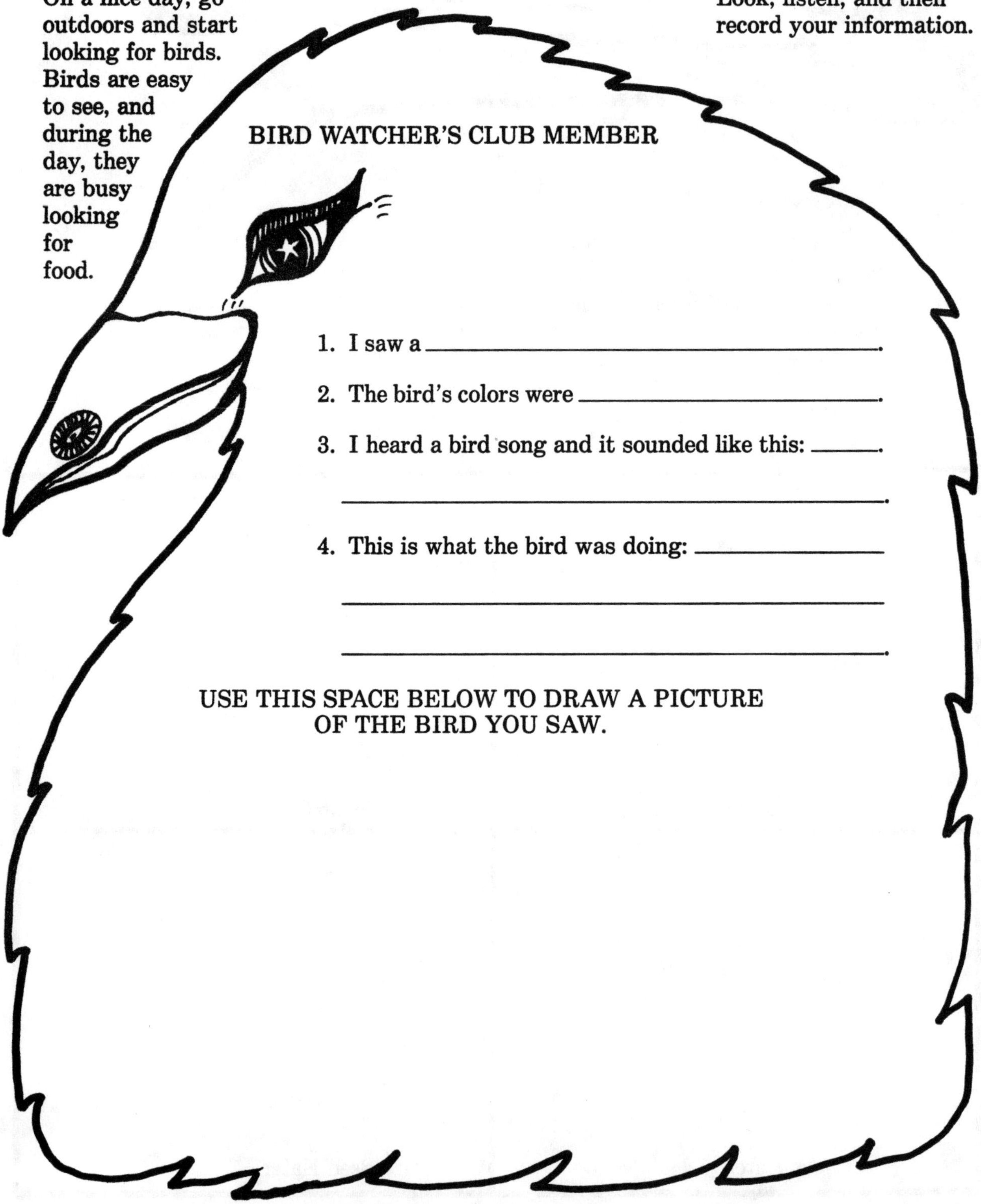

BIRD WATCHER'S CLUB MEMBER

1. I saw a _____.

2. The bird's colors were _____.

3. I heard a bird song and it sounded like this: _____.
   _____.

4. This is what the bird was doing: _____
   _____
   _____.

USE THIS SPACE BELOW TO DRAW A PICTURE
OF THE BIRD YOU SAW.

O
IS
FOR

OLLIE OCTOPUS

O IS FOR OLLIE OCTOPUS

BACKGROUND INFORMATION ABOUT OCTOPUSES: The octopus has eight (8) arms (tentacles) webbed together by a layer or cloak of skin called a mantle. Under this thin layer of skin there are color cells that change the tone of the octopus from orange to bright red to brown. This can be useful as a camouflage, since the colors attract and confuse other sea life. For example, an inquisitive sea creature may get too close and become the next dinner for the octopus. There are rows of suction cups fastened to the edge of the arms that stick to objects and help to pull the octopus along.

When in danger, the octopus can squirt a cloud of black ink from its siphon, which acts as a decoy while the octopus makes a hasty retreat. If a sea creature, such as a shark, should grab an octopus by the tentacle in a life-or-death grip, the octopus will let the tentacle be pulled off. In the life of a young octopus, it grows back in a few weeks.

READING/LANGUAGE ARTS:

1. **READ WITH OLLIE.** Make a classroom octopus by having students stuff a giant pillow for the body. Stuff eight kneesocks and sew them to the pillow. Glue on felt eyes and mouth. Spread out the eight legs in a circle and children can sit between the legs as they examine colorful picture books and magazines about sea life.

2. **SHORT AND LONG SOUND OF O.** The letter o is a vowel and has a short sound and a long sound. Octopus uses the short sound. List other words that begin with the sound of octopus (aaahhh). (Examples: October, olives, operator, otter, and so on). Then talk about the long sound—the letter says its name, (oooooo). Some words include: over, oaktree, odor, open, old, and so on.

3. **WHO ARE OUR VOWEL ANIMALS SO FAR?** The vowels are the letters a, e, i, o, and u. Let's list our vowel animals so far: A-Ashley Alligator, E-Eddington Elephant, I-Inky Insect, and O-Ollie Octopus. Work with lists of long and short names for these letters. Hmmm. . . . wonder what animal we will meet for the letter 'U'? Can we guess?

4. **OCTOPUS WINDSOCK.** Use 12″ × 18″ assorted colors of construction paper and have each student make a sea scene on one. Then roll it up and staple the ends together. Now we have a cylinder for our windsock. Next, we need eight crepe paper streamers (to represent legs). Students can make eight different sea creatures or shells from construction paper, and attach them to one end of the crepe paper. Glue the other end to the cylinder. Then, hang the windsocks from the ceiling with eight dangling, entangling sea creatures or shells on each one. CELEBRATE EIGHT!

MATH:

1. **LET'S WORK WITH EIGHT.** The word eight is from the Greek octo. Since Ollie Octopus has eight legs, we can do many activities using eight. Count eight beads;

point to eight items; bounce a ball eight times; click your tongue eight times; cut out eight circles; paste eight squares on a piece of paper and number them 1–8. Students may be able to think of more ideas for CELEBRATE EIGHT.

2. MICROSCOPIC MEANS VERY TINY. The octopus eggs are microscopic, probably no bigger than a tiny grain of rice. Yet, when 30,000 to 40,000 eggs are bunched together it looks like a lot. What else can we think of that is microscopic in size, yet when bunched together looks like a lot? Put on your thinking caps! (Examples: grains of sand form a beach, tiny raindrops form a big puddle, granules of sugar form a sugar-bowl full, and so on). This is an interesting concept—even a sweater is woven from tiny strands of yarn, and a whole head of hair is made up of single strands.

3. DOING THE OCTOPUS DANCE. Have four students huddle together facing outward. As a group, have them raise one arm up, then the other, then sway back and forth. Then lower one arm, then the other. Next, have one student raise one arm and call out "one" and raise his second arm and call out "two." His arms stay up. The next child raises one arm and calls out "three," and then "four," and so on until all eight arms are up. Octopus sways back and forth and moves along as a unit. Then, counting backwards (8, 7, 6, 5, 4, 3, 2, 1) all arms slither down to their sides. Link hands, and count "1,2,3,4,5,6,7,8" as arms are slowly raised up as a unit, and then count backwards as arms are slowly lowered as a unit.

SCIENCE:

1. OLLIE'S SUCTION CUPS. One worker who uses suction cups is the plumber. To get across the concept of suction, borrow a plumber's helper (rubber suction plunger on a stick) and have students use it on the floor to feel the pressure that comes from plunging it up and down. The octopus suction cups help it to move along the ocean floor.

2. WORKING WITH COLORS. The octopus can change colors for different moods. It uses red and brown to show excitement, orange for pleasure, and pale gray or white for fear. Ask students what color they would use to show these emotions:

happy	sad	excitement
fear	anticipation	pride
anger	surprise	let down

3. POETRY. Read from *Animals, Animals* by Eric Carle, and get the rhythm and rhyme of what is being said about the animals. Try writing poetry about any of the animals that we have investigated so far.

4. GETTING ALL TANGLED UP. Ollie Octopus would have a serious problem in the ocean because of pollution. Plastic and styrofoam are dangerous to all sea life. Some sea animals are attracted to the plastic because it floats and they think it is another sea creature and swallow it and choke or die slowly from it. Plastic rings on six-packs of cola drinks would be a hazard for Ollie if she got caught in them. Become aware of ocean pollution and don't throw garbage into the water. Have an "Ollie's Ocean Awareness Week" and learn about the dangers of water pollution. For a free brochure on recycling write to: Environmental Defense Fund, 257 Park Avenue South, New York, NY 10010.

The octopus has
Got a kink.
It's in leg number eight,
We think.

O

TALK AND TELL: OLLIE OCTOPUS

1. HI OLLIE OCTOPUS! WE CAN'T HELP BUT NOTICE YOUR ARMS. HOW MANY DO YOU HAVE?

    1-2-3-4-5-6-7-8. EIGHT ARMS. The correct name for my arms is *tentacle*. Can you say tentacle? (TENT uh kuhl) Good!

2. CAN YOU DESCRIBE YOUR TENTACLES FOR US?

    They are about 2 ft. long (that's two rulers put together end to end). There are double rows of powerful suction circles along the sides.

3. TELL US, OLLIE, WHAT DO YOU DO WITH YOUR POWERFUL TENTACLES?

    They help me to walk along the slippery ocean floor. Also, I can spread them way, way out and make a parachute. (Hushed voice): Then I can come floating down gently on top of some sea creature and SQUEEZE it for my dinner. Yummy! Yummy! Food for my tummy!

4. WHAT IS YOUR FAVORITE FOOD, OLLIE?

    I like seafood such as crab, crayfish, mussels, lobster—anything I can grab a hold of and pull apart.

5. MAYBE WE SHOULD BACK AWAY JUST A LITTLE BIT. ARE YOU BORN LIVE OR HATCHED FROM AN EGG?

    An octopus is hatched from an egg. An adult female octopus lays many, many (about 1,000) eggs at a time.

6. HOW BIG ARE ALL OF THESE EGGS?

    A teensy bit smaller than a grain of rice.

7. DID YOU HAVE A GOOD MOTHER?

    Yes, a mother octopus takes special care of her eggs. She builds a nest in a safe place under rocks, lays her eggs and tends them very carefully with her tentacles.

8. WHAT DO YOU MEAN WHEN YOU SAY THAT SHE TENDS THEM?

    Well, to tend something means to look after it with care. She glues the eggs together in long rows and hangs them to the side of her nest. Every day she brushes over them with her tentacles to keep them nice and clean. And, she doesn't leave her eggs alone for one second!

9. WHEN YOU ALL HATCH, HOW DOES SHE TAKE CARE OF EVERY BABY OCTOPUS?

    I'll let you in on a secret. Only three or four of us ever make it to the top of the water. The rest are eaten along the way by fish.

10. WELL, WE'RE GLAD YOU MADE IT, OLLIE! IS IT TRUE THAT YOU CAN SPURT WATER?

    Yes, I have a siphon.

11. A SIPHON? WHAT IS A SIPHON?

    Every octopus has a siphon, or tube, that sticks out through a slit in its skin. I can squirt water or even ink from it.

12. TELL US MORE ABOUT IT, OLLIE.

    When I squirt water, it helps to push (propel) me through the water just like a rocket. When I'm in real danger I squirt a purple liquid that I call ink. This misty ink clouds up the water and helps me to get away . . . fast!

13. OLLIE, HOW DO YOU SEE?

    I have two eyes that stick out a little from the top of my head.

14. OLLIE, HOW DO YOU EAT?

   I have a hard beak-like mouth at my center. Find a big picture book and take a good look at me.

15. HEY, OLLIE! ARE YOU MAGIC? YOU LOOKED PURPLE A MINUTE AGO AND NOW YOU LOOK ORANGE. HOW DO YOU DO THAT TRICK?

   I have color cells under my skin. To show that I feel good, I make myself orange. To show that I'm excited, I blush in waves of red and brown. When I'm afraid, I turn pale gray.

16. THAT'S WONDERFUL! IS THERE A SPECIAL NAME FOR ALL OF THAT SKIN THAT TURNS COLORS AND SEEMS TO HOLD ALL OF YOUR ARMS, OR TENTACLES, TOGETHER?

   Yes. It's called a *mantel*, or a protective coat (cloak).

17. YOU KNOW, OLLIE, I SAW AN OCTOPUS THE OTHER DAY WITH ONLY SEVEN TENTACLES. YOU SAID THEY HAVE EIGHT. WHY DID I SEE ONE WITH ONLY SEVEN TENTACLES?

   It's time for you to know something very special about an octopus. An octopus can lose a tentacle in a fight. It could be bit off or even ripped off. But, here's the special part, it grows back again in about six weeks!!

18. WOW! THAT'S AMAZING! DO YOU HAVE MANY ENEMIES IN THE SEA, OLLIE?

   Yes, the sharks and dolphins. And my worst enemy is the moray eel.

19. OLLIE, WHERE CAN WE GO TO SEE YOU?

   Marine Land in Florida is one place. Also, many Sea Museums and some zoos have octopus. Look me up in a book and read all about me!

THANK YOU FOR THIS TALK-AND-TELL TIME RIGHT HERE IN THE MARINE LIFE SECTION OF THE ZOO. TODAY OUR GUEST WAS OLLIE OCTOPUS. TUNE IN NEXT TIME WHEN WE WILL BE INTERVIEWING A(N)

_____. UNTIL THEN, TAKE GOOD CARE OF YOUR ARMS. DON'T EVER PUT ARMS OUTSIDE OF THE WINDOWS WHEN YOU'RE RIDING IN A CAR OR A BUS. NOW RAISE YOUR ARM, AND WAVE BYE-BYE.

INTERVIEW INFORMATION

What did you learn? Draw it, write it, or web it.

OLLIE OCTOPUS

OLLIE THE OCTOPUS

Ollie, the 8-armed octopus, can help you complete the names of these eight animals. Just put her letter (O) in the blanks. Then read the eight names.

Now Ollie wants you to learn to spell three of them. On the back of this sheet, she wants you to draw five of them. Ollie says, "3 + 5 = ____" She likes to change colors, too. What color will you make her?

f_x

alligat_r

g_at

h_rse

li_n

d_g

fr_g

m__se

Name —————————————

Date —————————————

OLLIE OCTOPUS LOVES EIGHT

One, two, three, four, five, six, seven, eight! An octopus has eight tentacles (or arms). Cut out eight long colorful streamers and paste them onto Ollie. You can cut Ollie out or leave her on the page surrounded by blue water.

I ♥ eight

1
2
3
4
5
6
7
8

THE MANY SOUNDS OF O

The letter O has a long sound, a short sound, and other sounds, too. Say the names of the items below. Look up the spelling in a dictionary for help. Put an X on anything that does not begin with one of the many sounds of O.

Name _____ Date _____

THE SHAPE OF THE LETTER O GAME

Take a good look at the letter O. What is it? That's right, O is a circle. Look at the items below. Some have already been made into something else. Color the items. Cut them into boxes. Shuffle the cards and place them face down. Pick up two at a time to see if you have a match. If so, set them aside. If not, return them (remember where you put them) and try again. What can you make using the O shape and your crayons to make your game special?

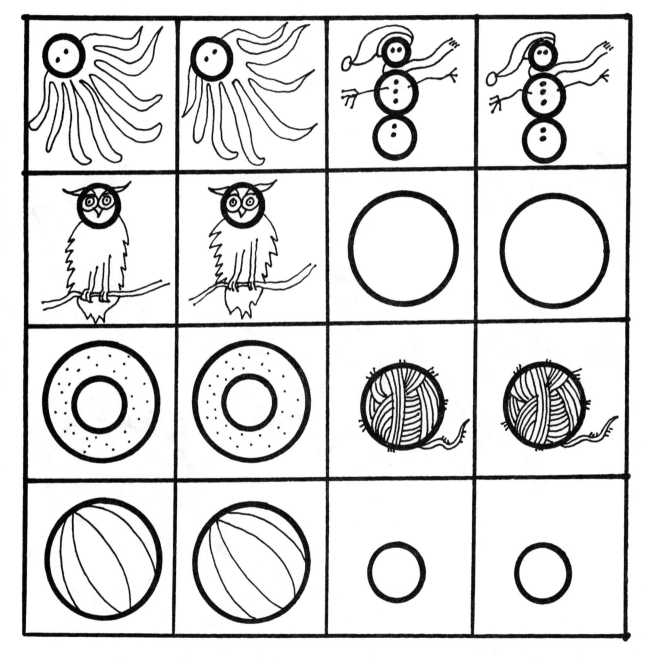

OLLIE'S OCEAN POLLUTION MESSAGE

Ollie Octopus says, "Don't throw garbage into lakes, rivers, streams, or oceans." Color only those items below that belong in the water. Put a big X on those that do not belong.

P
IS
FOR

PERCY PENGUIN

P IS FOR PERCY PENGUIN

BACKGROUND INFORMATION ABOUT PENGUINS: The penguin is a flightless bird that lives mainly in Australia and New Zealand. Its wings are flippers that allow the bird to dive and swim. Its short feathers are oily and water repellent. Penguins are primarily black and white, but some do have colorful patches on the side of the head. The largest is the Emperor Penguin, which is three feet tall, the smallest is the Little Blue, or Little Fairy Penguin, which is just over 12 inches tall.

Penguins are group birds. They crowd together in colonies called *rookeries*. The female lays a single egg in May or June, and gently rolls the egg to the waiting male bird who keeps the single egg in his incubator, which is a patch of skin located near his feet. The males fiercely guard their egg, especially from other males who might have a cracked or broken egg and who aggressively come looking for a replacement. During this time, the female penguins stay in the ocean and return to the rookery in time for the hatching eggs. Penguins have no need to migrate long distances, as the ocean offers an abundant supply of food.

READING/LANGUAGE ARTS:

1. PERCY'S NEW WORDS. Introduce *rookery*, a colony or group of penguins who gather together. Also introduce *incubator*, a warm place to keep fertile eggs while waiting for them to hatch. If possible, set up an incubator in the classroom, and purchase fertile duck or chicken eggs that can be hatched in the classroom.

2. PERCY'S PUPPET SHOW. Make penguin puppets from black and white socks, or from paper bags covered with black and white paper and added features. The new born chick is demanding and squawks out loud for food, while the mother and father penguin run and fetch food from the sea and feed it to the young penguin. This doesn't stop the squawking, but soon the tired mother and father stop running back and forth and back and forth and the young penguin waddles to the sea and begins to feed itself. Happy ending.

3. PENGUIN POEMS. Have students create penguin poetry on penguin shapes with information that they gain from the interview section. Also, have them learn Percy Penguin's rhyme on his picture.

4. CHANGING ENDINGS. Read several books about penguins and have the students predict the ending. Then have them write their own ending that is different from the storybook ending.

MATH:

1. LET'S MEASURE, PENGUIN STYLE. The largest penguin is the Emperor Penguin which is 3 ft tall. The smallest is the Little Blue, or Little Fairy, which is just over 12 inches tall. Make a wall measuring chart to see how tall the penguins are. Then,

have the students take turns standing with their back to the chart, and measure their height. Label it. That's how they compare to a penguin in height.

Students can check information books about the size of penguins in relation to other birds. Also, the size of penguins in relation to domestic and wild animals would make a good measurement survey.

2. TAKE A THREE-MINUTE PENGUIN BREAK. Penguins can stay underwater for about three minutes. Capitalize upon this 3-minute time period by taking a "penguin break" after a busy or strenuous activity. Children can rest for three minutes.

3. PREDICTION. Some day we will have another Alphabet Animal who is black and white like Percy Penguin. What letters are left? Can anyone predict what the animal will be? (Q, R, S, T, U, V, W, X, Y, Z—Zelda Zebra).

4. COMPARISON. How can we compare a penguin with a zebra from knowledge that we already have? Let's think about body markings (stripes), type of mouth, tails, feet, body parts, and so on.

5. THE CONCEPT OF OPPOSITES. Black and white are opposites. So are winter and summer, day and night, hot and cold, and so on. Have students think of many more opposites. For special book experiences with black and white, introduce students to *A,B,See!* and *Shapes,* both by Tana Hoban. Also, read *Reflections* by Ann Jonas.

SCIENCE:

1. WATERPROOF PENGUINS. The glossy look that penguins have is obtained with the aid of an oil sack at the base of its tail. With its beak, the penguin gets the oil and spreads it through its feathers. This is called *preening* and makes the bird clean and the feathers water repellent.

What other Alphabet Animals are waterproof (remember the frog talked about this).

2. HEALTH AND BEAUTY SECRETS. In the interview, Percy gives us a beauty secret by telling about its oil sack used for preening. Have a discussion about good grooming habits (hair care, tooth care, wearing clean clothes to school, and so on). Check the ingredients on several bottles of hand lotion. What can we learn from this?

3. BIRDS USE TOOLS. The Galapagos Penguin lives in the same area of the world (600 miles off the coast of Ecuador in South America) as the Galapagos woodpecker finch. The finch does not have a long tongue to catch insects, so it puts a stick in its mouth and pokes the stick into a crack in a tree looking for insects. For more information about birds and animals using tools, read *Animals That Use Tools* by Barbara Ford.

4. PENGUIN FEET. Most birds have four toes. These toes can point to the front or the back, depending upon how the birds moves around. The penguin has a webbed piece of skin between its three front toes, and this enables it to be a good swimmer. The small back toe on a penguin acts as a paddle. Use information book pictures to compare penguin feet to duck feet so that the size of the web can be determined. Now is a good time to check the feet of birds and a good resource book is *Some Feet Have Noses* by Anita Gustafson with pictures by April Peters Flory.

SOCIAL STUDIES:

1. LOCATION SKILLS. Find the equator on the map or globe. Locate Australia and New Zealand where most of the penguins live. Place a penguin sticker or cutout on

the map or globe as a reminder that penguins live there. Then, locate the Galapagos Islands off the coast of Ecuador in South America. One of the islands houses small penguins, and it is an endangered species, so add it to your list.

2. MIGRATION INFORMATION. Create a situation, such as a puppet show or a TV talk show, where the penguin has an opportunity to ask other birds all about the topic of migration. What does it mean? How far do birds travel? Why do they have a winter home and a summer home? There are four main aerial highways for birds that are migrating in North America and these routes are called the Pacific Flyway, the Central Flyway, the Mississippi Flyway, and the Atlantic Flyway. For more information read *Mysteries of Migration* by Robert M. McClung (Champaign, IL: Gerrard Publishing Company, 1983).

**PERCY'S TALK-AND-TELL
PICTURE AND RHYME**

I wear a suit of black and white
And look just like a waiter.
Today I'm serving tuna pie
And broiled alligator.

P

TALK AND TELL: PERCY PENGUIN

1. HI, PERCY! YOU LOOK LIKE YOU ARE ALL DRESSED UP AND READY TO GO TO A FANCY PARTY.

    I think that's why people like penguins. We sort of look like people since we stand up and walk, or waddle along. But a penguin is really a bird.

2. DO YOU FLY LIKE A BIRD?

    No. Our wings are called flippers and they help us to glide through the water. We're excellent swimmers.

3. PERCY, ARE PENGUINS BORN LIVE OR HATCHED?

    Penguins are hatched from eggs. After I was hatched, both of my parents took turns to go to the sea to get food for me until I was old enough to go for myself.

4. HOW MANY EGGS DOES A FEMALE PENGUIN LAY AT ONE TIME?

    The Emperor Penguin lays one. She rolls it across the ice to her mate who covers it with skin by his feet, and he keeps it warm until it hatches.

5. IF THE MALE TAKES CARE OF THE EGG, WHERE IS THE FEMALE DURING THIS TIME?

    She's out at sea, swimming, eating, and gaining weight.

6. HOW LONG DOES IT TAKE FOR THE MALE TO HATCH THE EGG, PERCY?

    It takes about two months for the chicks to hatch. All of the male penguins huddle together in a group for body warmth, and to keep the eggs warm. This group is called a rookery. That's a new word for you.

7. YES, IT IS. WE WILL HAVE TO LEARN IT. WHAT HAPPENS WHEN THE EGGS START HATCHING?

    It's an exciting time! When a chick is hatched, eager males go after it—especially a male who has lost his egg—and the males even fight over the newborn chicks. That's because they want to take care of the chick!

8. SOUNDS LIKE PENGUINS ARE PROUD PAPAS. WHAT DO PENGUINS EAT, PERCY?

    We eat seafood like shrimp, squid, lobster, or fish.

9. DO YOU HAVE ANY NATURAL ENEMIES IN THE WATER?

    Yes we do! Seals! Especially the leopard seal. They just can't seem to eat enough penguins.

10. PENGUINS SEEM TO LOOK ALIKE. ARE ALL PENGUINS ALIKE, PERCY?

    No. There are about 18 different kinds. The three main ones are the Adelie, the Ringed, and the Emperor. Maybe you can find pictures of us.

11. WE WILL LOOK FOR BOOKS ON PENGUINS. HOW TALL ARE PENGUINS?

    The smallest is 14 inches tall—just 2 inches longer than a ruler. It's called the Fairy Penguin. The largest is 3 ft tall—the same size as a yardstick. It's called the Emperor Penguin.

12. WHERE DO PENGUINS LIVE, PERCY?

    Most live south of the equator (the middle of the globe) in the southern part of the earth.

13. CAN YOU TELL US THAT AGAIN?

    Yes. Look for penguins especially in Australia and New Zealand.

14. WE'D LIKE TO ASK YOU SOMETHING PERSONAL, PERCY. WHY DON'T YOU FLY IF YOU'RE A BIRD?

    Penguins don't need to fly. Our food is always nearby in the water. We have adapted very well to the water. Other birds glide through the air with wings; we glide through the water with flippers.

15. IS IT TRUE THAT YOU EAT PEBBLES, OR SMALL STONES?

Yes. It makes us heavier and we can glide and dive in the water easier.

16. WHAT HAPPENS WHEN ICE FORMS ON THE WATER AND YOU'RE UNDER IT? HOW DO YOU GET OUT?

We dive down low, then swim straight up real fast and shoot right out of the water like a rocket!

17. THAT SOUNDS LIKE FUN. ARE PENGUINS NOISY BIRDS?

We have a loud call but mostly we communicate nonverbally, through body language.

18. WHAT IS BODY LANGUAGE?

Penguins use their body to bow very low to each other as a greeting. We threaten someone who is bothering us by raising our head feathers. And, if we don't want to fight we can press our feathers down flat and look much smaller than we really area. We send off signals with our bodies. I'll bet that you do too if you think about it.

19. PERCY, YOU REALLY SHAKE YOUR ENTIRE BODY FROM TIME TO TIME. IS THAT A SHIVER? ARE YOU COLD?

I shiver and shake automatically to remove things caught in my feathers. It puts me back in order.

20. WE'VE ENJOYED VISITING WITH YOU AT THE ROOKERY. IS THERE ANYTHING ELSE THAT WE SHOULD KNOW ABOUT PENGUINS?

I'll tell you a beauty secret. People like the way penguins look and we keep neat by preening ourselves. (Tell this in a hushed tone.) You see, I have an oil gland on my tail feathers and I remove the oil with my bill and rub the oil onto my feathers. It's called *preening.* This oil keeps me waterproof and shining with beauty. Now you know lots of things about penguins, don't you?

YES, WE DO! THANK YOU FOR THIS TALK-AND-TELL TIME RIGHT HERE AT THE ROOKERY. TODAY OUR GUEST WAS PERCY PENGUIN WHO LOOKED ALL DRESSED UP AND READY FOR A PARTY. NEXT TIME WE WILL BE

TALKING WITH A(N) _____ THIS IS STATION ABCD-EFG-HIJK-LMOP for PENGUINS.

INTERVIEW INFORMATION

P

PERCY PENGUIN

What did you learn? Draw it, write it, or web it.

ENDANGERED BIRDS

The Galapagos Penguin is on the endangered birds list. Use this page to record information you find about endangered birds, fish, and wildlife.

PERCY PENGUIN'S SNACK TIME

Percy Penguin is hungry. Today he will eat only those items that begin with his letter sound of p as in penguin. Color the items below that Percy will eat. Be sure to color Percy, too.

PERCY PENGUIN'S MATH FUN

Color all of the items in Percy's pie. Cut off the strip at the bottom of the page and cut out the spinner. Attach the spinner to the middle of the pie with a paper fastener. Spin three times and add the sum. Try again. Play with a partner. Each partner gets five turns and the high score wins.

POLLY IS A PUZZLE

Use your scissors and paste to help put Polly back together. Then use your crayons to make Polly look beautiful.

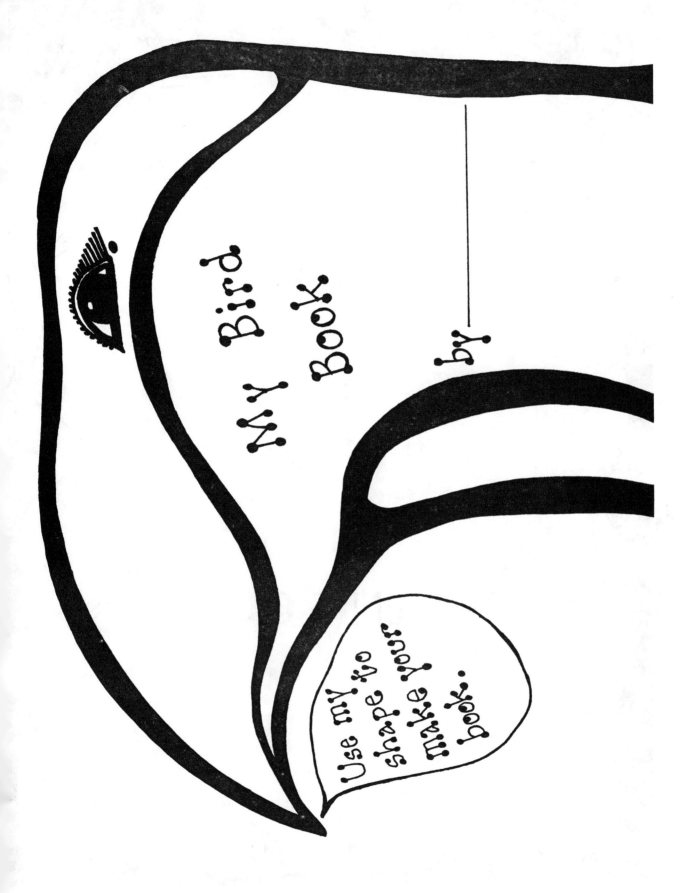

My Bird Book

by

Use my shape to make your book.

Q

IS
FOR

QUEENIE QUAIL

Q IS FOR QUEENIE QUAIL

BACKGROUND INFORMATION ABOUT QUAILS: Quails are the smallest of the chicken-like birds. The topknot feathers that stand erect on the top of the head are a distinguishing decoration of the quail. Quails belong to the order of birds called *gallinaceous fowl* that nest on the ground. This includes poultry, pheasants, and grouse. Probably the best-known quail is the bob-white. You can tell it from its song which sounds exactly like its name, "bob-white, bob-white." Originally this bird was found in woodlands in the eastern part of the USA but when the early settlers moved west, the quail went with them and today a great many are found in the Midwest, Arizona, and California.

READING/LANGUAGE ARTS:

1. THE "QU" CONNECTION.   In words that begin with the letter q, this letter is usually, if not always followed by the vowel u. The q does not stand alone. Explain to the students that the two letters are inseparable friends, and then think of words and look up words that begin with qu. Can we find a word that begins with "q" that is not followed by the u? Use great big letter cards to spell out simple words with the qu twins.

2. LET'S LOOK FOR PICTURES.   Locate a variety of colorful books on birds and have students look through them for differences and similarities. The quail is a gallinacious fowl (new term to learn), and children can locate its relatives such as the chicken and pheasant. Locate other ground feeders in your own backyard by noticing which birds come in to eat the seed that is spilled from a bird feeder. Set a birdfeeder outside the classroom window to observe the ground feeders.

3. QUEENIE HAS A TOPKNOT.   Make a long strip story showing Queenie engaging in some activity. The words that she is thinking can be written in the topknot shape above her head, much the same as a cartoon strip. This can be a humorous story strip.

MATH:

1. A COVEY OF QUAILS.   When quails gather together to live, we call this group a *covey*. They make their shallow ground nest from leaves and grass, so they are very difficult to locate. Discuss the concept of shallow as opposed to deep. (Example: A swimming pool has both a shallow and a deep end).

2. LET'S TAKE TURNS.   Both male and female work on the nest, and after the female has layed about 10 to 12 eggs, they both take turns sitting on the eggs. Let's take turns counting aloud to 12. Student A says "one," Student B says "two," Student A says "three," Student B says "four," and so on.

3. PLAY "SCRAMBLED EGGS."   Make egg shapes and put one numeral on each egg. Scramble the eggs all together. Now put them in order.

4. LET'S MAKE A QUAIL-STYLE CIRCLE. The members of the covey roost together in a circle with all heads and fronts facing out, and with their rear portion in the center. They form a circle quite naturally this way—all on the lookout, and all keeping warm.

Have five or six students join hands and form a circle. Then, have them drop hands to their sides and turn around slowly, facing outward. Now, have them back up until they are touching. Everyone keeps watch in a different direction. You can make small quail circles or large quail circles. Quails facing in different directions can tell what they see (example: those facing the window, those facing the front of the room, those facing the back, and so on).

SCIENCE:

1. MIGRATION? NO, THANK YOU. The quail does not migrate, although it does travel long distances on foot looking for food. Quails rarely fly, but can do so especially if they're being hunted. Queenie is a clever ground bird. When a predator (fox) comes along, Queenie will dart from her nest and crawl along with her wing dragging on the ground (pretending to be wounded). This diverts the attention of the fox who goes after Queenie rather than after her nest. Then, when she is a safe distance from the nest she flies off. Students can re-enact this nature story.

2. FARMERS LIKE QUAILS. Why? Because the quail is a helpful farm bird. It eats insects that are harmful to crops, as well as weed seeds before they get a chance to take hold. Write a journal entry from the point of view of the farmer today.

SOCIAL STUDIES:

1. THE CLASSROOM QUAIL CONNECTION. Since qu are very good friends, discuss the qualities that we look for in a friend. Then, have everyone print his or her name on a piece of paper and put it into a container. Since we're now in a friendly mood and know that we should only say nice things about another person, instruct the students to individually select a paper from the container, but not to tell who this friend is. (Encourage positive responses.)

Next, distribute 9″ × 12″ multicolored construction paper, and have each student draw a very nice picture of the person whose name is on their paper. Have them print or dictate something nice about the person. Now collect them and make Our Class from A–Z just like the Animals A–Z. (Arrange the names in ABC order by first or last name.)

2. THE A–Z ANIMAL CONNECTION. On small pieces of paper, print the name of each our A–Z animals that we have met so far. Put the pieces of paper in a little bag and shake the bag. Have a student reach in and select first one piece of paper (and read the name of the animal) and then another piece of paper (and read the name of that animal). These two animals are now a *pair* or have a connection. Have different students continue to do this until all of the animals have been connected. NOW, they have to compare the animals in terms of similarities and differences. (Reptile or mammal? Land animal or sea animal? Large or small? Domestic or wild? and so on.)

For an added incentive, have the students create a situation where the two animals play an important role. Will they cooperate? Will one lose out to the other? This should be extremely interesting, as the students engage in critical thinking and problem solving. How will they report their story? There are a variety of methods: script, a visual story, a cartoon, a cassette recording, a puppet show, and so on.

A quail has a topknot
　　On its head.
It doesn't fly
　　But walks instead.

Q

TALK AND TELL: QUEENIE QUAIL

1. HI, QUEENIE! WE LIKE THAT FEATHER STICKING OUT OF THE TOP OF YOUR HEAD. WHAT IS IT CALLED?
    It's called a topknot.
2. IS IT THERE FOR A SPECIAL REASON?
    It's just there to make me look nice.
3. QUEENIE, WE SAW YOU RUNNING UP THE ROAD. CAN YOU FLY?
    Yes, but . . . a quail would rather walk fast or run.
4. WHEN DO YOU FLY?
    I flew up into a tree last night when a fox was chasing me.
5. ARE YOU RELATED TO THE CHICKEN?
    Yes, I am in the chicken family. We are both ground feeders. I'm also related to the pheasant and the grouse.
6. WHAT DO YOU LIKE TO EAT, QUEENIE?
    I like those crunchy insects such as the beetles and grasshoppers. Also, I like to eat the seeds of weeds that grow in the gardens.
7. SINCE FARMERS DON'T LIKE WEEDS IN THEIR GARDENS, AND YOU EAT THE WEED SEEDS, DO FARMERS THINK YOU ARE HELPFUL?
    Yes, they love us. We eat the weed seeds and we also eat the insects that damage their crops.
8. QUEENIE, DO YOU HAVE A SPECIAL SONG THAT YOU LIKE TO SING?
    I do, and I'll sing it for you right now. "Bob-white! Bob-white!"
9. VERY PRETTY. DO YOU LIVE ALONE OR WITH OTHER QUAILS?
    We live together in flocks, called a covey, during the winter. You've heard about groups such as prides (lion), and litters (cat and dog), and rookeries (penguins), well, our group is called a covey.
10. WHERE IS YOUR NEST, QUEENIE?
    It's hidden in the fields. People usually can't find them.
11. WHO BUILDS THE NEST, THE MALE OR THE FEMALE?
    The male (cock) and the female (hen) quail both build the nest. They work together.
12. QUEENIE, WERE YOU HATCHED FROM AN EGG?
    Yes. The hen quail lays from 10 to 20 eggs, so we have a very big family.
13. WHO TAKES CARE OF YOU WHEN YOU ARE VERY LITTLE?
    Both the father (male) and the mother (female) tend to the babies and gather food for us. But, just as soon as baby quails hatch, we can run and peck for food, too.
14. WHERE DOES SUCH A BIG FAMILY SPEND THE NIGHT TO KEEP SAFE?
    (In a hushed voice). Under a big evergreen tree, or under a big bush. We form a circle to keep warm.
15. WE KNOW WHAT A CIRCLE IS. TELL US HOW QUAILS FORM IN A CIRCLE, QUEENIE.
    We back into the circle so that we're all facing out. It's warm and cozy and we can all keep watch in all directions.
16. DO YOU MIGRATE, OR FLY SOUTH FOR THE WINTER?
    No, but we sure do walk a long, long way for food. We usually find it.

17. WHERE DO QUAILS LIVE?

All over the world. In the USA you will find a lot of quail in Arizona and California. We went west with the settlers.

18. IS IT TRUE THAT YOU EAT PEBBLES AND GRAINS OF SAND?

It is true. They rub together in my stomach and help me to grind the food as I move around. You see, I have no teeth like you do. You can grind your food with your teeth before you swallow it, but I can't. It's nature's way.

19. WHAT DO YOU DO FOR EXERCISE, QUEENIE?

We run and chase each other. I think you call it playing tag.

20. BEFORE WE GO THERE'S ONE LAST THING.... HAS ANYONE EVER TOLD YOU THAT YOU'RE A PRETTY BIRD?

Yes, thank you. In Japan, people like our looks and our song and they put us in cages and keep us for pets.

THANK YOU FOR THIS INTERVIEW RIGHT HERE AT THE COUNTRY FARM. TODAY OUR GUEST WAS QUEENIE QUAIL WITH THE TOPKNOT FEATHER. TUNE IN NEXT TIME WHEN WE WILL BE INTERVIEWING A(N)

_____. REMEMBER: "BOB-WHITE," "BOB-WHITE."

INTERVIEW
INFORMATION

What did you learn? Draw it, write it, or web it.

Q

QUEENIE QUAIL

QUEENIE QUAIL MAKES A QUILT

There is work to be done! Queenie needs help. Trace the upper case Q's and the lower case q's with your pencil. Then use a different color crayon for each square to help make a beautiful quilt for Queenie.

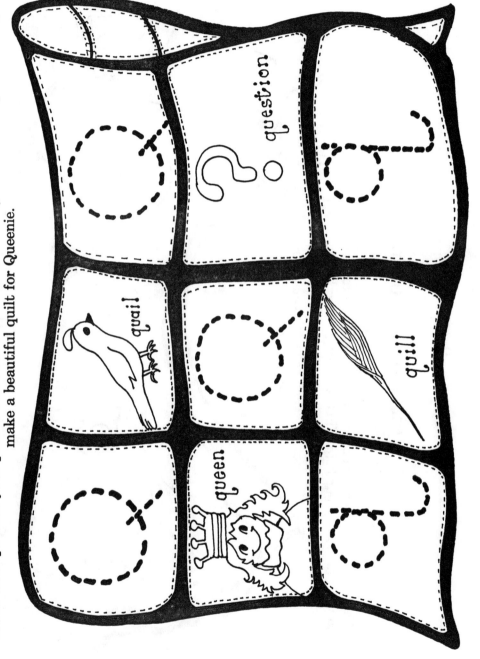

Name —————————

Date —————————

THE QUEEN IS COLLECTING QS

The Queen is gathering upper and lower case Qs for her gown. She needs your help. Circle all the Q and q letters and color them purple. Put an X on those letters that are not Qs. Then color the Queen and her quite gorgeous gown!

AN ANIMAL QUACKER PUPPET

Color this animal quacker (duck) and cut it out. On the back, list words that begin with qu. Quack them right out loud!

QUEENIE QUAIL LIKES QUESTIONS

Queenie wants to know which animals and birds are on the endangered species list. Can you answer her questions? Draw or print names of those you know about. She wants to know where you can go to find out more information. Can you help her?

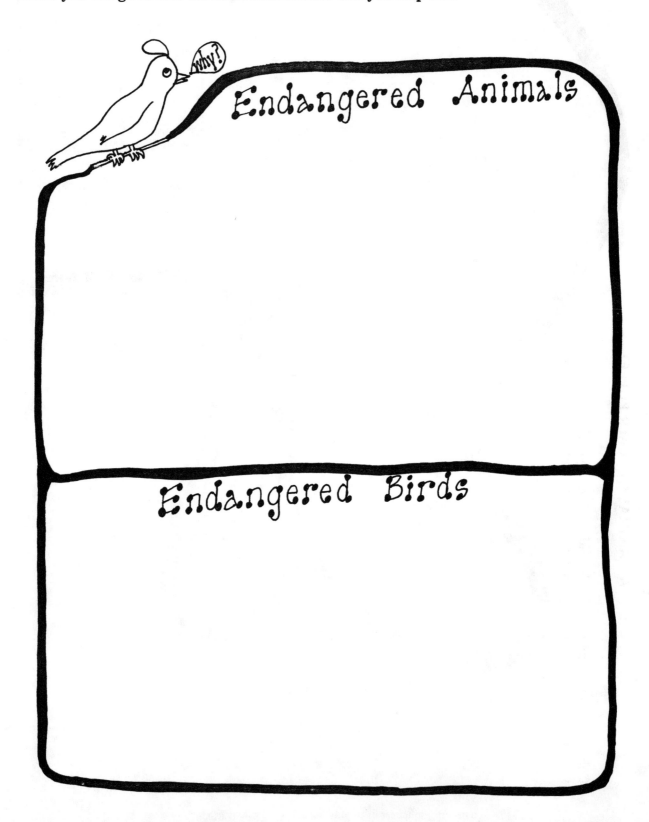

Name _____ Date _____

QUEENIE QUAIL LIKES RIDDLES

Queenie is giving you some clues. Draw your answer in each box. Compare your paper with others. How many different ones did you find for each riddle? Make up your own riddles.

I have feathers.
I am a _____.

I have fur.
I am a _____.

I have teeth.
I am a _____.

I have no teeth.
I am a _____.

My skin is smooth.
I am a _____.

My skin is rough.
I am a _____.

R
IS
FOR

RUDI RABBIT

R IS FOR RUDI RABBIT

BACKGROUND INFORMATION ABOUT RABBITS: Rudi the cottontail rabbit is very common. The rabbit is easily recognized by its fluffy cottonball of a tail which actually helps the animal to survive. During a chase, the cottontail will zig and zag, flashing its white tail and then will promptly sit down. When it sits, its coat blends in so well with the surroundings, that it can't be seen. Quite a cover up! While rabbits and hares look alike, upon closer examination the rabbit has a more rounded shape, whereas the hare is long and thin.

READING/LANGUAGE ARTS:

1. RABBIT EARS. Students can make long construction paper ears and glue them onto a headband. Wear the rabbit ears for good listening manners when talking about rabbit information, or when listening to the rabbit interview which can be taped on a cassette recorder by the teacher, by two students in the class, or by older students. These ears seem to work like magic when we're working on listening skills.

2. R-r-r-r AS IN RUDI RABBIT. How many items in the room begin with the same sound as rabbit? How many words can students think up that begin just like rabbit? List them on the chalkboard or on chart paper. Suggest to students that you make up a sentence where almost every word begins with r. (Example: Rudi rabbit ran in road ruts). Some students may be able to make up sentences for other animals also, just using their special sound. This is a focus on alliteration and some of the sentences can be downright funny!

3. RABBIT TALES. Many rabbits appear in storybooks and become favorites of students. *Peter Rabbit* and *The Tale of Benjamin Bunny*, both by Beatrix Potter can launch the students on an indepth study of the works of Beatrix Potter. They will meet up with a wide array of animals and fanciful tales that make for good listening, good story telling, and good story writing.

4. WHY THE RABBIT HAS LONG EARS. Read some of *Aesops Fables* to students to learn fanciful accounts of why certain animals look or behave the way they do. Then, encourage students to create their own WHY TALE.

MATH:

1. JUMPING JACK RABBIT. A jack rabbit can jump 20 feet. Be sure to measure this with a ruler. Outside on the playground, have students run along the 20-foot area. Also, a jack rabbit can run faster than 30 mi/h. That's faster than the school bus travels in a school zone.

2. PRACTICE ZIG AND ZAG. Lines come in all shapes and sizes. Today, practice making zigzag lines like Rudi the Rabbit. Have students zig and zag on the playground to get the general idea.

3. ZIGZAG CHA-CHA.   Play a cha-cha record and have students zig and zag to the music (kinesthetic experience). Wear the rabbit headbands for the dance. Incorporate counting, so that students do three zigs and six zags, or seven zigs and nine zags. Keep changing the count so that students gain practice with focusing their attention in conjunction with auditory directions.

4. MULTIPLICATION WITH RABBITS.   Rabbits have multiple births, and keep multiplying. Introduce the term multiply to young children in conjunction with rabbits, and in conjunction with numerals. Have multiplication facts on rabbit shapes so that students can use them as flashcards. (Make addition facts flashcards also, since multiplication is repeated addition.)

SCIENCE:

1. SWIVEL EARS.   Discuss the word *swivel.* A rabbit can swivel its ears to the left and to the right. Is there a swivel chair in the room? Students can put on their rabbit ears and sit in the swivel chair and swivel to the left and to the right, just like the rabbit. What else can swivel?

2. ANIMAL EARS.   So far Rudi has the longest ears of any of our Alphabet Animals. Probably the elephant ears are the largest. Look through the flashcards and pictures of the animals that we have met so far, and take note of their ears. How can we classify them? (Big, little, floppy, flat to the head, can't see, and so on). In what way are ears important to each of our ABC animals?

3. RABBITS MAKE NICE PETS.   A tame rabbit makes a very nice classroom pet. Keep the cage clean, and feed the rabbit according to instructions. The pet can be named by the students, and can be let out for periods of the day. The students enjoy holding and petting the rabbit, and it can help to cheer up students. It may even help a reluctant student come to school. It provides many learning opportunities, and is an avenue for creative expression with art and writing.

SOCIAL STUDIES:

1. GETTING A RUNNING START.   Hounds chase rabbits and jackrabbits can run very fast. Also, they are clever. When a hound is getting very, very close, a jackrabbit can jump high up into the air and the hound keeps right on running. Then the jackrabbit turns around and runs the other way and finds a safe place to hide. This is a form of survival behavior and using one's intelligence and instinct for survival.

2. JACKRABBIT TEAMS.   Rabbits have been known to cooperate in order to outsmart a hound. One rabbit will run until it becomes tired, then the second rabbit takes over while being pursued by the same dog. Rabbits can run a hound into the ground through this cooperative effort. The dog gets exhausted and gives up, and the rabbits go on about their business. Let's try some team learning.

3. RABBITS ARE NOT IN DANGER OF BECOMING EXTINCT . . . YET. That is the good news. The bad news is that many animals are endangered, and some day the rabbit may join this list. Perhaps, because rabbits are so prolific, they can be put to work in our classroom to help form committees to study reasons why animals are endangered. We can have the Acid Rain Rabbit Committee, the Ozone Layer Rabbit Committee, the Anti-Hunting Animals for Parts and Pelts Committee, the Toxic Waste

Rabbit Committee, the Ocean Pollution Rabbit Committee, and so on. Put on those investigative ears and get going!

Students can become informed on these topics and inform each other. They can write letters to the President of the United States. The White House, Washington, D.C. 20501, and the Mayor and Zookeeper of their own city or town. Be sure to get a copy of the book entitled *Fifty Simple Things Kids Can Do To Save the Earth* by The Earthworks Group (Andrews and McMeel, Kansas City, MO 64112), and *The Kids Nature Book: 365 Indoor/Outdoor Activities* by Susan Milford (Williamson Publishing Co., Charlotte, VT 05445).

I know a rabbit
    That's quick as a wink
She's got long ears.
    That are lined with pink.

R

TALK AND TELL: RUDI RABBIT

1. HELLO THERE, RUDI! WE HAVE A QUESTION FOR YOU. CAN YOU TELL US IF RABBITS AND HARES ARE THE SAME?

    People think we're the same but we're really different.
2. IN WHAT WAY ARE YOU DIFFERENT?

    Bunny rabbits have a round shaped body. Hares look long and lanky, or skinny.
3. RUDI, ARE YOU BORN LIVE OR HATCHED?

    I'm a mammal, which means that . . . (pause and have children join in) "I'm born live." Good. When a baby rabbit is born, it has no fur and is helpless. A hare is born with all of its fur and it can see and hop right away.
4. RUDI, ARE YOU SHY? WHY DO YOU ALWAYS RUN AWAY FROM EVERY-BODY AND EVERYTHING?

    Sigh . . . I'm probably the most hunted animal you can name. Just about every animal, and even large birds, are out to catch me and eat me. Rabbits are very, very tasty!
5. AND YOU MAKE A NICE PET TOO, DON'T YOU?

    Yes I do. There are wild rabbits and there are tame rabbits. A tame, pet rabbit can live side by side with many of the same animals that would attack it in the wilds—like cats and dogs.
6. HMMM-MM-M! CAN YOU TELL US SOMETHING ABOUT YOUR VERY, VERY, VERY LONG EARS, RUDI?

    Aren't they wonderful? I can hear someone coming from a long way off. I can twist and turn my ears in different directions to pick up sounds. I can twist one ear to the right and at the same time twist the other ear to the left. Try it.
7. THAT'S NOT EASY TO DO! HOW DO YOUR EARS HELP YOU TO KEEP COOL?

    My body heat travels up through my ears and out into the air, which cools me off in hot weather. Isn't that great?
8. IT IS! IF YOUR EARS KEEP YOU COOL, CAN YOUR EARS HELP YOU TO KEEP WARM?

    They sure do! In cold weather not as much heat escapes through my ears and so my body stays warmer.
9. YOU HAVE LOVELY EYES, RUDI. DO YOU SEE WELL?

    Very well, thank you. My eyes are high on the side of my head and I can catch sight of an enemy coming from all directions.
10. WHAT DO YOU LIKE TO EAT?

    Rabbits are not meat eaters. We like vegetables, fruits, and grains.
11. RUDI RABBIT, DO YOU MAKE SOUNDS?

    I'm very quiet. But if a predator catches me, I can let out such a loud scream that it can really scare you.
12. OTHER ANIMALS HAVE MENTIONED THAT WORD PREDATOR. CAN YOU TELL US AGAIN WHAT PREDATOR MEANS? WE'RE LISTENING CARE-FULLY.

    The predators are the ones who keep chasing after other animals in order to catch them for supper. The ones being chased are called the prey.

13. THANK YOU, RUDI. WE'LL TRY TO REMEMBER. ARE RABBITS CLEAN ANIMALS?

We wash our fur and paws and ears just like the cats do.

14. WHERE DO COTTON TAILS LIVE?

Along borders of fields or woods where the bushes are thick. Rabbits make a shallow spot to lay in. This home is called a form. The word sounds like farm, but has the letter o in it.

15. YES, FARM AND FORM. RUDI RABBIT, DO RABBITS MAKE GOOD MOTHERS?

Excellent! The female rabbit digs a nest in a sheltered spot. She lines the nest with grass and with fur that she pulls from her very own chest. She wants a soft, comfortable spot for her babies.

16. DO BABY RABBITS STAY IN THE SAME NEST WITH THEIR MOTHER?

No, it's not safe. A female rabbit has her litter of 4 or 5 babies and covers them with a blanket of grass. Then, she watches them from her form (home) and visits them in the night, so that the babies can nurse.

17. HOW HIGH CAN RABBITS JUMP, RUDI?

Jack rabbits can jump 20 feet. That's high! Measure it on the wall today.

18. WHEN COTTON TAILS ARE BEING HUNTED, HOW DO THEY GET AWAY?

They're tricky! They run in a zigzag path and flash their cotton tail, and then, all of a sudden, they sit down. When they sit, they hide that fluffy white cotton tail, and blend in with the woods. It's hard to see the rabbit then.

19. IS IT TRUE, RUDI, THAT YOU CAN BE SO-O-O-O STILL THAT A WOLF COULD WALK RIGHT BY AND NOT EVEN SEE YOU?

It's true. We freeze.

20. DO YOU MEAN THAT YOU GET COLD?

No. Freeze means to stay perfectly still and not to move a muscle. Even our whiskers don't twitch! Did you ever play Freeze? Try it, it's a good game. Well, I have to run along now, I smell an animal coming. Bye-bye.

WHERE DID HE GO? HE WAS JUST HERE. OH WELL, THANK YOU FOR THIS TALK-AND-TELL TIME RIGHT HERE AT THE EDGE OF THE WOODS. TODAY OUR GUEST WAS A BUNNY RABBIT NAMED RUDI, WHO PLAYED FREEZE AND SEEMS TO HAVE DISAPPEARED. TUNE IN NEXT TIME WHEN WE WILL

BE INTERVIEWING A(N) _____. AND NOW, LET'S ALL GET UP AND STRETCH AND HOP LIKE A BUNNY UNTIL I SAY FREEZE.

R

INTERVIEW INFORMATION

What did you learn? Draw it, write it, or web it.

RUDI RABBIT

Name _____ Date _____

RUDI RABBIT GOES A-HUNTING

Rudi Rabbit hunts without a gun. Today he was hunting for four items that begin with his sound of r as in rabbit. He has four items, but do they all begin with his sound? If not, you can add another drawing so that he has all four.
Then color Rudi so that he looks proud!

ruler

rooster

rocket

basket

RUDI RABBIT'S BOARD GAME

For one player, name an animal or bird for every letter shown here so that Rudi Rabbit can reach home. For two players, roll one die. If it is a 3, for example, you must name three animals beginning with the letters M and P before you can go to the next letter. Take turns. The first player to get Rudi home is the winner.

RUDI RABBIT'S ABC OVERALLS

Color the As green.
Color the Bs red.
Color the Cs blue.
Color Rudi with a color you
think is ravishing!

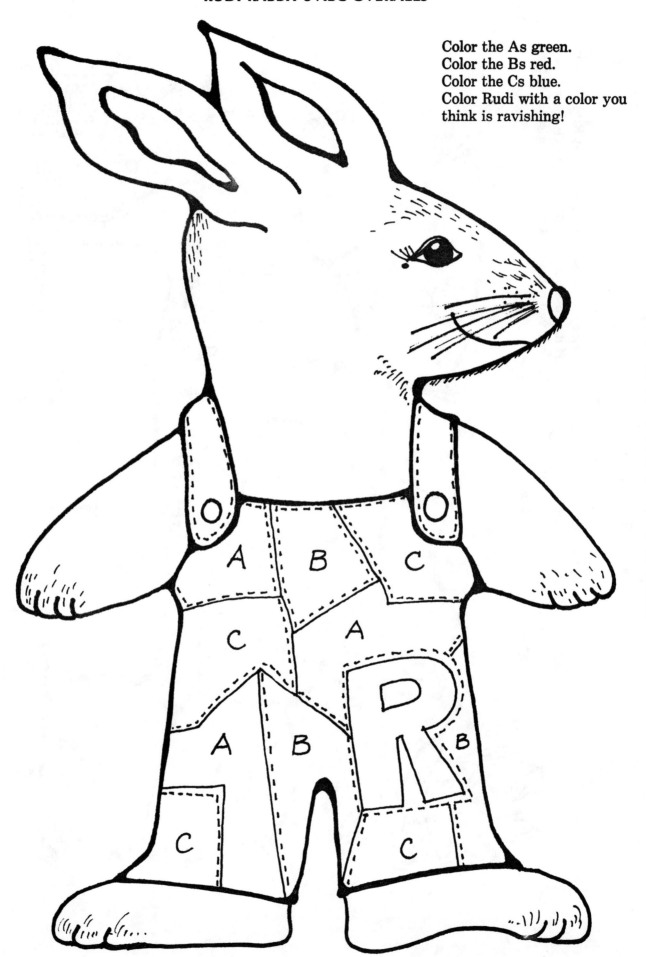

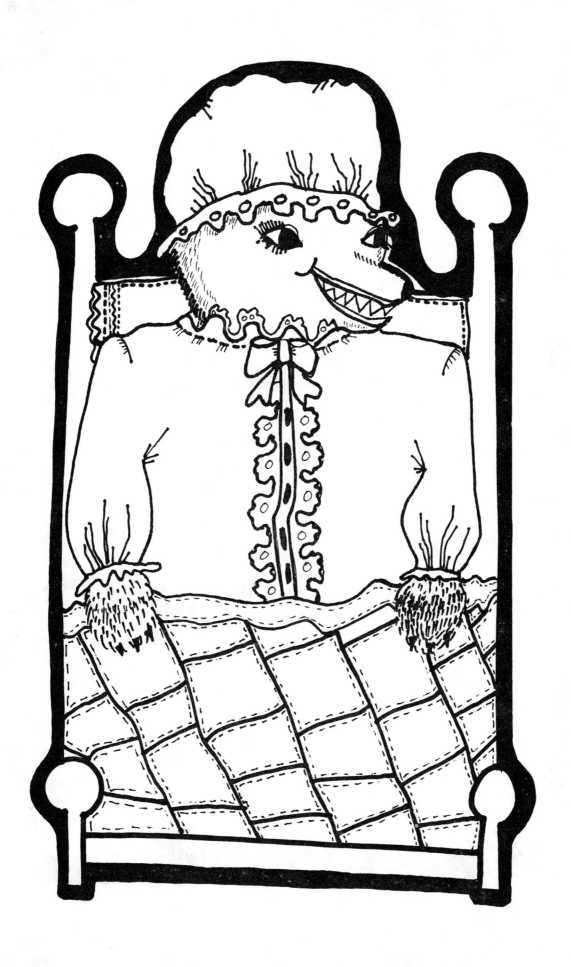

S
IS
FOR

STACY SQUIRREL

S IS FOR STACY SQUIRREL

BACKGROUND INFORMATION ABOUT SQUIRRELS: Squirrels have been called the acrobats of the forest and they are also high wire artists, performing amazing feats on communication lines in suburban areas. The tail, which is about half the length of the squirrel's body, is useful to the animal. The tail can fan out like a parachute to break a fall, it covers the animal to keep it warm, and it covers the back and head to provide shade from the heat and an umbrella in the rain. Squirrels flick and jerk their tails to show anger. They use their teeth, claws, and tongue to keep this amazing tail clean.

READING/LANGUAGE ARTS:

1. A-HA! CINDERELLA'S SLIPPERS WERE NOT GLASS—THEY WERE MADE FROM SQUIRREL FUR! Now it can be told. In the original story, told in Norman, the French word VAIR (meaning squirrel fur) was used to describe Cinderella's slippers. In the retelling, the word was changed to VERRE, which sounds the same, but it is the word for glass! Alas, Cinderella has been condemned to a storybook life dancing in glass slippers instead of soft, squirrel fur slippers. Note that the word slippers remains, and slippers denote something soft and comfortable. Glass slippers and furry slippers are two very different slippers. (Source: *Tree Squirrels*, by Colleen Stanley Baro. New York: Dodd, Mead & Co. 1983). Give this startling bit of information to the students. Have them decide how, or if, it would make the story different. Let's take this opportunity to rewrite this magic tale and give the squirrel the credit it has long deserved!

2. SOFT-SLIPPERS BY STACY. Get some fake fur at a fabric shop, and students can help Stacy Squirrel design and create wonderful fur slippers for Cinderella. For dramatic play, a squirrel could present the slippers to Cinderella and tell her of the vair/verre mistake. The squirrel has missed its place in this wonderful fairy tale!

3. COMPARE CINDERELLA TALES. There are many versions of the Cinderella tale. Read some of the traditional tales and be sure to include *The Egyptian Cinderella* by Shirley Climo with illustrations by Ruth Heller, and *Cinderella* retold by Barbara Karlin with illustrations by James Marshall, and *Princess Furball* by Charlotte Huck with illustrations by Anita Loebel. How are they the same? Where do they differ? What do the slippers look like and how are they described in each tale? Have students compose their retold tale.

4. CINDERELLA MAY BE FROM THE ORIENT. The oldest Cinderella tale dates back to China and the T'ang Dynasty (618-907 A.D.). The oldest European version of Cinderella was found in an Italian version from 1634. Obtain a copy of *Yeh-Shen, A Cinderella Story from China*, retold by Ai-Ling Louie and illustrated by Ed Young. Follow the gorgeous illustrations from page to page to note the flowing lines. How does this story differ from the rest? How is the slipper represented? Note that in this tale, as in the others, Cinderella is really not a waif but is linked to royalty. She is actually a charac-

ter who is restored to her rightful place in society, rather than a character who is rescued by chance.

MATH:

1. HOW LONG IS THREE MONTHS? Check the calendar to see how long the mother squirrel stays with her babies. After three months go by, the mother moves out of the nest and the squirrels are on their own.

2. STACY BUILDS MORE THAN ONE HOME. Tree squirrels generally prefer to live alone and will build two or three nests. If they sense that one nest is in danger, they can get to another for safety. They build their nest with an escape hatch (a back door) to run from the raccoon who is a squirrel hunter. Use plasticene to built three nests with the escape hatch.

3. SQUIRRELING ACORNS. A squirrel may hide as many as hundreds of nuts daily in the autumn in preparation for winter. In winter, very little squirreling of nuts goes on. Have students review their counting of 1-100 by ones, twos, fives, and tens as they count actual items, perhaps nuts.

SCIENCE:

1. LET'S TAKE A CLOSER LOOK AT AN ESCAPE ROUTE. Discuss the concept of an escape hatch. The squirrels have planned ahead in anticipation of danger because they usually build their nest with a front and a back door. This could lead to a discussion about "WHAT IF . . . THEN WHAT?" Some specific topics could be: "What if you smelled smoke in the night, then what? What if you are being pestered by a playground bully, then what?

2. THE INDIANS APPRECIATED STACY. The Indians honored squirrels because they reforested the land. This amazing ability to plant trees is truly a gift from the squirrel. During creative play, have the students scamper around and dig and bury nuts. How can they honor these tree planters?

SOCIAL STUDIES:

1. THAT USEFUL TAIL. Make a large cutout of a squirrel shape and have students add features with a felt pen. Use a new, clean fluffy mop as a bushy tail and students can show the squirrel how to use its tail for an umbrella, a parachute, a sun screen, and a blanket. A student, holding Stacy's mop tail, can lead a discussion about how people protect themselves in all kinds of weather.

2. WHAT WOULD SQUIRRELS DO WITHOUT TREES? They would have to *adapt.* That means, they would have to change in order to survive. Squirrels find a good home in trees because they can travel faster going up and down than over a flat ground area. Claws on the ends of their toes help them to cling to trees. So squirrels have an interest in keeping our earth's great resource of trees in a healthy state. Learn more about what can be done by reading *Going Green, A Kid's Handbook to Saving the Planet* by John Elkington, Julia Hailes, Douglas Hill, and Joel Makower, with illustrations by Tony Ross. (NY: Viking, 1990).

3. WHO SHARES THE TREES WITH SQUIRRELS? What other animals and birds inhabit our trees? They are very busy places at various times of the year. For your information, read *Tree Trunk Traffic* by Bianca Lavies (NY: Dutton, 1989).

A squirrel buries acorns
In the ground.
Then digs them up
When we're not around.

S

TALK AND TELL: STACY SQUIRREL

1. HI THERE BUSHY TAIL! IS IT TRUE THAT THERE ARE TWO TYPES OF SQUIRRELS?

    Yes, it's true. There are tree squirrels and there are ground squirrels.

2. WHAT IS THE DIFFERENCE BETWEEN A TREE SQUIRREL AND A GROUND SQUIRREL?

    Tree squirrels build nests from twigs and leaves high up in a tree in order to catch the breezes that blow. Ground squirrels burrow (dig) underneath the ground to make a home.

3. STACY SQUIRREL, ARE YOU HATCHED FROM AN EGG, OR ARE YOU BORN LIVE?

    I'm a mammal which means that . . . (encourage children to join in) "I'm born live." When a squirrel is born, it's pink and has no hair.

4. HOW BIG ARE YOU WHEN YOU'RE BORN, STACY?

    I'm very tiny, only about 2 inches long. Check it out with your ruler.

5. WHEN DO YOU GET HAIR?

    By the time a squirrel is 3 weeks old, it has all of its hair.

6. STACY, HOW MANY TREE SQUIRRELS LIVE IN ONE NEST?

    Only one squirrel lives in each nest. Squirrels like to live by themselves. We like to run and chase each other and play together, but we each have our very own nest.

7. WHAT DO YOU USE TO MAKE YOUR NEST, STACY?

    If I can't find an old dead tree trunk, I use leaves and branches to build my nest. I build it way up high, and it's about 12 inches long (as long as a ruler).

8. WHAT DO YOU DO ALL DAY?

    I look for food. Squirrels are ALWAYS searching for berries, insects, nuts, and especially those acorns. We love those acorns!

9. DO YOU EAT A LOT, STACY?

    What we don't eat, we bury in the ground. That way we can come back and get it later. We're always busy digging and burying nuts in the ground.

10. TELL US, STACY, HOW CAN YOU REMEMBER WHERE YOU BURIED THE NUTS?

    Squirrels have a pretty good sense about where the nuts are. For one thing, we can smell them. But, you know, sometimes we do forget, or we don't need them, and some of the nuts sprout and grow into trees.

11. THAT'S GOOD TO HEAR. THE AMERICAN INDIANS HONORED SQUIRRELS FOR BURYING ACORNS AND OTHER NUTS, DIDN'T THEY?

    Yes, the Indians appreciated squirrels. The Indians said that we were good planters, and that we helped to make forests grow.

12. HOW DO SQUIRRELS LEARN TO CLIMB TREES? YOU MAKE IT LOOK LIKE FUN.

    The mother squirrel teaches her little ones to climb trees and to jump from branch to branch and from tree to tree. We just do what she does, and it works.

13. DO YOU HAVE ANY ENEMIES, STACY?

    Sigh! There are snakes that crawl into the nest looking for food. And the raccoons like to reach inside the nest and try to grab a squirrel. That's why we build an escape hatch.

14. WHAT IS AN ESCAPE HATCH?

We have a front door and a hidden back door in our nest. The hidden door is the escape hatch. But that's not all . . .

15. THIS IS EXCITING! WHAT ELSE DO YOU DO TO GET AWAY FROM YOUR ENEMIES?

(In a hushed voice) Squirrels build two or three nests at a time. That way, if we see that one is in danger, we just go to another nest where it's safe!

16. THAT'S CLEVER, BUSHY TAIL. CAN YOU TELL US SOMETHING ABOUT YOUR GREAT BIG TAIL?

I like to swish it around. I can use it like an umbrella in rainy weather; I can use it for shade in hot weather; and I can wrap it around me just like a blanket if the weather gets too cold.

17. YOUR TAIL IS VERY USEFUL, ISN'T IT?

Yes it sure is. When I run across a high wire or go way, way out on a tree limb, my tail helps me to keep my balance so I don't fall off.

18. I THINK YOUR TAIL IS WONDERFUL. YOU CARRY YOUR VERY OWN UM-BRELLA AND BLANKET WITH YOU ALL THE TIME. YOUR TAIL MAKES YOU SPECIAL, STACY.

Yes, it comes in very handy. I can use it for a fan too when it's extra hot outdoors.

19. WHAT IF PEOPLE HAVE NEVER SEEN A REAL, LIVE SQUIRREL. WHERE SHOULD THEY LOOK FOR YOU?

Go to a wooded area or an open park. If you see nutshells under a tree, it's a sign that a squirrel is living up there.

20. ONE LAST QUESTION—WHAT IF I STILL DON'T SEE YOU?

Be patient and wait. Don't sit too close to the tree. After awhile, I'll get used to you and I'll come around, especially if you bring some nuts with you and put them on the ground.

THANK YOU FOR THIS TALK-AND-TELL TIME RIGHT UP HERE IN THE TREE TOP. TODAY OUR GUEST WAS A GRAY TREE SQUIRREL NAMED STACY. TUNE IN NEXT TIME WHEN WE WILL BE MEETING A(N)

—————————————————————————. LET'S CHECK THE WEATHER AND SEE IF THIS IS AN UMBRELLA DAY OR A BLANKET DAY FOR BUSHY TAIL. BYE FOR NOW.

INTERVIEW INFORMATION

S

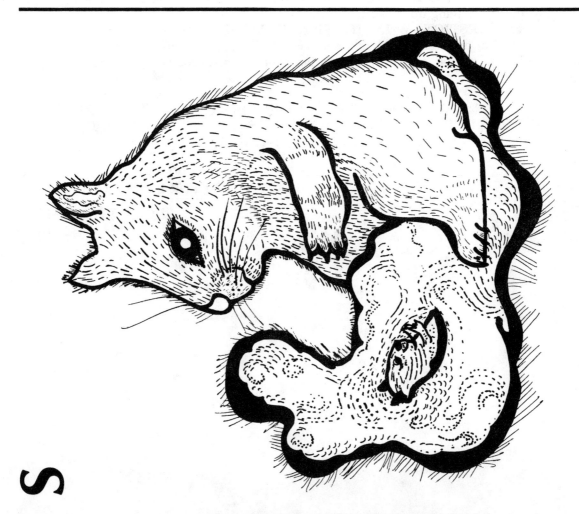

STACY SQUIRREL

What did you learn? Draw it, write it, or web it.

STACY SQUIRREL IS PACKING FOR S TOWN

Stacy is going to S Town. There you can only use things that begin with the sound of s as in squirrel. How many items can you pack into Stacy's bag? Then color Stacy and describe her by using two s words.

sweater

STACY SPINS A TALE WITH HER TAIL

Cut out Stacy's tail at the bottom of this page and use a paper fastener to put it in the middle of the story wheel. Spin Stacy's tail for four story elements so that you can spin your tale.

A—character
B—setting
C—more characters
D—type of story

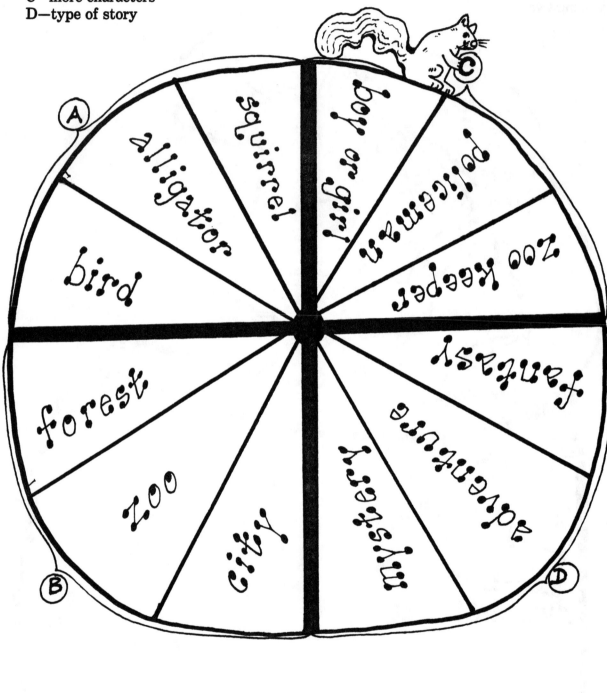

Name _____

Date _____

SAMMY SPIDER'S SURPRISE PARTY

Sammy Spider invited five guests for a party. Only those beginning with the s sound get a red circle around them. The others get a blue circle. While you are coloring Sammy's guests, think of a game they could play. For example:
They could slither like a snake, or slide like a _____, or _____ like a _____, and so on.

CLAWS, PAWS, AND FOOTPRINTS MATCHING GAME

Cut the squares on the lines so that you have 16 squares. Notice that you have two of each, or a total of eight sets. Lay the cards face down (four rows of four cards) and turn over two cards at a time. If the cards match, you may keep them. If the cards don't match, turn them back over again. Go on to the next player, and repeat. Try to concentrate and remember where each picture is hidden as each player takes a turn. The player with the most matches is the winner. Then, set up the cards face down and begin a new game.

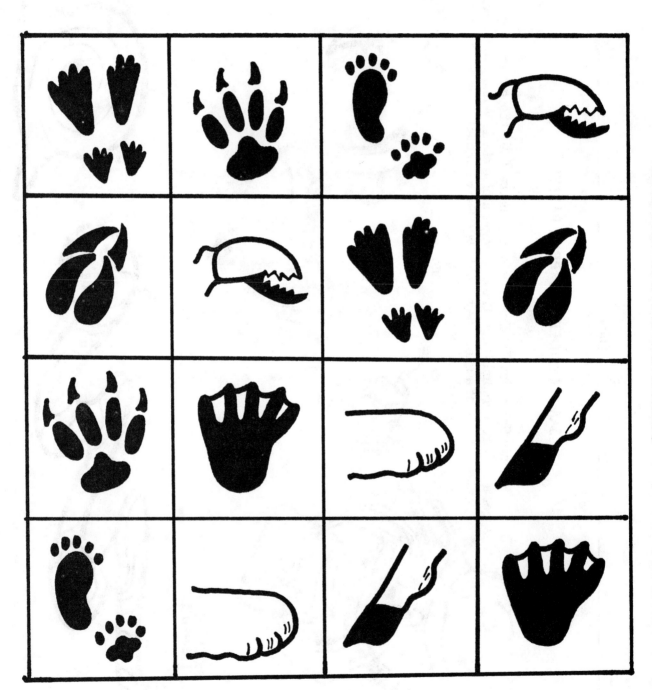

Name _____ Date _____

CALLING ALL RODENTS! CALLING ALL RODENTS!

Some animals are called rodents. Stacy Squirrel is calling other rodents today. Who, besides the mouse, will answer the call? Use information books to help you. Show the animals and label them.

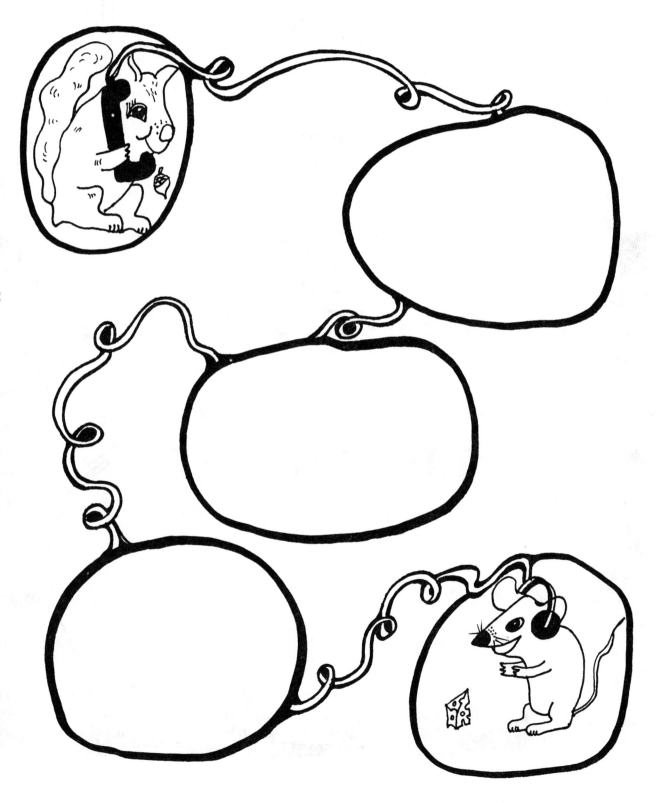

T
IS
FOR

TRACY TURTLE

T IS FOR TRACY TURTLE

BACKGROUND INFORMATION ABOUT TURTLES: Scientists use the word tortoise when referring to land-dwellers and turtle when referring to sea-dwellers. There are five types of sea turtles and in order of size from largest to smallest they are: Leatherback, Green, Loggerhead, Hawksbill, and Ridley. The largest ones can weigh a ton. The shell of the turtle is made from very large scales, and it serves as a suit of armor for the turtle. When it pulls in its head, tail and four legs, it looks amazingly like a rock. Both the tortoise and turtle lay their eggs in a sandy pit near the water's edge. They cover them with dirt to hide them and keep them safe. Only the female turtle comes ashore. When the turtles are hatched, they instinctively seek the water.

READING/LANGUAGE ARTS:

1. THE ABC OF TURTLES. Have students put the names of turtles in alphabetical order: Green, Hawksbill, Leatherback, Loggerhead, and Ridley. Find books about turtles so these five can be located and identified. Make a turtle-shaped fact book.

2. THE HARE AND THE TORTOISE. Read this fable with the underlying message that slow and steady wins the race. Discuss the value of doing some things slowly and well, and not always rushing just to finish first. Students can practice moving slowly like a turtle. Re-enact the story.

3. THAT'S TURTLE WITH A T. Make a large construction paper turtle for the bulletin board. Make round egg shapes and print words that begin with the letter t on them. (Elicit the words from the students.) Hang the words on the shell, and play the game "I'm thinking of something that begins with Tracy Turtle's sound of t and the elephant has one" (trunk or tusk).

4. TRACY TURTLE SCRAMBLE. Use the chalkboard or ABC cards to scramble the name of one turtle at a time (Example: diryel for ridley). Challenge students to unscramble the name. When the word is scrambled, the turtle is hiding in its shell. Try to bring it out of its shell by unscrambling the word.

MATH:

1. CAN YOU COUNT TO SIXTY? It takes 60 days for baby turtles to hatch and it is quite a sight to see them struggling against the surf to make their way to the ocean. Have students waddle to the count of 60 by tens, by fives. What music would be appropriate for waddling?

2. THE TURTLE COUNT. Turtles may live to be over 100 years old! Count to 100 by 1, 2, 5, and 10. Print numerals on turtle shapes for review and reinforcement.

3. TRACY LIKES FIVE.   There are five kinds of sea turtles. Call attention to five fingers on each hand, and five toes on each foot. Count from 1–5 and backwards from 5–1. Make a "Tracy Turtle Treasure Box" and have students help decide what to put into the box. There must be five of each item. Then, they can help Tracy with the concept of five. (Example: paper clips, crayons, seashells, toy turtles).

SCIENCE:

1. REPTILE RELATIVES.   Turtles, along with alligators and crocodiles, are classified as reptiles. The snake and lizard are also in this group. That means that Tracy Turtle and Ashley Alligator are related. Perhaps a meeting of the two is possible, using hand puppets.

2. A TURTLE VISIT.   Arrange to have a pet turtle visit the classroom so that students can examine its shell and body parts. The land turtle can retract its head and body parts, but the sea turtle cannot do this. Get information books from the library on turtles and examine the pictures and read about them.

3. GALAPAGOS MEANS TORTOISE.   Galapagos is the Spanish word for tortoise. The Galapagos Islands off the coast of Ecuador, South America, at one time were home for hundreds of thousands of giant tortoises. Today, they are an endangered species. What happened? The islands became a stopping place for ships, and the tortoises were a good supply of fresh meat. Ship rats began to inhabit the islands, too, and feasted on tortoise eggs and the babies. Today, the islands have been declared a wildlife refuge and national park and the tortoises are being protected. For more information, read *And Then There Was One, The Mysteries of Extinction* by Margery Facklam with illustrations by Pamela Johnson (Boston: Little, Brown, & Co., 1990).

SOCIAL STUDIES:

1. BACKPACKING.   Survey your students to find out how many have gone backpacking or camping. What would we need to take along for an overnight in the woods? List the items. Bring in a real backpack, and have students take turns wearing it. For some, it may be the first time they have worn a backpack. The turtle or tortoise is a backpacker, also. Have students keep track of the weight they can carry with comfort and ease. Also, how long can they continue to carry this weight around?

2. CRAWL-IN AND READ.   For a total school project, or a grade-level project, have students spend the night at school with ample parent and teacher supervision. This can be done in the school gymnasium. Students can come back to school in the evening with their animal books, stuffed animals, and other belongings in a backpack or a bag of some sort. They can bring their own sleeping bag, or school mats can be used. The evening would be planned with silent reading time, quiet play time, snack time, quiet reading time, getting ready to settle down time, and lights dim time. (This requires a great deal of advance preparation in terms of planning, but it is an event that students will always treasure.)

3. TURTLE CHANTING.   Remember the chant "There was a little turtle . . ."? Teach this variation of it:

There was a little turtle
Who lived in a box
He dreamed about seashores
He dreamed about rocks.
I took the little turtle
To the edge of the sea
Now he swims all day
And he can thank me!

Have students compose their own Turtle Rhymes. Write them on green paper cut in turtle shapes.

A turtle takes a backpack
    Wherever he does roam.
And that is why a turtle
    Is never far from home.

T

TALK AND TELL: TRACY TURTLE

1. TAP, TAP, TAP! TRACY TURTLE, WE LIKE YOUR HARD SHELL. DOES YOUR SHELL KEEP YOU SAFE?

    Yes, it's my suit of armor. A fresh water turtle can pull in its head, legs and tail and feel safe. A sea turtle cannot do this.

2. DO YOU TAKE YOUR SHELL WITH YOU WHEREVER YOU GO OR CAN YOU LEAVE IT?

    Where I go, my shell goes.

3. IS IT FUN TO CARRY IT ON YOUR BACK?

    It slows me down, but I'm used to it.

4. TRACY TURTLE, ARE YOU BORN LIVE OR HATCHED?

    I'm hatched from a hard-shelled egg. Both sea turtles and land turtles lay their eggs on land. When the young turtles hatch, they head straight for the water.

5. AMAZING! HOW DO TURTLES FIND A PLACE ON LAND TO LAY THEIR EGGS?

    The female just digs a pit, or a hole, in the sand near the water. She lays her eggs and covers them over with dirt to hide them and keep them safe.

6. THAT'S JUST ABOUT THE SAME THING THAT THE ALLIGATOR DOES WITH HER EGGS. ARE YOU TWO RELATED, TRACY?

    Oh, yes. Turtles are related to alligators and crocodiles. We're called reptiles. We're from the same family.

7. SO! TURTLES ARE RELATED TO ALLIGATORS AND CROCODILES!! DO YOU HAVE ANY OTHER WELL-KNOWN REPTILE RELATIVES?

    The snake and the lizard are my relatives too.

8. WOW! WHAT IS THE DIFFERENCE BETWEEN A TORTOISE AND A TURTLE?

    Tortoise means a land-dweller, and turtle means a sea-dweller.

9. STACY, HOW MANY DIFFERENT TYPES OF SEA TURTLES ARE THERE?

    Hold up one hand. Count your fingers. Ready? 1-2-3-4-5. Five. There are five types of turtles. From biggest to smallest they are: Leatherback, Green, Loggerhead, Hawksbill, and Ridley. Maybe you can find some pictures of them in library books.

10. THAT'S A GOOD IDEA, TRACY. HOW BIG IS THE LEATHERBACK?

    About 6 ft in length. That's two yardsticks put end to end.

11. WHY IS THE BIGGEST CALLED LEATHERBACK?

    It's the only sea turtle without a shell. Its back is covered with brown, tough leathery skin.

12. TELL US ABOUT THE NEXT LARGEST, THE GREEN TURTLE.

    Well, it's a green color, just like its name. And it eats sea grass, not meat. All the other turtles are meat eaters, but not the green turtle.

13. IS IT HARD TO TELL THE LOGGERHEAD AND THE GREEN TURTLE APART?

    They look alike and they are the best swimmers, but their shells have a different number of scale shapes, called scutes.

14. DOES THE HAWKSBILL LOOK LIKE A HAWK?

    The upper jaw hooks down and over the lower jaw just like a hawk or a parrot. That's how it got its name.

15. THE SMALLEST ONE IS LEFT, THE RIDLEY. WHAT IS DIFFERENT ABOUT THE RIDLEY?

> For one thing, this sea turtle has a nasty temper. The others are more gentle.

16. WE ARE LEARNING A LOT ABOUT TURTLES, TRACY! HOW FAST CAN A SEA TURTLE SWIM?

> About 20 mi/h. That's a lot faster than you can ride your bike.

17. TRACY, WHY ARE YOU CRYING? ARE YOU SAD?

> No. Sea turtles cry a lot. We get rid of sea-salt that way. But, we're really not at all sad.

18. WE'RE GLAD TO HEAR THAT. TRACY, DO PEOPLE HUNT FOR SEA TURTLES?

> Yes. We must be protected or there won't be any more of us left. We could become extinct like the dinosaur!

19. WHAT DO PEOPLE WANT WITH SEA TURTLES?

> Well, we make delicious turtle soup. Also, people like our shell to make combs and eyeglass frames and jewelry. And turtle fat oil is used for making perfume and soap. We're very much in demand.

20. TRACY, DO YOU HAVE ANY MESSAGE FOR US TODAY FROM THE SEA TURTLES?

> Yes. We're endangered wild life. Please do not hunt for us—give sea turtles some protection. You know, we could live to the ripe old age of 100 years if people would let us. Thank you for letting me give this message.

THANK YOU, TRACY TURTLE, FOR THIS INTERVIEW RIGHT HERE AT THE EDGE OF THE ATLANTIC OCEAN ALONG THE COAST OF FLORIDA. TODAY WE MET A BIG SEA TURTLE WHO WAS VERY FRIENDLY. OUR NEXT INTERVIEW WILL BE A(N)

_____. GOOD-BYE FOR NOW FROM STATION ABCD-EFG-HIJK-LMNOP-QRS T for TURTLE.

INTERVIEW INFORMATION

T

TRACY TURTLE

Name ———————

Date ———————

DESIGN A TURTLE IN A SHELL

Use construction paper to make the head, tail, and feet for your turtle. Then use bright crayons to make a beautiful shell design. My, this is going to be something special!

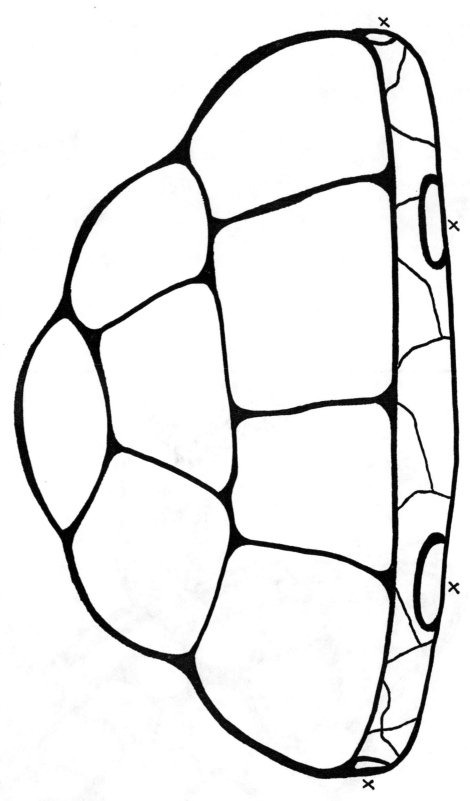

Name _____ Date _____

TRACY TURTLE'S MYSTERY SHAPES

Use your pencils and crayons to complete what Tracy has started. Use real books to examine special features.

Tortilla Turtle Treat

1. Two tortilla chips.

2. One scoop tuna salad!

3. Four celery stick legs.

4. One carrot tail.

5. One olive head.

6. Yummy!

Name _____

Date _____

TRACY TURTLE'S RELATIVES

The turtle is a reptile. Find Tracy's relatives and color them to make them look healthy.
Color Tracy, too. Oops! Who does not belong with the reptile family?

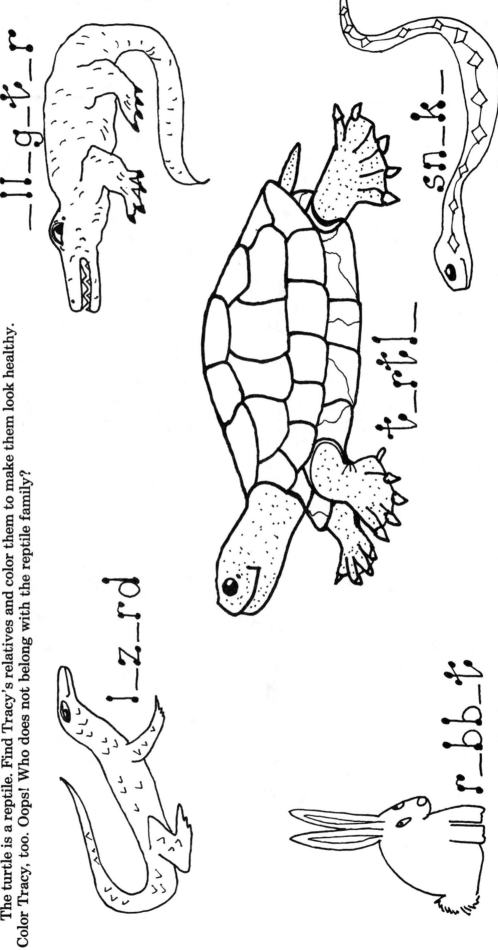

ll _ g _ t _ r

sn _ k _ _ us

t _ rtl _

l _ z _ rd

r _ bb _ t

TORTOISE AND HARE BOOKMARK

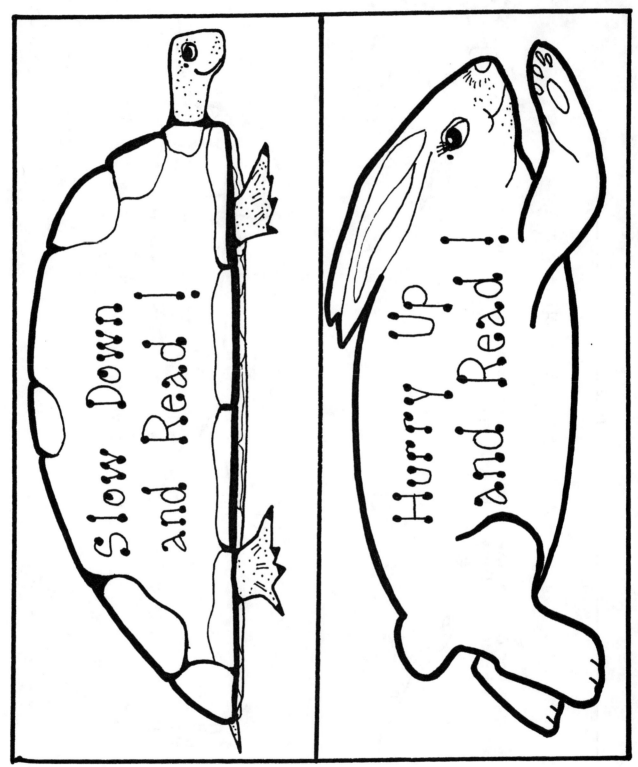

U
IS
FOR

UNI UNICORN

U IS FOR UNI UNICORN

BACKGROUND INFORMATION ABOUT UNICORNS: The unicorn is a beautiful, mythical animal with the head and body of a horse, the legs of a deer, and the tail of a lion. It also has a long, cylindrical horn that protrudes from the tip of its head. It is usually depicted in woven tapestries and in literature as being all white, for purity. Reports of seeing the unicorn in forests date back to biblical times, but catching a unicorn has never been accomplished. For centuries, people believed that the unicorn contained magic in its horn. It was thought that to capture a unicorn and grind the horn into a powder would enable man to create a powder that could magically cure all illness.

Ironically, the same thing is thought of the rhinocerous. The African rhino has a single or double horn protruding from its forehead. Also, there are some white rhinos, although they are rare. One theory is that the unicorn is an idealized version of the white rhino who roams the forests looking for vegetation. The rhinosaurus is an endangered specie because it is hunted for its horn which is ground into powder and used as a cure for many ills.

READING/LANGUAGE ARTS:

1. STORYBOOK UNICORNS. Locate storybook pictures and art pictures of unicorns so that children can examine them. There are many storybooks that contain unicorns. The bibliography at the end of the book will help you to locate some stories about unicorns to read to the students. Since many unicorns are located in tapestries and paintings in art galleries, an excellent read-aloud book that takes the reader on an adventure in an art gallery with famous paintings is *The Girl With the Watering Can* by Ewa Zadrzynska.

2. CREATE FANCIFUL ANIMALS. The unicorn is horse-like, yet has the horn of a rhinocerous, the feet of a deer, and the tail of a lion. Have students work together to create other fanciful animals with different body parts. Try using some of the favorites from the ABC animals we have met. What name can be given to these strange creatures? What tales do they have to tell? This is a good language experience opportunity.

3. U IS FOR UNICORN. The letter u is the last vowel that we will meet. It has a long and a short sound. List words for each. Review the other vowel animals that we have met for a,e,i, and o.

4. A TIME FOR FANCIFUL STORIES. Since unicorns are magical, this would be a good time to launch a unit on fairy tales. Read aloud several versions of some of the favorite tales from the Brothers Grimm for comparisons. For example, read several versions of *The Three Little Pigs, Red Riding Hood, Snow White,* and *Beauty and the Beast.* Take special note of the illustrations to find fanciful creatures. Make comparison charts for each main story. Remember to look for some of the characteristics of fairy tales, such as: magic potions, magic objects, magic spells; the use of the number three;

wicked versus good characters; the opening line; the ending line; how good conquered evil, and so on. This unit can be done during the month of March or April when leprechauns and fairies are in the air. Uni Unicorn can be in charge of the festival of fairy tales.

MATH:

1. UNI MEANS ONE.   Have students make a "uni farm" picture with one of each item (such as one barn, one horse, one wagon, one garden, and so on) or a "uni city" picture with one of each item (such as one skyscraper, one taxicab, one big bus, one traffic light, and so on). Perhaps the pictures could have a unicycle in it—a bike with one great big wheel.

2. UNICORN IS TWENTY-ONE.   The unicorn starts with the twenty-first letter of the alphabet—two tens and a single one. Add on until you get to twenty-six, the last letter. Work with tens and ones, in terms of which animal owns that number. Who is one ten and three ones? (Mike MacMoose) Who is two tens and zero ones? (Tracy Turtle) Use flashcards or pictures of the animals to make a chart, and print the number beneath the animal picture (Animal I.D.) so that students can work with tens and ones.

3. UNICORNS AND RAINBOWS.   Work with cutouts from construction paper and put number sentences on unicorns and the answers on rainbows. Students can match up the correct pairs.

4. THERE'S SOMETHING MAGICAL ABOUT THE UNICORN.   Unicorns love math. They enjoy seeing how many ways we use math. They like to "catch us using numbers." Make a bulletin board with a huge unicorn stirring a pot. On the pot, students can print all the ways that math is used every day (example: lunch count, time for special classes or recess, how many papers need to be distributed, measuring with a ruler, putting on the correct size shoes and clothing, and so on).

SCIENCE:

1. MAKE A UNICORN ENDANGERED SPECIES CHART.   Make a large shape of a unicorn, and print the names of endangered animals or birds on it. Make sure to start with the rhinocerous. In Kenya, Africa, where the rhino roams, schoolchildren have made "Save the Rhinocerous" posters. Students can select a particular animal and make a "Save the _____" poster and display them in the room, out in the hall, or have a parade. Many zoos have an "Adopt an Animal" Program. Perhaps this is something the class is interested in pursuing by calling the local zoo for information.

2. MAKE UNICORN STEW.   You will need water in a container, a prism, and a sunny window ledge. When the prism is positioned just right, the sun rays create a mini-rainbow that will dance across the water (unicorn stew) when you stir it. See reproducible activity pages.

3. GET REAL.   Have students make a Unicorn Board Game. They can choose to print statements of fact or fancy about animals on the board spaces. Use a spinner or dice to determine number of spaces to move. When a student lands on fancy, he or she must go back to a fact space. First one to the end wins. Have students make several versions of this game. For help, use the animal interview sections.

4. FANCIFUL ENVIRONMENTS.   If the unicorn is fanciful, make a fanciful environment for it. Use a large box and create a diorama. Make fanciful trees, fanciful plants, and even more fanciful animals. Hang a fanciful sun, fanciful moon, and fanciful stars from the top of the box to help create the environment. What colors would a unicorn like in its magical forest? Remember, it doesn't have to be green! For help with color, read *Color Dance* by Ann Jonas.

SOCIAL STUDIES:

1. VISIT AN ART GALLERY.   Arrange to visit a local gallery or museum. Search for a unicorn and while you're at it, note specific painting styles, tapestries, and sculpture.

2. A UNICORN VISIT TO MY TOWN.   Suppose that Uni Unicorn should visit your city. Secure a large city map, and locate points of interest such as parks, zoo location, the main street, and so on.

3. WRITE TO THE CHAMBER OF COMMERCE.   Have students compose a class letter to send to the local Chamber of Commerce for information that is available on your city or town.

4. GOOD LUCK CHARM.   Since a unicorn is a good luck charm, let's talk about other good luck charms that are a part of our heritage. Do students have a rabbit's foot? Do they ever knock on wood for good luck? What else?

Did you ever see a unicorn
    With dreamy eyes and pointed horn?
Well, if you did, you're safe from harm
    A unicorn's a good luck charm.

U

TALK AND TELL: UNI UNICORN

1. UNI, YOU ARE A BEAUTIFUL ANIMAL. ARE YOU REAL OR MAKE BE-LIEVE?

    I'm make believe.
2. BUT THEN, WHERE DO YOU LIVE?

    In storybooks, legends, and beautiful tapestries woven by artists.
3. WHERE DID YOU GET THE NAME UNICORN?

    It comes from one (uni) horn. I have a horn sticking out of my forehead.
4. YES, WE CAN SEE IT. CAN YOU TELL US ABOUT YOUR MAKE-BELIEVE BODY?

    I have the head and body of a horse, the legs of a deer, and the tail of a lion.
5. THE HEAD AND BODY OF A HORSE, THE LEGS OF A DEER, AND THE TAIL OF A LION? WHO THOUGHT UP THAT COMBINATION?

    Long ago, in a place called Europe, people began to talk of seeing an animal in the forests that looked just like me.
6. DID THEY TRY TO CATCH YOU, UNI?

    Yes, but they never could.
7. DID THEY SAY AND WRITE NICE THINGS ABOUT YOU, UNI?

    Always! They said I was truthful, and good and pure!
8. UNI, DID PEOPLE BELIEVE THAT YOU HAD MAGIC POWERS?

    Yes, People said that if you caught a unicorn, you could take its horn and grind it into white powder. This chalk-white powder was thought to cure all kinds of illness.
9. DO YOU THINK YOU WERE EVER REAL? AFTER ALL, MANY PEOPLE DID SAY THAT THEY SAW YOU.

    Some folks believe that people may have been seeing the white rhinocerous from far away. The rhino is a real animal, and sometimes the white ones are surprisingly gentle.
10. THE RHINOCEROUS DOES HAVE A HORN STICKING OUT OF ITS FORE-HEAD, TOO, DOESN'T IT, UNI?

    Yes, and people believed that if you ground up the horn of a rhinocerous the chalky powder could be used as medicine to cure many illnesses. So the stories sort of match.
11. UNI, WHERE CAN WE SEE A REAL RHINOCEROUS IN THE WILD?

    Find Africa or India on the map or globe. That's where you can find a rhinocerous. But I'm going to tell you a sad thing. They are in danger of becoming extinct. They need protection. People are killing the rhino and selling the horns.
12. WHY ARE THEY STILL SELLING THE HORNS?

    Many tribes in Africa still believe that the horns have the power to cure certain illnesses, such as fever. Also, the horns are used as decorations on swords. Before you know it, there won't be any rhinos left unless people do something to protect them.
13. WE HOPE THEY HELP THEM OUT! GETTING BACK TO THE UNICORN, WHAT IS IT LIKE TO LIVE IN LEGENDS AND STORIES AND TAPES-TRIES?

    It's wonderful. When people read about me and talk about me, it makes me feel like I'm real.
14. IN THE STORYBOOKS, DO THE REAL ANIMALS LIKE YOU, UNI?

    Yes, because I help them with my magic powers.

15. CAN YOU TELL US SOMETHING ABOUT YOUR MAGIC POWERS?

In the forest, I look for my reflection in the waters and streams (like looking into a mirror). If the water is too muddy, and I can't see myself, I dip my magic horn into the water and it becomes clean and pure. Then, all of the animals come and drink and stay healthy.

16. THAT'S WONDERFUL! WHAT ELSE?

If there's been a forest fire and everything is black, I stomp my deer legs 3 times, and switch my lion tail 3 times, and the flowers bloom and the trees blossom.

17. YOU ARE AMAZING! DO YOU HELP HUNGRY ANIMALS IN WINTER, TOO?

Yes, in winter I touch the ground with my magic horn and the food begins to grow. All of the animals come and have a feast, just like Thanksgiving.

18. NO WONDER THE ANIMALS LOVE YOU, UNI. DO YOU HAVE A FAVORITE COLOR?

The rainbow follows me wherever I go, so I love all of the colors of the rainbow!

19. CAN YOU TELL US THE COLORS IN THE RAINBOW?

Red, orange, yellow, green, blue, violet. You can learn them too.

20. ONE LAST QUESTION, UNI. WHY DO YOU THINK MAN CREATED THE UNICORN?

It was an act of love. I am probably the only imaginary animal that *always* does good, pure, noble deeds! I am just too good to be true!

THANK YOU FOR THIS TALK-AND-TELL TIME RIGHT HERE AT THE ART MUSEUM. WE HAVE BEEN TALKING WITH A BEAUTIFUL UNICORN IN A PICTURE PAINTED BY AN ARTIST. THE UNICORN TOLD US THE MOST WON-DERFUL STORIES, WE JUST MIGHT LIKE TO HEAR IT ALL OVER AGAIN. TUNE IN NEXT TIME WHEN OUR GUEST WILL BE A(N)

_____. HAVE A MAGICAL DAY!

INTERVIEW INFORMATION

What did you learn? Draw it, write it, or web it.

U

UNI UNICORN

LONG AND SHORT SOUNDS OF THE VOWEL U

Long u sounds like the u in *unicorn*. Short u sounds like the u in *under*. Can you hear the difference? Put a circle around those that have the unicorn sound. Color all of the items.

ŭmbrella

unicorn

ūniform

ŪSA

ūnicycle

ŭpside down

THE UNICORN AND THE UMBRELLA

The letter u has a long sound (unicorn) and a short sound (umbrella). Look through magazines and cut out pictures that begin with the letter u. Select a long sound item and a short sound item. Paste them in the appropriate raindrops. Then use your crayons to brighten up this rainy day!

Name _____ Date _____

CREATE AN ANIMAL

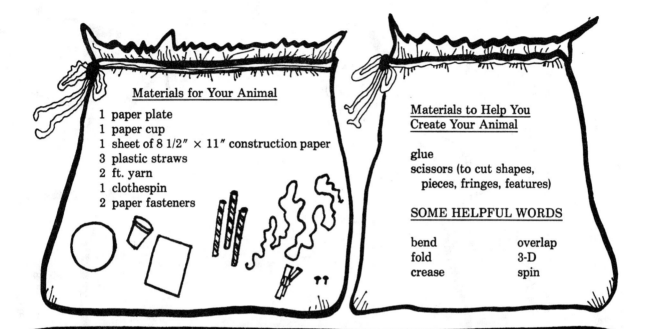

Materials for Your Animal

1 paper plate
1 paper cup
1 sheet of 8 1/2″ × 11″ construction paper
3 plastic straws
2 ft. yarn
1 clothespin
2 paper fasteners

Materials to Help You
Create Your Animal

glue
scissors (to cut shapes,
    pieces, fringes, features)

SOME HELPFUL WORDS

bend   overlap
fold   3-D
crease   spin

NOW, tell us something, in writing, about this very special animal.

NAME of animal _____

FOOD it eats _____

HOW does it get this food? _____

WHAT sound does it make? _____

WHEN does it make its sound? _____

WHERE DOES IT LIVE? HOW DOES IT TRAVEL? DOES IT EVER CHANGE SHAPE? DOES IT MIGRATE? DOES IT HIBERNATE? Use this space, and the back of the sheet, to let us know much more about your special animal!

Name ————————

Date ————————

DO I LOOK LIKE A UNICORN?

Some people think the rhinocerous is really the unicorn. Others say, "Rhinocerous? Preposterous!" What do you think? Write your answer on the rhino below and use the back of this sheet too.

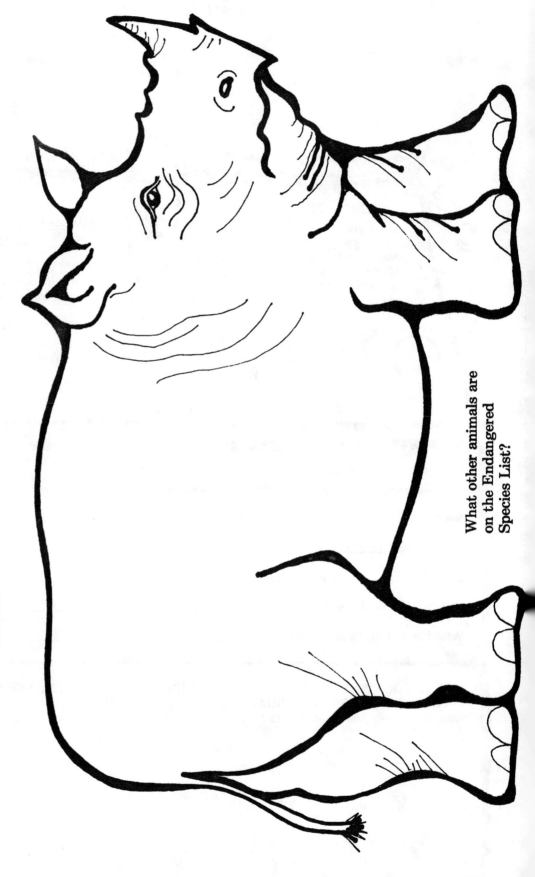

What other animals are
on the Endangered
Species List?

Name —————————————————— Date ———————————————

UNI UNICORN HAS A PARTY

Use your crayons to invite one (uni) animal or bird that begins with the letter in the box.

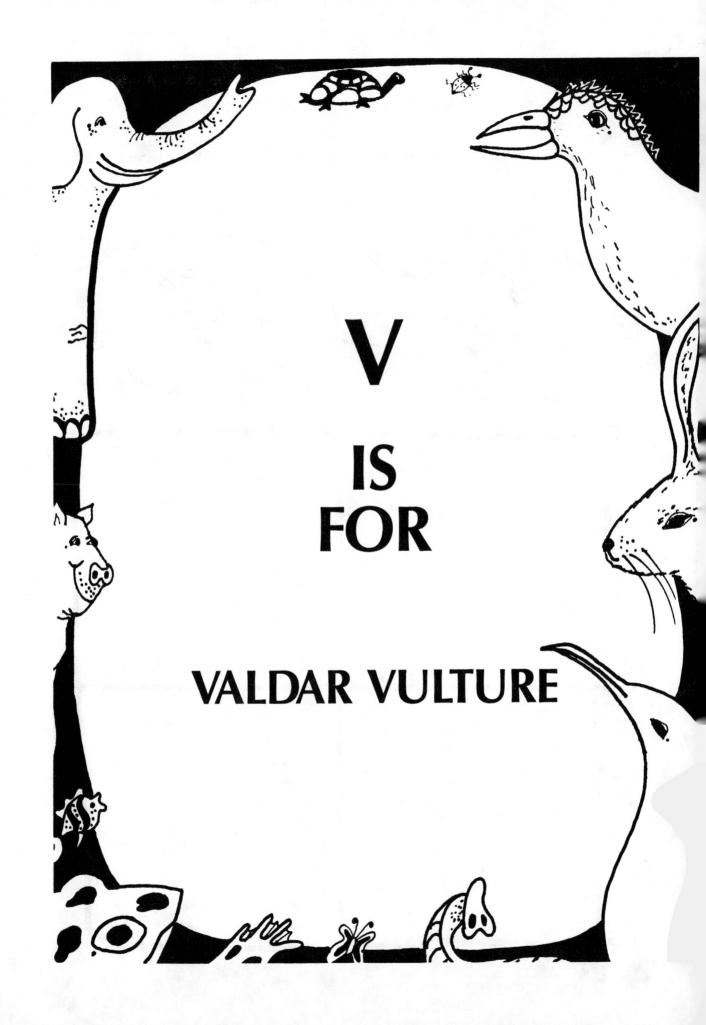

V

IS

FOR

VALDAR VULTURE

V IS FOR VALDAR VULTURE

BACKGROUND INFORMATION ABOUT VULTURES: Vultures like Valdar belong to the same order of birds as eagles and hawks. They have a nose hole, but cannot smell. Their beak, while strong enough to tear apart old meat, is not as strong as that of the eagles and hawks. The vulture is a *scavenger* bird which feeds on old, dead meat. They don't usually kill, but go in for the carcass. In this way, they do clean up the environment and are extremely helpful in preventing the spread of germs and disease.

Vultures have a large, bald, orange head and a bare neck. Nature designed the bird in this way in order to prevent germs from forming on them. The sun and rain help to clean them and to kill the germs from the decaying meat they devour. They are often seen bathing in streams. They have very long feathers at the wing tips which stabilizes the bird in strong wind currents. While they are not a favorite bird such as the robin, the American Indians recognized the value of vultures in helping to clean up the environment. The Indians believed that they took messages to heaven and back on their mighty wings.

READING/LANGUAGE ARTS:

1. SCAVENGER HUNT. Let's go on a scavenger hunt for words that begin with v. Then, let's go on a scavenger hunt to help clean up the floor and deposit waste in the proper container. That's what Valdar does—helps dispose of waste. He is an *environmentalist* and we can learn this word from him, as well as the importance of what he does.

2. MYTHS AND LEGENDS. Give a definition of myths and legends as stories that have been handed down through the ages, and they may or may not be totally accurate. There are some myths, for example, about the vulture. For a long time farmers believed that vultures killed their animals which is a myth. Vultures do not actually kill animals, but they do eat the carcass of dead animals. This act serves a purpose, since it is nature's way of helping to stop the spread of disease. Also, west coast Indian tribes in America believed that the California Condor was a thunder god who caused lightning and storms. Other Indians believed that the vulture carried messages to the gods on its tremendous wings.

3. NATIVE AMERICAN FOLKTALES. Collect folktakes that are available in the library, and then have a Native American legend and folktale festival for reading, writing, and storytelling. Indians were noted for their ability to tell good stories. Who are some of the famous Native Americans that we can read about? Learn their names, and learn about their ways. This is an opportunity to practice telling stories with strings, too. (Throw a ball of string or yarn around the room to different children, who start and continue a story when they catch the string.)

MATH:

1. CALIFORNIA CONDOR MATH.   The California Condor is a large vulture. It has a wing span of 10 feet across. (That's approximately three yardsticks and one ruler put end to end.) Have students measure this in the room, and tape a piece of bright colored yarn from one end to the other. It's long! How many students can stand side-by-side to fit under the vulture wings?

2. VALDAR GETS A SPEEDING TICKET.   Vultures can fly at 100 mi/h. That's speeding in the sky! Students might want to see how fast they can count to 100 by 10s, 5s, 2s, and even 1s. Perhaps they can be given a "speeding ticket" (a little flash card with a number fact on it that they must find the answer for in a designated number of seconds).

3. LONG AND SHORT DISTANCES.   A robin may have a territory that is in your backyard. There would be enough food there for robins to build a nest and have a family. But, the condor of South America has a huge territory. Food is scarce in the Andes Mountains (locate this mountain range on the map or globe) and so this bird must travel miles and miles to find food.

SCIENCE:

1. NATURE'S GARBAGE CAN.   Alas! This bird is on the endangered species list. It does do helpful environmental work. It is now protected by law, even though it is almost extinct. If the bird doesn't clean up the environment, then who will? The message that we want to convey to students is that this bird is very important (and undervalued). When people say that they work as a garbage collector, do we say, "UGH"? Of course not! They are doing important work. We must get this message across about the vulture, as well.

2. SING OUT FOR THE VULTURE!   The vulture has no voice, nor no need of one in nature, since it has no territory. The Indian tribes in South America make flutes from the hollow wing bones of condors, so perhaps the vulture has a sweet song after all! Have students create an environmental song for the condor (either a call for helping to clean up the land, or an actual song with words). Perhaps a flute accompaniment would be appropriate.

SOCIAL STUDIES:

1. WEAR THE VULTURE BADGE.   See the reproducible Activity Pages for a badge that promotes the vulture and its clean-up-the-earth program. What can you do to help Valdar? Many things, such as picking up trash and putting it in a bin where it belongs. Write to Greenpeace, 1436 U Street NorthWest, Washington, D.C. 20009 for more information.

2. SURVEY YOUR TERRITORY WITH FIELD GLASSES.   That is what the vulture does. The vulture has excellent eyesight, about seven times as strong as human eyesight. Set up an Environmental Station on your window ledge, and use field glasses to get a close look at tree bark, blades of grass, stones, and so on. Also, be on the alert for items left by people that will not recycle naturally. List all of these items. Your class may be able to patrol the playground area with Environmental Gloves and Bags.

3. STUDY THE ENVIRONMENT WITH A MICROSCOPE. Examine natural items from the environment, such as a tree leaf, tree bark, blade of grass, and so on. Have students draw diagrams of their environmental items.

4. LIFE IN THE AIR. What other animals fly? Let's begin to look for some answers. It's not just birds that swoop through the air. (Example: flying squirrel, flying lizard, flying frog, flying insects such as butterflies, bees, and so on).

I do my best
    To pick up litter.
I'm the earth's
    Best baby sitter.

V

TALK AND TELL: VALDAR VULTURE

1. HOW DO YOU DO, VALDAR? HOW DOES IT FEEL TO BE CALLED "NATURE'S VACUUM CLEANER"?

Well, someone has to clean up! We eat what others won't eat and this keeps germs from spreading.

2. BUT, DON'T YOU GET GERMS ON YOUR FEATHERS IF YOU'RE EATING GARBAGE?

See my bare head and bald neck with no feathers? They keep germs from sticking to me. Also, the rain washes me and the sun dries me.

3. PEOPLE THINK OF VULTURES AS DIRTY BIRDS, DON'T THEY, VALDAR?

Yes, but I'm here to tell you that we're really clean birds. We take baths often in streams and rivers. We do valuable work for you by cleaning up waste.

4. DO YOU HAVE A STRONG BEAK?

Not as strong as my relatives, the hawks and eagles, but strong enough to tear old meat apart.

5. IS YOUR EYESIGHT GOOD, VALDAR?

It's about 6 times as good as human eyesight. Think of yourself as always looking through a pair of binoculars—that's how well I can see.

6. DO YOU HAVE A SONG TO SING, VALDAR?

No, I have no voice since I don't have a territory. Bird songs and bird calls are needed by birds who have territories to protect. I roam all over.

7. DO YOU HAVE ANY NATURAL ENEMIES?

Yes. Are you listening carefully? My enemies are long winters, starvation, and man.

8. TELL US, VALDAR, WHY IS MAN YOUR ENEMY?

Because man thinks that vultures kill animals, but we don't really. We just eat them if they're already dead. Cattle farmers don't like to see us flying around; they get worried.

9. WHAT IS YOUR FAVORITE FOOD?

Cow or deer. If I can't find that, I eat from garbage heaps and dumps. It helps stop the spread of disease, you know. It's the good work that vultures were put here to do.

10. WHAT IS THAT BULGING POUCH THAT'S JUST UNDER YOUR THROAT?

That's called my crop. I store extra food there for a day or two in case I can't find any food to eat.

11. VALDAR, CAN YOU FLY?

Very fast! I fly between 60-100 mi/h. I can keep up with a highway truck!

12. WHAT COLOR ARE YOU?

My main color is black, but notice that I do have some orange, purple and white on my feathers. People don't like the looks of me, though.

13. WHO IS THE LARGEST VULTURE?

The California Condor. It has a wing span of 10 ft across! Measure that and you will be surprised! It's over 3 yardsticks long!

14. WHERE DO YOU BUILD YOUR NEST?

Vultures don't build a nest. The adult female lays her one egg on a rock ledge high up off of the ground.

15. DOES SHE JUST LEAVE HER BABY THERE?

Oh, no! Both parents, male and female vultures, pay a lot of attention to the baby bird. They bring it food and teach it to flap its wings. It stays on that rock ledge for about 5 months—that's a long time. Vultures are good parents!

16. HOW LONG DOES IT TAKE A VULTURE TO BECOME FULLY GROWN?

Six years, and that's a long time.

17. WHERE DO MOST VULTURES LIVE, VALDAR?

In mountains and valleys in Southern California and Northern New Mexico. Look for those places on the map or globe.

18. WHAT IS YOUR FLIGHT TAKEOFF LIKE?

Because of my heavy weight, about 20 lb, I have to run, hop, and flap my wings before I can take off. I do look very awkward. Probably you'd laugh at me if you saw me take off.

19. NO, I DON'T THINK WE WOULD LAUGH! AFTER ALL, YOU CAN FLY. ARE VULTURES PROTECTED BY LAW?

Yes, because we're almost extinct. That means there aren't very many of us left to do the clean-up work.

20. WELL, VALDAR, AT LEAST THE AMERICAN INDIANS APPRECIATED YOU, DIDN'T THEY?

Yes. They said the vulture could fly to heaven and back again with messages and prayers. Bless the Indians! They appreciated the clean-up work that vultures do! I hope you do, too.

THANK YOU FOR THIS TALK-AND-TELL TIME RIGHT HERE IN SUNNY CALIFORNIA. TODAY WE HAVE BEEN TALKING TO A GOOD HOUSEKEEPER FOR PLANET EARTH—VALDAR VULTURE. WE HAVE TO LEARN TO APPRECIATE THE WORK THAT THE VULTURE IS DOING FOR US. WOULD WE WANT TO DO IT? TUNE IN NEXT TIME WHEN WE WILL BE INTERVIEWING

A(N) _____. UNTIL THEN, YOU BE A GOOD HOUSEKEEPER TOO!

INTERVIEW INFORMATION

What did you learn? Draw it, write it, or web it.

V

VALDAR VULTURE

NATURE'S GARBAGE CAN

Cut out this badge and wear it to show that the vulture does good work! The vulture is on the Endangered Species List. Vultures care about the environment. Do you? How can you show it?

Name _____ Date _____

COUNTDOWN WITH A CONDOR

The condor has a wing span of 10 feet. Use a measuring tape and find something in the classroom that is the same length as the number of feet shown below. Print or draw that item.

1 foot	4 feet
2 feet	5 feet
3 feet	10 feet

20   feet

FABULOUS FEET

We take feet for granted. Animals use feet as tools for digging and scratching. They also use them to run, climb, kick, and walk. Some animals are flat-footed and some walk on their toes.

Find out more about animal feet and list 10 FEET FACTS below. Share the facts with your classmates.

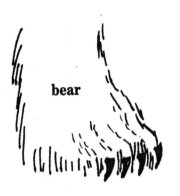
goat

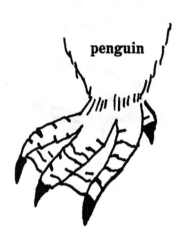
penguin

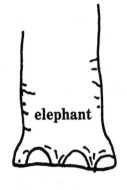
bear

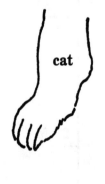
cat

elephant

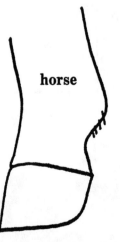
horse

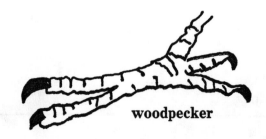
woodpecker

THE VULTURE'S ANIMAL BOOK

Vultures can see very well. Have you ever looked through binoculars? That's how good the vulture's eyesight is. This vulture sees three animals or birds. What are they? Cut out each circle. Place it on a sheet of paper and draw the rest of the animal or bird around it. Make a colorful book cover, too.

THE VULTURE HELPS IDENTIFY BIRDS

Cut the strip at the bottom. Cut out each of the six names for the bird's body parts. Paste the word next to the appropriate number. Did you do it? Good! Now use your crayons to make a colorful, healthy bird.

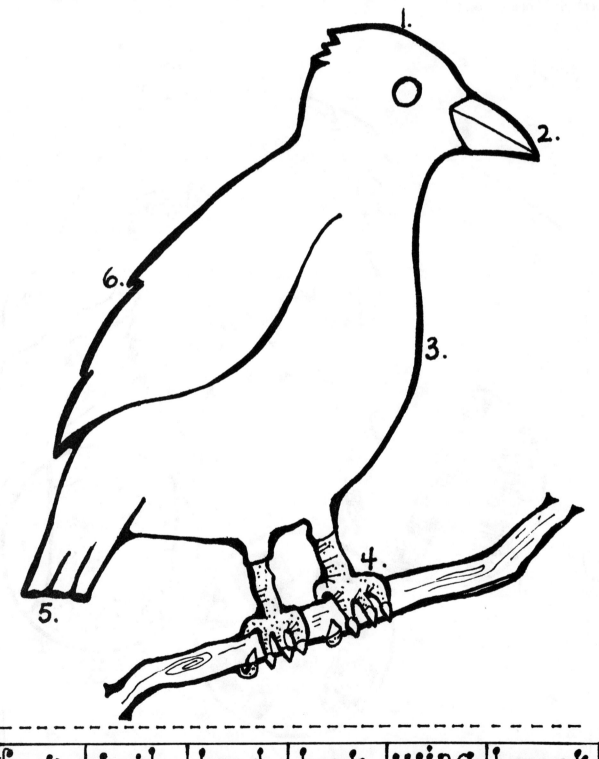

| feet | tail | head | beak | wing | breast |

W

IS
FOR

WALDORF WHALE

W IS FOR WALDORF WHALE

BACKGROUND INFORMATION ABOUT WHALES: Whales are shaped like huge fish, but they are huge mammals. Mammal comes from the Latin word *mammary*, which is the name of the milk-producing gland by which the adult female feeds her young. Whale milk tastes fishy. Whales have large brains and large hearts. Biologists think they are very intelligent creatures. Whales breathe air, and when they surface they create a water spout as they breathe.

The dolphin is a member of the whale family. Dolphins are social animals who play, fight, and care for their young. They like to be in groups. The mother carefully trains her young and they are punished for disobedience (wandering too far away) by a slap with a flipper or a nip. Dolphins can establish a relationship with their human trainers and can be trained to jump through hoops and do other things because they want to please and because they seem to enjoy it. They catch on very quickly to hand signals. Man is still studying the dolphin to find out more about this wonderful sea creature. However, whales are endangered by ocean pollution and there is a need to work to save this creature of the deep.

READING/LANGUAGE ARTS:

1. CRACK THE CODE. Dolphins are vocal animals and make sounds that resemble clicking, whistling, squawking, and squealing. Have students make these sounds. How can we interview a dolphin to find out what it is trying to tell us?

2. A WHALE OF A HEART. The whale has a very large heart (see math section). There are many heart sayings and songs that have the word heart in the title or in the lyrics. Let's try to think of some. Here are some heart-starters: "You're a sweetheart!" "Waldorf is big hearted." "Her heart is in the right place." "I left my heart in San Francisco." One state has the word heart in its state slogan—"Ohio, the heart of it all." Print these sayings on a big heart shape. (Also, whale is used in sayings to indicate a great amount, such as, "That's a whale of a big helping of potatoes" and "That's a whale of a pumpkin!") Try using language in this colorful way, and have a whale of a good day!

MATH:

1. WALDORF HAS A WIDE HEART! Waldorf Whale's heart is 6 feet wide. That's two yardsticks placed end to end. Measure it. Cut a piece of string that is that length. Have one person hold it at one end and another person hold it at the other end. How many people can stand in between?

2. STOVEPIPE ARTERIES. See if you can get a sample piece of large stovepipe from a builder's supply store. That's how large the whale arteries are. Get a little stovepipe too for comparison of big/little. People's arteries are even much smaller. Now we can get into the concept of small, medium, and large.

3. LET'S MEASURE.   We can have ABC soup for a class treat today. How many cans will we need to purchase, how much water goes into each can, how long will it take to heat it, what will we use for dishes and spoons, and how many? There are many ways to use math when we have a soup group.

SCIENCE:

1. TWO TYPES OF WHALES.   There are two kinds of whales—the toothed whale and the baleen whale. The toothed whales catch fish with their teeth and swallow them whole. The baleen whales eat plankton and sea life that float on the top of the water. Baleen whales have no teeth, but have strings of baleen (material made from keratin just like our fingernails) that hang from the top of their mouth. The sea life gets caught up in the baleen strings, similar to a net.

2. EYELASH APPRECIATION TIME.   Have students slowly blink their eyes, and then gently feel their eyelashes. Explain that eyelashes are a protection for the eye since they help to screen out dust and dirt. On a windy day, we are especially lucky to have eyelashes. Our eyes are also protected by lids, eyebrows, and bones that surround the eye socket. Whales do not have eyelashes (as we learn in the interview).

3. THE SENSE OF HEARING.   Whales can hear high and low sounds miles and miles away. By using the piano, triangle, bell, and drum, have students identify high and low sounds. Have students tap items in the room (they can use their keratin fingernails) to determine sounds that are high, higher, low, lower. Make a dolphin headband so that students can wear them to help establish good listening habits. (Record the whale interview on a cassette tape and have students listen individually.) Get a record from the library of recordings made by sea animals, and listen carefully.

4. WHALES HAVE MORE IN COMMON WITH PEOPLE THAN THEY HAVE WITH FISH.   Whales are mammals. Their young are born live and they nurse them. Fish are cold-blooded creatures. That is, when the water gets cold, they get cold. When the water gets warm, they get warm. They do not maintain a regulated body temperature as does the whale and people. Also, fish lay eggs from which their young are hatched.

SOCIAL STUDIES:

1. PLANET EARTH IS TWO-THIRDS WATER.   How much water do we use in a day? Have students do some sleuthing by asking questions and observing at home. They should know how much one gallon is by having a gallon container in class. (One washing machine load uses from 25 to 40 gallons, and one dishwasher load uses approximately 10 gallons of water.) Have students vow to turn off the faucet while they are brushing their teeth because gallons and gallons of water are going down the drain. Become a water conservationist!

2. DOLPHIN-FREE TUNA.   Many dolphins are caught in the nets of fishermen who are fishing for tuna, and the dolphins are killed. There has been an outcry from the public on this matter and now new techniques for fishing are being carried out so that dolphins are not caught along with tuna. Many cans of tuna fish carry the words "dolphin free" on their labels. Check your labels in the grocery story for this message.

I wish I could ride
    On a water spout,
Made from the ocean
    When a whale breathes out.

W

TALK AND TELL: WALDORF WHALE

1. HI, WALDORF! YOU ARE VER-R-RY BIG! SOME PEOPLE CALL YOU THE "GIANT OF THE OCEAN." HOW BIG ARE YOU?

   The Blue Whale is over 100 ft long. That's as long as six cars parked along the curb.

2. VERY LARGE! HOW HIGH ARE YOU?

   I'm about as high as a two-story house.

3. YOU MUST WEIGH MANY TONS. HOW CAN YOU SWIM AND NOT SINK?

   Well, the water supports my weight. Water holds me up when I swim. For me it's no problem to weigh even 50 or 100 tons, and to swim well.

4. IS IT TRUE, WALDORF, THAT YOU HAVE AN EXCELLENT SENSE OF HEARING?

   Yes, it's true. My ears are like tiny holes and they're right here behind my eyes on each side of my head. I can hear for miles and miles and miles.

5. DOES THE WATER HURT YOUR EYES WHEN YOU SWIM AND DIVE, WALDORF?

   No. I have eyelids to protect my eyes, just like you do. I don't have the protection of eyelashes though. Boys and girls are lucky to have eyelashes. Eyelashes help keep dirt out of the eyes.

6. TELL US, WALDORF, ARE WHALES BORN LIVE OR HATCHED?

   See if you can guess. (Pause). OK? Here's the answer. I'm a mammal, which means that . . . (children can join in) I'm born live. GOOD!

7. HOW BIG WERE YOU WHEN YOU WERE BORN?

   I was about 20 ft long. It's about as long as a big living room.

8. IS THE ADULT FEMALE A GOOD MOTHER, WALDORF?

   Yes! Every day she nurses her baby with milk that is creamy white and tastes fishy! Baby whales grow fast, and a mother will really fight to protect her baby.

9. WALDORF, ARE ALL WHALES ALIKE?

   No. There is the toothed whale and the baleen whale.

10. WHAT IS THE DIFFERENCE BETWEEN A TOOTHED WHALE AND A BALEEN WHALE?

    The *toothed whale* is a hunter and goes after other big sea creatures. The *baleen whale* has long strings hanging from its upper jaw, and it uses these strings to catch small sea creatures floating on top of the water.

11. WHAT IS BALEEN?

    Pretend you don't have teeth, but that you do have long tough strings hanging from your upper gums. When this whale opens its mouth, you don't see teeth but you do see these long strings. The strings are called *baleen*. They're about as tough as your fingernails. Click your thumbnails together and listen for the sound.

12. YES. WE CAN HEAR IT. TELL US, WALDORF, IS A DOLPHIN NICE?

    Dolphins make friends with man in a controlled environment where they're well fed. They can be trained to jump through hoops and to throw balls. Dolphins are very intelligent and they seem to like people.

13. CAN MAN COMMUNICATE, OR TALK WITH, DOLPHINS?

    Dolphins are able to learn from people. Scientists are trying to learn from the dolphins, especially what their different squeals and squeaks mean.

14. WHY DO SCIENTISTS STUDY DOLPHINS, WALDORF?

To learn how they communicate; to learn how they use their very large brain. Scientists always investigate and ask lots and lots of questions. It's their job.

15. WHEN DOLPHINS LIVE IN THE OCEAN, DO THEY LIVE IN GROUPS OR ALONE?

They're very social, which means that they like to be together. Dolphins can play and care for each other and train their young.

16. WHAT IS THAT HOLE RIGHT THERE ON THE TOP OF YOUR BODY, WALDORF?

It's my blow hole. It's like your nostrils in your nose.

17. HOW DOES YOUR BLOW HOLE WORK?

It's the first part of my body to come out of the water and it let's me take a deep, deep breath. I make a real fountain spray, sort of like a spout.

18. HOW LONG CAN YOU STAY UNDER THE WATER?

From 5 to 10 minutes. Did you know that a whale stores oxygen in its muscles? That's why we can stay underwater for so long. Don't you try it, though.

19. NO, WE WON'T. WALDORF, YOUR SKIN LOOKS NICE AND SHINY. IS IT THICK?

No, my skin is thin and this might surprise you, but whales can even get a sunburn. Underneath my outer layer of skin is my fat layer, or blubber.

20. ONE LAST QUESTION, WALDORF. YOU LIVE IN THE SAME OCEAN WITH THE FISH. ARE YOU RELATED TO FISH?

No, we are not related. Fish are cold-blooded and hatched from eggs. Whales are warm-blooded and are born live. I have more in common with humans that I have with a fish!

THANK YOU FOR THIS TALK-AND-TELL TIME RIGHT HERE AT THE ZOO SEA WORLD. TODAY OUR GUEST WAS A FRIENDLY, WELL-FED WHALE NAMED WALDORF. NEXT TIME WE WILL BE TALKING WITH A(N)

——————————————————————. I"M GOING SWIMMING! BYE FOR NOW.

INTERVIEW INFORMATION

What did you learn? Draw it, write it, or web it.

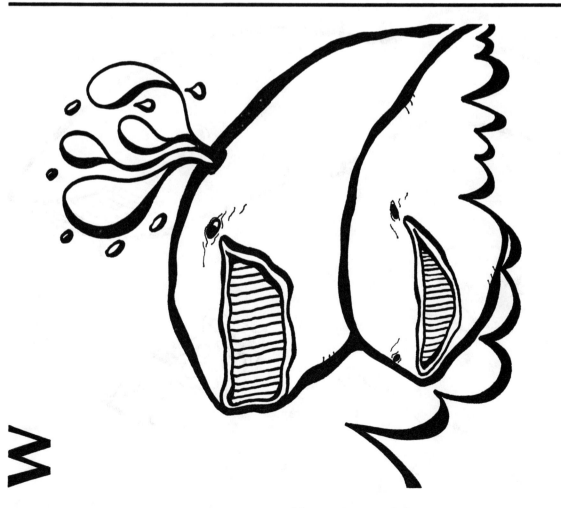

W

WALDORF WHALE

Name _____ Date _____

WALDORF WHALE'S DANGEROUS WATER

The oceans are becoming polluted. Put a big X on those things that do not belong in the ocean. Color the living things that do belong in the ocean and make them look healthy. Remember: Don't pollute!

THE WONDERFUL W WORLD OF WALDORF WHALE

Draw six different items that begin with Waldorf's sound in the sections of this great big enormous W. Doesn't Waldorf look happy? That's because he likes your work!

Name _____ Date _____

THE WHALE'S WATER MESSAGE

Do you leave the water running
when you're not using it?
Become more WATER AWARE
and help save water.
List five ways that
YOU can help.

Don't Waste Water

1. _____

_____

_____

2. _____

_____

_____

3. _____

_____

_____

4. _____

_____

_____

5. _____

_____

_____

Share your ideas and add to your list!

THE ENORMOUS/TINY WHALE GAME

Color the enormous (big) and tiny (little) matching sea creatures with matching colors. Cut them out on the straight lines. Shuffle the cards. Place them face down and select two. Do they match? If so, keep them. If not, put them back and REMEMBER where they are. Try again. *For two players:* The first player to get more matched sets is the winner.

WHALE BOOK REPORT COVER

Make a shape book.

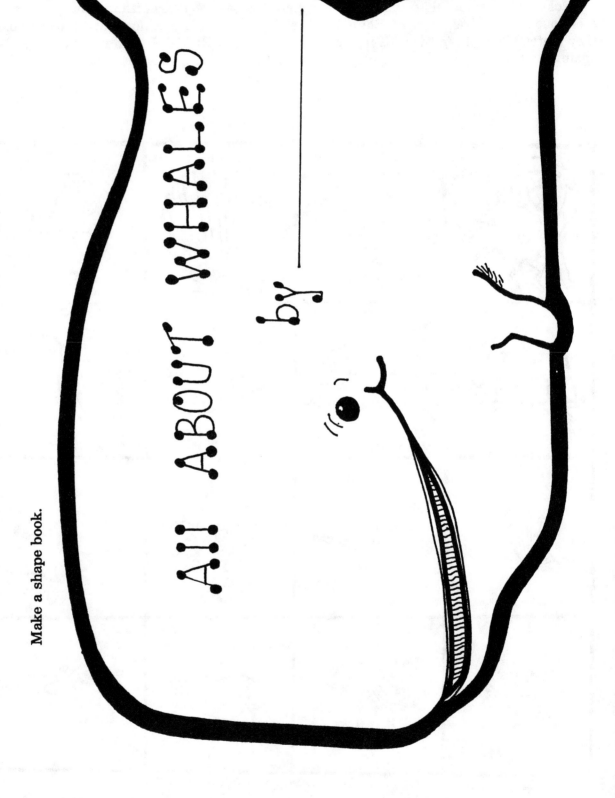

All ABOUT WHALES

by
_____

X

IS

FOR

FO-X-Y FOX

X IS FOR FOXY FOX

(TEACHERS, PLEASE NOTE: There is no familiar animal that begins with the crispy sound of the letter x. Therefore, the fox was selected because it ENDS with the letter x.

The fox was in the ABC lineup for the letter f but Francine Frog was selected. Did the fox give up? Never! The sly fox went to the end of the alphabet line and stood by the letter x. When no other animal showed up, the fox got the job. Pretty tricky!)

BACKGROUND INFORMATION ABOUT FOXES: The fox is one of the smartest wild animals. It is clever, and is blamed for a great deal of mischief, especially by farmers who raise chickens. When enemies pursue the fox, it will make a zigzag path, or it may jump on top of a fence and walk along the fencetop so that its tracks disappear. It will go into a river and come out farther up. The gray fox climbs trees to escape enemies. And the fox has been known to freeze or play dead when other animals get too close, and then at just the very moment when the animal thinks that it has a fox for dinner, the fox will jump up and go on the attack.

The fox is a predator and eats mice, squirrels, snakes, and a variety of insects as well as some plants. It is a relative of the wolf and the domestic dog. The beautiful fox fur (red, gray, black, silver blue, yellow) feels thick, and the animal is hunted and trapped for the fur, called *pelts*.

READING/LANGUAGE ARTS:

1. FOXY PREDATOR.   Review the vocabulary words predator and prey, noting that the fox is in the predator category. Additional vocabulary words include *vixen* (adult female) and *dog* (adult male).

2. THE TRICKY LETTER Y.   We refer to the vowels as a,e,i, o, and u, and sometimes y. The letter y often takes on the sound of long e or long i. In this case, Foxy sounds like "Fah ks ee." Let's take a good look at two-syllable words that end with the letter y and see what sound the letter makes. Can we identify any patterns for one sound or another?

3. ENDING SOUNDS.   Print the alphabet in a vertical line. Go through the ABC animals looking for their ending sounds, and print that letter after the beginning alphabet letter. For example, after the letter A, print the letter R for the ending sound in alligator. Do this for the other letters. These will get you started:

A . . . R (alligator) B . . . R (bear) C . . . T (cat) D . . . G (dog) After all of the ABC animals have their beginning and ending sounds accounted for, try to think of an animal that begins with their ending sound. Tricky, isn't it? (For example A . . . R (rabbit), B . . . R (roadrunner), C . . . T (tiger), and so on.

4. LET'S TAKE A GOOD LOOK AT THE SOUND OF X.   As the fox instructs in the interview section, when the letter x is at the ending of a word it borrows the crispy sounds of the letters "ks" and blends them together. And, when the letter x is at the

beginning of a word it borrows the sound of the letter z. What happens when the x is in the middle of a word. Let's find out. Here are some words to get us started:

Alexander (ks)   taxes (ks)   taxi (ks)

5. TRICKY THREE-PART PICTURE BOOKS.   Use 9″ × 12″ pieces of paper and place the paper with the longer side going horizontally. Then divide the page into three equal sections. Sketch an animal so that the head is in section one, the body of the animal is in section two, and the tail end of the animal is in section three. Then carefully cut the page into three sections (do not cut all the way to the top). Do this again for another animal, and another and another. Place the pages on top of one another and staple them at the top of each section, or use a ring holder at the top of each section. Then, students can flip the book so that the head of one animal is showing, the body of another is showing, and the tail end of another is showing. Who are these new animals? Make up names for them using parts of the letters from their real names. Tricky, isn't it? Have students interview these jumbled animals.

MATH:

1. TRICKY FOX MATH.   At birth a fox may weigh from 2 to 4 ounces. It's tricky to find scales that will record ounces and it's tricky to find small things that weigh ounces, but we can try.

Weigh a ball of clay. If it is 8 ounces, that could be two 4-ounce babies or four 2-ounce babies. Mold them and weigh them again.

2. REVIEW OVAL AND ROUND.   Fox eyes are oval, whereas their dog relatives have round eyes. Check this in books that have photos of real animals. What are the shapes of other animal eyes? Make sketches of a variety of eyes and learn to identify which animal, bird or fish they belong to. A helpful resource book is *Eyes* by Judith Worthy, with illustrations by Beba Hall.

SCIENCE:

1. TRICKY FOXY GOES TO THE EASEL.   New mixtures of colors, such as red-orange and silver-blue tempera paint would be very inviting for creating beautiful fox paintings. Black and white can also be used for features and highlights. (Students can examine pictures of a variety of foxes and do the paintings when all pictures have been removed.)

2. MAGIC TRICKS are fun to learn. Have Foxy be in charge of teaching some magic tricks that we find in library books about magic.

SOCIAL STUDIES:

1. WHERE DOES EVERYONE LIVE?   Foxy is interested in this information and you can help to classify animals by habitat (for example, caves, plains, ocean, trees, and so on).

2. WHO IS MORE INTELLIGENT?   Scientists seem to think that it's either the whales (dolphins) or the chimpanzees. What would the fox think about this? The fox is known for outsmarting other animals. Challenge students to write a story to see if the fox can outsmart the dolphin and the chimpanzee or if the fox is outfoxed.

**FOXY'S TALK-AND-TELL
PICTURE AND RHYME**

I lost the F
    To the frog, you see.
That's why the X
    Belongs to me!

X

—X. (HEY WHAT IS A FOX DOING UNDER THE LETTER X? DON'T YOU BELONG UNDER THE LETTER F?)

TALK AND TELL: FOXY FOX

1. EXCUSE ME, BUT I'M LOOKING FOR AN ANIMAL WHOSE NAME BEGINS WITH THE LETTER X. CAN YOU HELP ME, FOXY?

    I'd be glad to help you, but there is no animal here whose name begins with the letter X.

2. DID YOU SAY THERE IS NO ANIMAL HERE WHOSE NAME BEGINS WITH THE LETTER X?

    Correct. I am a fox, and my name ends with an X. It's spelled F - O - X.

3. OH, WHAT AM I GOING TO DO? THESE BOYS AND GIRLS ARE HERE TO LEARN ABOUT THE SOUND OF X.

    I can help you with the letter x. It's a tricky letter.

4. WHAT DO YOU MEAN BY TRICKY?

    Well, one sound of X is sort of crispy, like putting the letters k and s together. Say "k-k-k-s-s-s-," "k-k-k-s-s-s-." You can hear it in the words "fox," (fok-k-s-s-), or "box," (bok-k-s-s-), or "taxi," (tak-s-s-eee) or "Max," (Ma k-k-s-s). It sounds crispy, crashy!

5. THAT'S NOT TOO TRICKY, IS IT?

    There is more! When the letter X is at the beginning of a word, it borrows its sound from Z and sounds like z-z-z-z-z-.

6. DO YOU MEAN THAT X CAN SOUND LIKE THE BUZZING SOUND OF A BUMBLEBEE?

    Yes. Listen to this. "Xylaphone. . . . Z-z-z-z-ylaphone." And Xylograph. . . . Z-z-z-z-zylograph." Do you hear that buzzing sound? (*Teacher:* It would be helpful to write the word on the chalkboard). And in the word *Xerox* (Z-z-z-z- er o-k-k-s-s-s) the letter X uses both the z sound and the ks sound. Tricky, eh?

7. THAT LETTER X IS TRICKY AND WE'RE GLAD YOU TOLD US SO. SPEAKING OF TRICKY ISN'T A FOX SUPPOSED TO BE TRICKY?

    Yes! I'll tell you a secret. I wanted to be chosen for the letter F (my beginning sound) but Francine Frog leaped in ahead of me. So, I waited around the alphabet corner until the X interview, because fox ends with the letter x. And here I am! Nobody else showed up.

8. THAT IS TRICKY! WHILE YOU'RE HERE, WE MIGHT AS WELL FIND OUT SOMETHING ABOUT YOU, OK?

    Yes. I'm a relative of the wolf and of the domestic dog. But dog's eyes are round, and mine are oval shaped. Do you know the difference between something that's round like the sun and oval like an egg?

9. YES, WE PRACTICED OVAL SHAPES WITH ALLIGATOR EGGS. ALLIGATORS ARE HATCHED FROM EGGS. ARE YOU BORN LIVE OR HATCHED?

    I'm a mammal, so I'm born live. When a baby fox is born it's called a *kit*.

10. HOW MUCH DID YOU WEIGH WHEN YOU WERE BORN, FOXY?

    About 2 ounces. Try that on a scale and you will see that it is very, very tiny!

11. WHAT ARE THE MOTHER FOX AND THE FATHER FOX CALLED?

    The adult female (mother) is called a *vixen*, and the adult male (father) is called a *dog*.

12. FOXY, WHERE DO YOU LIVE?

I live in a fox den. The mother fox digs out a hollow spot in a hillside. It has one opening but many tunnels underneath. Some of the tunnels are used to store food. Some connect and some are dead-ends.

13. IS THE ADULT FOX A GOOD MOTHER?

Yes! Both parents pay attention and feed the kits. The family stays together through spring, summer, and autumn and then splits up in winter.

14. WHY DO THEY SEPARATE IN WINTER? WHY DON'T THEY STAY TO-GETHER?

For survival. It's easier to go it alone when we look for food. It's nature's way!

15. A FOX HAS BEEN CALLED ONE OF THE SMARTEST WILD ANIMALS. IS THAT TRUE, FOXY?

Yes it it. We're blamed for a lot of mischief. We can freeze, or play dead, and when another animal comes close we can jump up and catch it! On the run, we zig and zag a lot so it's not too easy to pick up our scent, or smell. It's hard to catch a fox!

16. WHO ARE YOUR ENEMIES IN THE WILDS?

The wolves, coyotes, and wild cats.

17. WHAT DO YOU EAT IN THE WILDS?

We like meat and plants too. Our favorite meat includes juicy mice, fat squirrels, squishy snakes, and crawly insects. Sounds yummy to a fox.

18. IS IT TRUE THAT YOU HUNT IN THE FARMER'S CHICKEN COOP AND GET HIS CHICKENS?

Yes, if I'm hungry enough I will do that. That's why Farmer Brown is not happy to have a fox around the chicken coop and sets traps.

19. WHAT COLOR IS A FOX?

Some are red, or gray, or yellow, or even a beautiful silver-blue. We're hunted and trapped for our fur to make clothing. Our fur is called a *pelt*.

20. DO YOU HAVE ANY ADVICE TO GIVE US ABOUT THE TRICKY FOX?

Don't ever go near a fox, and don't let your pet go near one. A fox can play dead and then when you get very close, will jump up and get you! If you ever, ever, ever see a fox in the woods, run the other way!

THANK YOU FOR THIS INTERVIEW AT THE EDGE OF THE WOODS. TODAY OUR GUEST WAS A TRICKY FOX, WITH X AS THE LAST LETTER IN ITS NAME. TUNE IN NEXT TIME WHEN WE WILL INTERVIEW A(N)

—————————————————————————. UNTIL THEN, DO YOU KNOW ANY MAGIC TRICKS?

INTERVIEW INFORMATION

X

FO-X-Y FOX

What did you learn? Draw it, write it, or web it.

THE FOX HUNT

Foxy Fox went on a hunt for an X-ray, an ox, and a . . . Well, he forgot. Can you help Foxy out? He needs one more item that has the letter X in its name.

Name _____ Date _____

DIAL AN A B C ANIMAL

The cunning fox is dialing
flattering words! Which
animal will answer? What
other words can the fox use?

DIAL A WORD   **WHO WILL ANSWER?**

DIAL A FOR ____acrobat____   _____
DIAL B FOR ____beautiful____   _____
DIAL C FOR _____clever_____   _____
DIAL D FOR ____dangerous____   _____
DIAL E FOR ___entertaining___   _____

Fox is running out of words and needs your help to play this game. Think up some
fancy words. Who will answer?

DIAL F FOR _____   _____
DIAL G FOR _____   _____
DIAL H FOR _____   _____
DIAL I FOR _____   _____
DIAL J FOR _____   _____
DIAL K FOR _____   _____
DIAL L FOR _____   _____
DIAL M FOR _____   _____
DIAL N FOR _____   _____
DIAL O FOR _____   _____
DIAL P FOR _____   _____
DIAL Q FOR _____   _____
DIAL R FOR _____   _____
DIAL S FOR _____   _____
DIAL T FOR _____   _____
DIAL U FOR _____   _____
DIAL V FOR _____   _____
DIAL W FOR _____   _____
DIAL X FOR _____   _____
DIAL Y FOR _____   _____
DIAL Z FOR _____   _____

CAN THE FOX TRICK YOU?

Foxy Fox started drawing three animals and then stopped still in his tracks. He's trying to see if you can finish the animals. Can you?

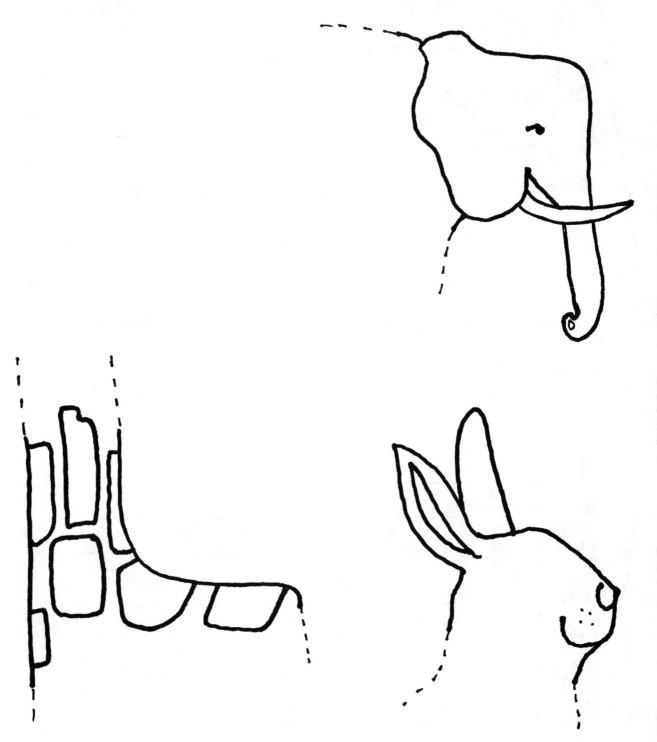

FOX MASK

Color this mask, cut it out, and use it for dramatic play.

Name _____

Date _____

FOX AND GEESE GAME

Foxy Fox sees the geese and wants to play with them. Can you help him find his way?
Good luck!

Start

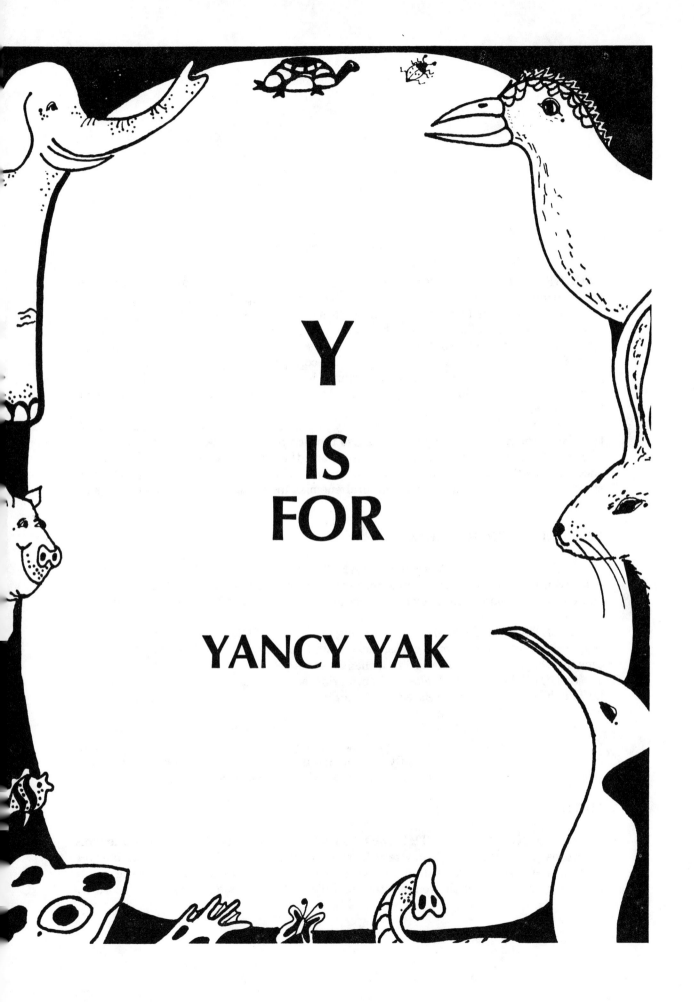

Y

IS

FOR

YANCY YAK

Y IS FOR YANCY YAK

BACKGROUND INFORMATION ABOUT YAKS: The yak is a member of the bovine family (oxen, cows, buffalo) that lives on the highlands (plateau) of Tibet. This sure-footed expert climber lives higher than any other mammal in the world. The yak is the largest of the cattle tribe. Its long, thin horns point straight out sideways and then turn upward. They can grow to 3 ft in length and are useful as weapons. The very long shaggy coat of the yak almost sweeps the ground. This coat protects it from the cold and snow. The more it snows, the higher the animal climbs in order to reach plant food. Yaks travel over high peaks in a single file, walking in the tracks made by the animals that went before them.

Yaks are used as pack animals and carry people, mail, and other items from village to village. The mountain people of Asia use the rich milk to drink and to make cheese. The fur of this ox is used for weaving cloth, and the hide is useful for building tents, shoes, and clothing. This wild ox can slide down icy slopes, swim rapid rivers, and cross steep rocks. It defends itself from natural enemies (bears and wolves) by charging at them.

READING/LANGUAGE ARTS:

1. **DOES THE YAK MAKE A YAKETTY YAK SOUND?** No, the yak doesn't yak and it doesn't moo, but the yak does grunt to communicate. Let's review our ABC animals to see what sounds they make in order to communicate. Which one has no voice? (vulture)

2. **LET'S EXPLORE SHAGGY.** Bring in samples of shaggy material, and shaggy tree bark. Check the linings of coats, jackets, and boots for shaggy textures. Some mittens are shaggy. Is anyone wearing a shaggy sweater?

3. **BOVINE BOOK.** Make an information book about the yak, the cow, and the buffalo. These animals are related. Make a diagram of each, tell about the similarities and differences of this big animal.

4. **YANCY YAK MEETS CHRISTIE COW AND BUFFALO BILL BISON.** After we have made the information book about these animals, now we can do some creative writing. Let's have a family reunion and have the animals tell about where they live, and what they do. This can be performed with puppets too.

MATH:

1. **WORKING WITH A THERMOMETER.** In Asia where the yak lives, the temperatures get to 30 degrees below zero. That's frigid! Have a thermometer available and a tub of warm water and a tub of cold water. Place the thermometer into the warm tub and leave it there until the temperature stabilizes. Then take a reading and record it.

Move the thermometer to the other tub and repeat. Also, take the thermometer outdoors and place it in the sun (or snow), leave it, and return in 20 minutes to note the change.

2. CLASSIFY HORN SHAPES. Yancy Yak has horns that are horizontal and then vertical. They also have a curved line. Let's take a good look at animal horns in picture books and books with real photographs and trace the shape of horns with the tip of a finger. Some look like branches. List the animals that have horns. Classify the horn shapes.

SCIENCE:

1. MORE WORK WITH TEMPERATURE. Begin to chart the temperature daily so that students know that the higher the numeral, the warmer it gets and vice versa. Listen to the radio and TV weather reports for their *predictions* and then check the next day with the thermometer to see if they are accurate. Students can begin to make their own predictions and check them the following day.

2. AN ALMOST-EXTINCT FAMILY MEMBER. Yancy Yak is a member of the bovine family, and its cousins include the cow and buffalo. The cow has been protected and is not an endangered specie, but the Bison Buffalo is another story. At one time when the west was being settled, millions of buffalo roamed the plains in herds. However, when the railroad was put through, buffalo were killed by hunters. Today there is an American Bison Association which has enabled laws to be passed to protect the buffalo. A small herd of about 200 buffalo lives within the protection of Yellowstone National Park (locate the park on a map or globe). Locate photographs of the bovines—yak, cow, buffalo and note similarities. For a good information book on this topic, find *And Then There Was One, The Mysteries of Extinction* by Margery Facklam with illustrations by Pamela Johnson (Boston: Little, Brown, 1990).

SOCIAL STUDIES:

1. PACK ANIMALS. What animals do work for people—carrying, pushing, pulling? Make a Yak-Pack List of Animals That Work. In which cities or countries do they work? Do circus animals work? Do zoo animals work?

2. FOLLOW IN SOMEONE'S FOOTSTEPS. Tape cutouts of yak hoofprints on the floor and have students try to follow the pattern without losing their balance. Keep practicing (large motor development). Yaks move along in lines, following in the footsteps of those that have gone before.

3. TIP-TOE THROUGH THE ABC ANIMALS. Tape laminated pictures or flashcards of the ABC Animals to the floor. Have students move from one to the other (jump or tiptoe) as steady as a yak when the animal name or alphabet letter is called out.

Weather that's cold
    Won't make me sick.
Because my coat
    Is very thick.

Y

TALK AND TELL: YANCY YAK

1. HELLO, YANCY! BR-R-R! IT'S BELOW FREEZING! THE THERMOMETER IS AT ZERO. AREN'T YOU COLD?

   No. I don't get cold when it gets to zero degrees. I get a little chilly when it gets about −30 degrees.

2. BR-R-R! HOW DO YOU STAY WARM?

   My nice, shaggy fur coat really helps. In winter, I also grow an undercoat of hair . . . just like some of you put a lining in your coat in winter.

3. WE ARE ON A VERY HIGH HILL UP HERE, AREN'T WE YANCY?

   Yes. This hill in Tibet is called a *plateau.* Maybe you can find it on a map or globe. I live higher up on hills than any other mammal on Planet Earth.

4. DO YOU LIKE TO CLIMB UP THOSE GREAT BIG HILLS?

   Yes I do. It's easy for me. I'm what you call *surefooted* which means that I don't stumble around.

5. IT'S SNOWING VERY HARD TODAY. HOW DO YOU TRAVEL IN THIS SNOW?

   Yaks move through the snow in a single file—one long line. Each yak uses the hoof tracks made by the yak in front of it. Did you ever try to follow in someone's tracks in the snow? Try it.

6. DO YAKS LIVE TOGETHER IN GROUPS, YANCY?

   Yes. Our groups are called *herds* just like cows live in herds. Our herds can go all the way up to 100 yaks. That's a lot of yaks in one place.

7. WHEW! I'M HUFFING AND PUFFING! WHY ARE WE CLIMBING EVEN HIGHER TODAY?

   Because it's snowing. When it's snowing we move to the high ground in order to get food.

8. WHAT DO YAKS EAT UP HERE, YANCY?

   We eat all kinds of grasses, and twigs taste good too.

9. YANCY YAK, DO YOU HAVE ANY RELATIVES?

   Yes. Yaks are related to the cows.

10. YAKS AND COWS ARE COUSINS? DO YOU GIVE MILK JUST LIKE A COW DOES?

    We sure do. Yak milk is rich and creamy, and it makes good butter too.

11. DO YOU CHEW YOUR CUD JUST LIKE A COW DOES?

    I'm always chewing my cud, just like a cow. Chewing my cud helps me to crunch and munch those twigs and tough grasses that I love to eat.

12. DO YOU "MOO-O-O" JUST LIKE A COW DOES?

    No I don't moo, but I do grunt.

13. IT'S REALLY SNOWING HARD! HOW DO YOU FIND FOOD WITH ALL OF THIS SNOW HERE?

    Yaks are used to lots of snow. We just brush it aside with our nose or with our hoof and get at the patches of grass underneath.

14. IT'S SO COLD HERE, HOW DO YOU FIND WATER? DOESN'T IT FREEZE?

    When we can't find water, or when it is frozen, we just eat the snow. The melted snow becomes water.

15. YANCY, I LIKE YOUR GREAT BIG HORNS. WHAT DO YOU DO WITH THEM?

Horns are used as weapons to fight the enemies. Yaks charge together in a herd with their heads lowered. We can put up quite a fight.

16. DO YOU HAVE MANY ENEMIES HERE?

Mainly the wolves and the bears.

17. BRR-R-R. IT'S WINDY. I HEARD THAT YOU ARE HELPFUL TO THE PEOPLE HERE, IS THAT TRUE?

Yes. The mountain people use yaks as a pack animal. They put heavy loads on our back and we carry it over the hills for them.

18. WHAT ARE YOU CARRYING TODAY, YANCY?

Today I have a big load of mail, so I'm a mail carrier.

19. HOW ELSE DO YAKS HELP THE MOUNTAIN PEOPLE WHO LIVE HERE?

My owner uses my long hair to weave cloth and make clothing. Yak hide makes good leather for boots and gloves, and yak skin is used to make tents.

20. IT'S TIME FOR US TO LEAVE NOW. YANCY, YOU LIKE LIVING IN THESE COLD, SNOWY MOUNTAINS, DON'T YOU?

Sure! I can slide down icy slopes, and swim in swift, freezing cold rivers! It's a winter wonderland! I've learned to live here very well. I don't get very many visitors, though, so thanks for coming to meet me!

WELL, THANK YOU FOR AGREEING TO MEET WITH US RIGHT HERE IN THE MIDDLE OF A SNOWSTORM. TODAY WE'RE HIGH ON A GREAT BIG HILL IN TIBET. YANCY YAK IS BRAVE TO LIVE WHERE IT'S SO COLD. BOYS AND GIRLS, GUESS WHAT? ONLY ONE MORE TALK-AND-TELL TIME TO GO. OUR LAST ANIMAL BEGINS WITH THE LETTER "Z". CAN YOU GUESS WHAT IT IS? SEE YOU SOON.

INTERVIEW INFORMATION

What did you learn? Draw it, write it, or web it.

Y

YANCY YAK

YANCY YAK LIKES YELLOW

Yancy Yak is in a grocery store and wants to buy four yellow items. Yancy has found two. Can you find two more and draw them? This is going to be a bright yellow page, isn't it?

YAK YAK ABOUT HORNS AND ANTLERS

Hello! I'm Yancy Yak. I'm having a party for animals with horns and antlers. Can you come? Use your crayons to diagram and label other animals that can come to the party.

MAKE A YAK HAT

Decorate your Yak Hat. When you wear it, these are some things you can do. You can think of others, too.

- Walk one behind the other in the same footprints.
- Make a circle. Then turn around and back up so that everyone is facing out.
- Deliver mail packages. Write a letter and deliver it.

A, E, I, O, U and sometimes Y describes the vowels. Color the animal that goes with each vowel. Cut each card out on the straight lines and place them face down. Try to get matching pairs by picking up two cards at a time. If they match, keep them. If not, return them and remember where they are. If you play with a partner, the first player to get more matching pairs is the winner.

YANCY YAK DELIVERS THE MAIL

Make an animal post card. The animal interviews, stories and picture books can help.
Do the following: (1) Address the post card; (2) Write an interesting message about an animal; and (3) Turn the page over and make a bright attractive picture on your post card from edge to edge.

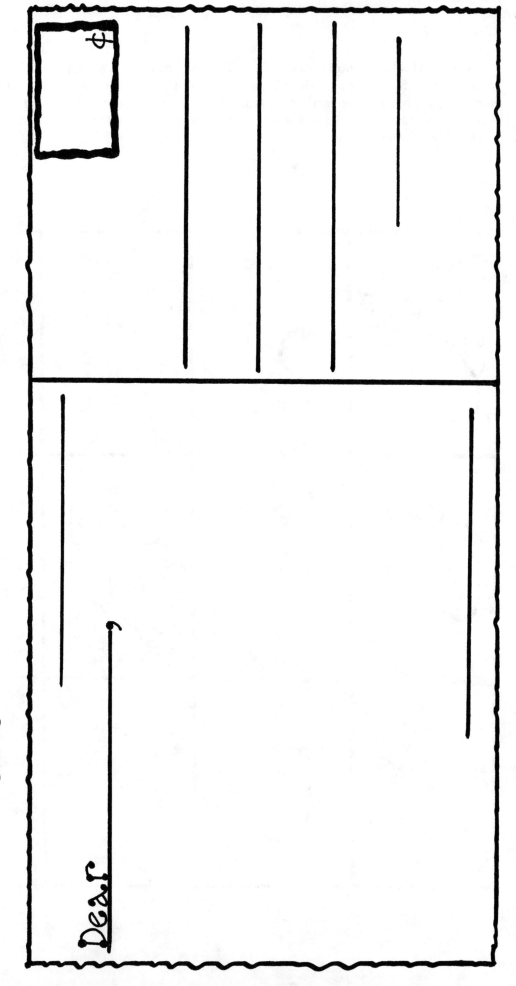

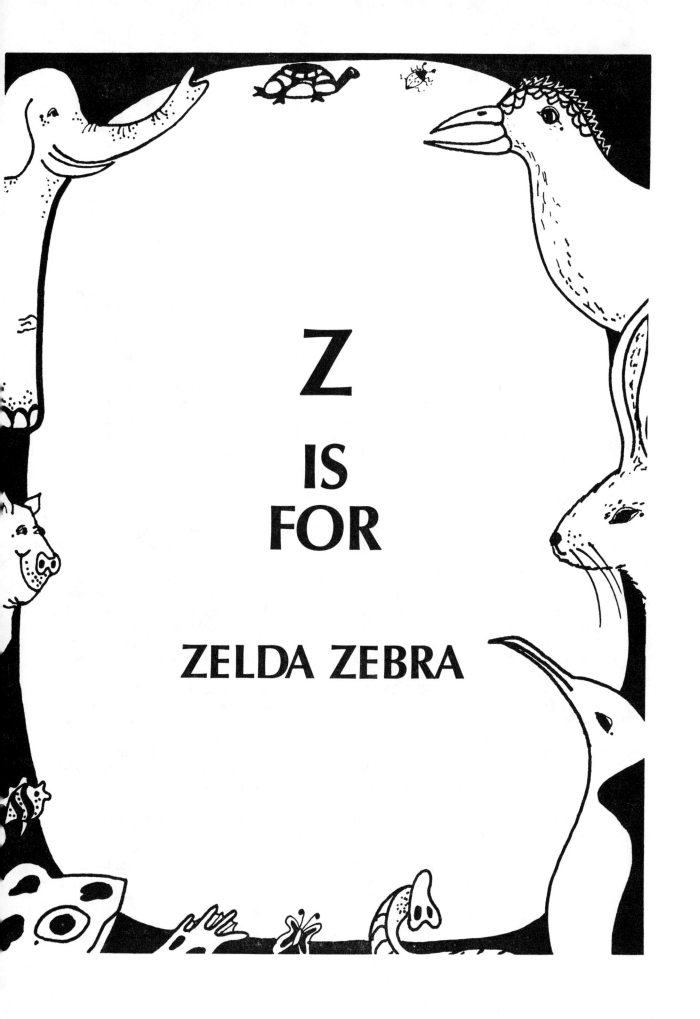

Z
IS
FOR

ZELDA ZEBRA

Z IS FOR ZELDA ZEBRA

BACKGROUND INFORMATION ABOUT ZEBRAS: At one time people referred to the zebra as a horse tiger because of the shape of its body, which looks similar to a horse, and because it has stripes like a tiger. However, scientists who study animals (zoologists) claim that the zebra is not a combination animal. Zebras are from the same family as horses and donkeys (Equidae).

Zebra stripes are as unique as fingerprints. Some are thick and some are thin. Some zebra have many stripes whereas some have only a few. Zoologists don't claim to know if the animal is white with black stripes or black with white stripes. Interestingly, some zebras have stripes of reddish yellow, gray or even brown. Several zebras together create an optical illusion and confuse their enemies. They like to gather in groups and rest their head on each other's back, but they are not still for very long. It has been said that zebras were born to run, and they have been clocked at 60 mi/h.

READING/LANGUAGE ARTS:

1. ZELDA'S FAMILY LANGUAGE LESSON. The same terms used to describe Handkerchief Horse are used to describe Zelda Zebra: stallion (adult male), mare (adult female), colt (young male), filly (young female), and foal (baby).

2. THE HORSE TIGER. Even though the zebra is not a combination animal, horse tiger was a name given to the zebra long ago because of its shape (horse) and stripes (tiger). Can we take a good look at some of ABC Animals and think of some combination names for them? Think in terms of body shape, markings, hide, hoofs, and so on. Look through books for other animals that could have interesting names. The hippopotamus has been called the water horse and some common house cats are referred to as the tiger cat and calico cat.

3. Z IS FOR THE END. The letter z is the last letter of the alphabet, and the zebra brings up the rear. See if students can name the animals from alligator to zebra. And perhaps students can make a "Book of Animal Tails" and identify the animal by the shape, color, and use of the tail.

4. I'M THINKING OF AN ANIMAL THAT.... Play the "I'm Thinking" game and give away a big clue for that animal. Students raise their hand if they think they know. Call upon a student. If the answer is correct, that student gets the chance to call out the next clue.

5. EVERYBODY GETS A FLASHCARD. Distribute ABC animal flashcards face down so that each child has one. Then, one by one students get up and tell a fact that they learned about the animal. Students guess which animal by asking a question, such as "Does it have stripes and sharp teeth? (tiger) "Does it use its tail for an umbrella?" (squirrel) "Did the Indians like it?" (vulture) and so on.

MATH:

1. LET'S WORK WITH STRIPES.   Young students can paint stripes from top to bottom at the easel. When dry, cut out a big zebra shape, and add eyes, lashes, nose, mouth, tail.

Paint white stripes on black paper. Paint black stripes on white paper. Make zebra puppets.

Students can practice cutting long strips of white paper and paste them on black paper. Place a cutout of several black and white zebras on this background and see if we can find them—they create an optical illusion.

2. LET'S COMBINE STRIPES AND OTHER PATTERNS.   Although the zebra is not a combination animal, combination animals using stripes, plaids, polka dots, checks, and so on, are fun to make. Combine this with story telling, and let the animal tell its own story.

SCIENCE:

1. WE CAN'T SEE ZELDA ZEBRA.   Let's work with camouflage. Using construction paper, have students cut a red circle. Have them hold it up against a blue background, green background, and then a red background. When do we have the most difficulty seeing it? (Red figure on red background). Some animals change coats with the seasons (rabbit, deer) in order to remain camouflaged. What animals, birds, and fish have stripes and dots so that they blend in with the background? Find colored pictures of different animals, birds, and fish that show a variety of colors in their coat, skin, or feathers. How do these colors camouflage certain animals?

2. MAKE CAMOUFLAGE BOOKS.   Use wallpaper samples or material with tiny, overall patterns. Students can make animals and background pages from the same design. Glue on something (whiskers or nose) that gives the animal away.

SOCIAL STUDIES:

1. Z IS FOR ZOO.   The zoos in our country are becoming more of a home for animals. Naturalists are trying to recreate the natural environment of the animal in order that it will feel more at home in a zoo, rather than being caged in a concrete cell. Design a perfect environment for your favorite zoo animal. Make a diagram or a diorama.

2. MAKE A ZOO MURAL.   Have students paint the background of rolling green hills and beautiful trees. Then, section off the zoo for the home of Eddington Elephant, Zelda Zebra, Lollipop Lion, and so on. Make construction paper cutouts of the animals and place them in their zoo environment. Take a trip to the local zoo to see how they divide the space, and who the animal neighbors are.

3. ZOO WEBS.   As we conclude our study of animals with Zelda Zebra, have students divide into groups and make a variety of webs (survival web, habitat web, character web) and display these on large charts.

4. ADOPT A ZOO ANIMAL.   Zoos help to keep many animals alive and healthy. In this safe environment, they can thrive and even have families. But this is costly. To

help with the cost, there are "Adopt An Animal" plans in many zoos around the United States. For more information about adopting a zoo animal, write to The American Association of Zoological Parks and Acquariums, 4550 Montgomery Avenue, Bethesda, MD 20814. Also, obtain the National Geographic videotape entitled "The Urban Gorilla" which shows the effort being made to put zoo animals in more natural habitats.

I've got wide stripes
   Of black and white.
I'm very hard
   To see at night.

Z

TALK AND TELL: ZELDA ZEBRA

1. HI, ZELDA! WE LIKE YOUR STRIPES. ARE YOU BLACK WITH WHITE STRIPES, OR ARE YOU WHITE WITH BLACK STRIPES?

    That's a very old question, and there is no right or wrong answer. But I'll tell you something that might surprise you. Not all zebras are black and white.

2. THEY AREN'T? WHAT COLOR ARE SOME OTHER ZEBRAS?

    Some have brown stripes, some have yellow stripes, some have red stripes, and some have gray stripes.

3. WOW! ARE ALL ZEBRA STRIPES MADE THE SAME, ZELDA?

    No. Some stripes are thick and some are thin. Some zebras have many stripes and some have few stripes. We have different patterns too.

4. HOW CAN YOU TELL WHO EVERYBODY IS WITH ALL THOSE DIFFERENT STRIPES?

    Well, even though each zebra's stripes are as different as people's fingerprints, we look for patterns.

5. ARE YOUR STRIPES HELPFUL TO YOU IN THE WILD, ZELDA?

    Yes, they sure are. They serve as a *camouflage*.

6. THAT WORD IS FUN TO SAY. LET'S SAY IT BOYS AND GIRLS. "KAM-OH-FLA-ZH." WHAT DOES CAMOUFLAGE MEAN?

    It's like a cover up. A black and white zebra is hard to see in the shadows. When 3 to 4 of us are together, you can't tell where one begins and the other one ends.

7. ZELDA, YOU HAVE VERY LONG EYELASHES. DO ZEBRAS SEE WELL?

    My eyes are on the side of my head so I have a little trouble seeing in front of my face unless I turn my head. But I can see for a long, long way off.

8. ZELDA, ARE YOU RELATED TO THE HORSE?

    Yes. Zebras are from the same family as horses and donkeys (Equidae).

9. PEOPLE SAY THAT YOU LOOK LIKE A HORSE WITH STRIPES, DON'T THEY?

    Yes, but zebras are not as tall as horses, and our hoofs are smaller. The horses are domesticated or tame animals, and zebras are wild animals. Zebras are born to run. We're very good at running!

10. HOW FAST CAN YOU RUN, ZELDA?

    We can keep up with your car on the open highway (40–60 mi/h).

11. THAT'S VERY FAST. ARE YOU BORN LIVE OR HATCHED?

    I'm a mammal which means that . . . (encourage the students to join in) I'm born live." Most adult females have a baby zebra every 3 years.

12. ZELDA, WHAT CAN BABIES DO WHEN THEY ARE BORN?

    A baby zebra (foal) can usually stand right up in just a few minutes. Within one hour, we're running around!

13. DO ZEBRAS GET GOOD CARE FROM THEIR MOTHER?

    Oh, yes. She lets us drink her warm milk. She always stands up and watches over her baby.

14. YOU MEAN SHE DOESN'T EVEN LAY DOWN TO SLEEP?

    When she stands up, her leg muscles LOCK automatically and support her, so she can stand up and relax and sleep. At the slightest sound, she's wide awake.

15. THAT'S AMAZING, ZELDA. TELL US, WHERE DO ZEBRAS LIVE?

We live in the wilds of Africa in *herds*—that's a group that stays together. We're very loyal. Can you find Africa on a map or globe?

16. WE WILL LOOK FOR IT. TELL US, WHAT DO YOU EAT, ZELDA ZEBRA?

Mainly grasses and plants. Zebras are not meat eaters.

17. DO YOU HAVE ANY ENEMIES IN THE WILDS?

Those lions are out to get us! We always have to be on guard. The wild dogs and hyenas are after us too. We put up a good fight with our hoofs and teeth.

18. IF YOU COULD TELL US ONE MAIN THING ABOUT ZEBRAS, WHAT WOULD IT BE?

A zebra is not a combination animal such as part horse and part something else. Zebras are animals in their own right!

19. SHOULD WE BE AFRAID OF YOU, ZELDA ZEBRA?

Yes, because I'm a wild animal! You never know what a zebra is going to do next. If my ears go straight back, it means that I sense danger and I will go on the attack with my hoofs and teeth. So, I can be ferocious.

20. ONE LAST QUESTION, ZELDA. WHERE CAN WE GO TO SEE YOU?

Well, you can come to Africa for a visit. Or, you can see me at the zoo where I eat all of my vegetables, and you should too. Veggies are good for you!

THANK YOU FOR THIS TALK-AND-TELL TIME RIGHT HERE AT THE LOCAL ZOO. WE'VE JUST MET ZELDA ZEBRA WITH ZIGZAG STRIPES. BOYS AND GIRLS, THIS IS OUR LAST ANIMAL TALK-AND-TELL TIME. I HOPE THAT YOU HAVE ENJOYED LEARNING ABOUT ALL OF THESE ANIMALS. I THINK I'LL MAKE AN ABC BOOK OF ANIMALS WITH DRAWINGS AND INFORMATION ABOUT EACH ONE. WHY DON'T YOU MAKE AN ANIMAL ABC BOOK, TOO? GOOD-BYE FOR NOW.

INTERVIEW INFORMATION

What did you learn? Draw it, write it, or web it.

Z

ZELDA ZEBRA

THE EYE OF THE ZEBRA

Cut out the circle and look through the zebra eye. Find ten things that have stripes. Then place the eye on top of pictures. Look carefully. Can you guess what the picture is?

UNZIP A POCKET FULL OF Z'S

There are four things inside this pocket that begin with the sound of z in zebra. Use your crayons to show us what they are. Share your pocket items with your classmates.

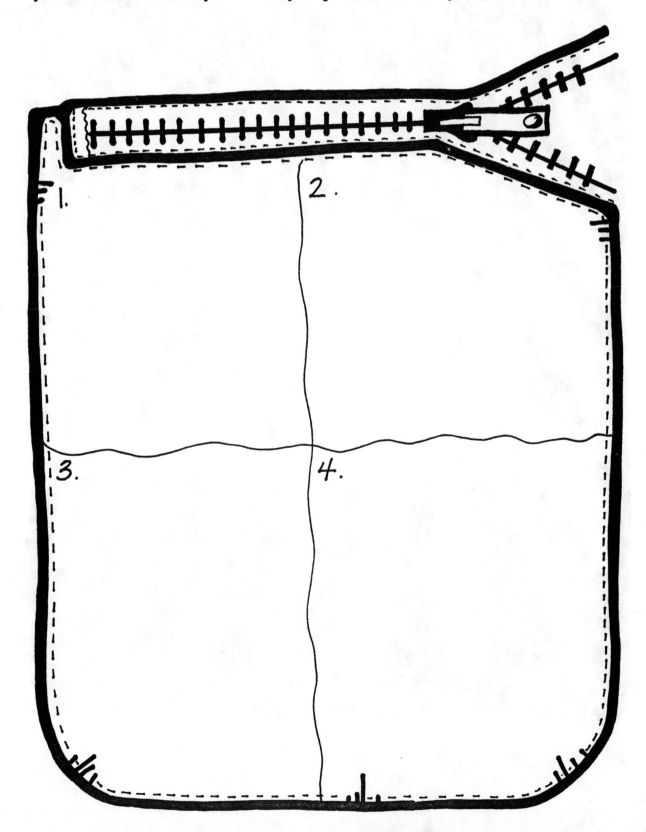

ZEBRA LINES WRITING PAPER

ZOO SIGNS

Some signs have no words, but we know what they mean. Make four more zoo animal signs.

A REBUS ZOO STORY

You can write a rebus zoo story using words and pictures. The pictures below can help you with your story, but you can make your own, too! After your story is written and drawn, cut apart the pictures below and use them as flashcards.

RECOMMENDED CHILDREN'S BOOKS

ASHLEY ALLIGATOR'S FAVORITE CHILDREN'S BOOKS ABOUT ALLIGATORS:

Christeltow, Eileen. *Jerome the Baby Sitter.* New York: Clarion Books, 1985.

DeGroat, Diane. *Alligator's Toothache.* New York: Crown Publisher, 1977.

Dorros, Arthur. *Alligator Shoes.* New York: E. P. Dutton, 1982.

McPhail, David. *Alligators Are Awful and They Have Terrible Manners, Too.* Garden City, NY: Macmillan, 1980.

Stevenson, James. *No Need for Money.* New York: Greenwillow Books, 1987.

BRANDI BEAR'S FAVORITE CHILDREN'S BOOKS ABOUT BEARS:

Asch, Frank. *Bear Shadow.* Englewood Cliffs, NJ: Prentice-Hall, 1985.

Bunting, Eve. *Valentine Bears.* Illustrated by Jan Brett. New York: Clarion Books, 1983.

Hague, Kathleen. *Alphabears, an ABC Book.* Illustrated by Michael Hague. New York: Holt, Rinehart and Winston, 1984.

McCue, Lisa. *Corduroy Goes to the Doctor.* New York: Viking Kestrel, 1987.

Vincent, Gabrielle. *Breakfast Time, Ernest and Celestine.* New York: Greenwillow Books, 1985.

CLANCY CAT'S FAVORITE CHILDREN'S BOOKS ABOUT CATS:

Calhoun, Mary. *High-Wire Henry.* Illustrated by Erick Ingraham. New York: Morrow Junior Books, 1991.

Carle, Eric. *Have You Seen My Cat?* Natick, MA: Picture Book Studio, 1987.

Larrick, Nancy. *Cats Are Cats Poems.* Illustrated by Ed Young. New York: Philomel Books, 1988.

Selsam, Millicent E., and Joyce Hunt. *First Look at Cats.* New York: Walker & Co., 1981.

Simon, Norma. *Cats Do, Dogs Don't.* Illustrated by Dora Leder. Niles, IL: A. Whitman Co., 1986.

DUKE THE DOG'S FAVORITE CHILDREN'S BOOKS ABOUT DOGS:

Bunting, Eve. *Jane Martin, Dog Detective.* Illustrated by Amy Schwartz. San Diego: Harcourt Brace Jovanovich, 1984.

deHamel, Joan. *Hemi's Pet.* Illustrated by Christine Rose. Boston: Houghton Mifflin Co., 1985.

Kellogg, Steven. *Pinkerton, Behave.* New York: Dial Books, 1990.

Tafuri, Nancy. *Do Not Disturb.* New York: Greenwillow Books, 1987.

Williamson, Jane. *The Trouble with Alaric.* New York: Farrar, Straus & Giroux, 1975.

EDDINGTON ELEPHANT'S FAVORITE CHILDREN'S BOOKS ABOUT ELEPHANTS:

Cutler, Ivor. *Elephant Girl.* Pictures by Helen Oxenbury. New York: William Morrow & Co., 1976.

deBrunhoff, Jean. *The Story of Babar the Little Elephant.* New York: Random House, 1933, 1984.

Kasza, Keiko. *When the Elephant Walks.* New York: G. P. Putnam's Sons, 1990.

Mahy, Margaret. *17 Kings and 42 Elephants.* Pictures by Patricia MacCarthy. New York: Dial Books, 1987.

Pearce, Philippa. *Emily's Own Elephant.* Illustrated by John Lawrence. New York: Greenwillow Books, 1987.

FRANCINE FROG'S FAVORITE CHILDREN'S BOOKS ABOUT FROGS:

Lobel, Arnold. *Days with Frog and Toad.* New York: Harper & Row, 1979.

Priceman, Marjorie. *Friend or Frog.* Boston: Houghton Mifflin Co., 1989.

Solotareff, Gregoire. *The Ogre and the Frog King.* New York: Greenwillow Books, 1986.

Velthuijs, Max. *Frog in Love.* New York: Farrar, Straus & Giroux, 1989.

Wildsmith, Brian. *Animal Games.* Oxford, England/New York: Oxford University Press, 1980.

GOLDIE GOAT'S FAVORITE CHILDREN'S BOOKS ABOUT GOATS AND OTHER ANIMALS:

Brown, Margaret Wise. *Baby Animals.* Illustrated by Susan Jeffers. New York: Random House, 1989.

Chouinard, Roger, and Mariko Chouinard. *The Amazing Animal Alphabet Book.* New York: Doubleday, 1988.

Hazen, Barbara Shook. *Hello Gnu, How Do You Do?* Illustrated by Dora Goldman. New York: Doubleday, 1990.

Stadler, John. *Animal Cafe.* Scarsdale, NY: Bradbury Press, 1980.

Wildsmith, Brian. *Goat's Trail.* New York: Knopf, 1986.

HANDKERCHIEF HORSE'S FAVORITE CHILDREN'S BOOKS ABOUT HORSES AND OTHER ANIMALS:

Boegehold, Betty D. *A Horse Called Starfire.* Illustrated by Neil Waldman. New York: Bantam Books, 1990.

Dennis, Wesley. *Flip and the Cows.* Hamden, CT: Linnet Books, 1989.

Gobel, Paul. *The Girl Who Loved Wild Horses.* New York: Bradbury Press, 1978.

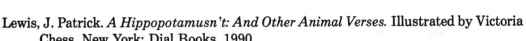

Lewis, J. Patrick. *A Hippopotamusn't: And Other Animal Verses.* Illustrated by Victoria Chess. New York: Dial Books, 1990.

Machotka, Hana. *What Neat Feet!* New York: Morrow Junior Books, 1991.

INKY INSECT'S FAVORITE CHILDREN'S BOOKS ABOUT INSECTS:

Carle, Eric. *The Grouchy Ladybug.* New York: Thomas Crowell Co., 1977.

Carle, Eric. *The Very Hungry Caterpillar.* New York: Philomel Books, 1979.

Cohen, Miriam. *Jim Meets the Thing.* Illustrated by Lillian Hoban. New York: Dell, 1989.

Howe, James. *I Wish I Were a Butterfly.* San Diego: Harcourt Brace Jovanovich, 1987.

Sundgaard, Arnold. *Lamb and the Butterfly.* New York: Orchard Books, 1988.

JACKSON JAGUAR'S FAVORITE CHILDREN'S BOOKS ABOUT JAGUARS AND OTHER BIG CATS:

Selsam, Millicent E., and Joyce Hunt. *Animals That Eat Other Animals.* Illustrated by Harriett Springer. New York: Walker and Co., 1989.

Small, Terry. *Tails, Claws, Fangs and Paws, An Alpha Beast Caper.* New York: Bantam Books, 1990.

Stone, Lynn M. *The Jaguar* (The Big Cat Discovery Library). Vero Beach, FL: Rourke Enterprises, Inc., 1989.

Tafuri, Nancy. *Junglewalk.* New York: Greenwillow Books, 1988.

Taylor, Kim. *Too Clever to See.* New York: Delacorte Press, 1990.

KELLY KANGAROO'S FAVORITE CHILDREN'S BOOKS ABOUT KANGAROOS:

Cole, Joanna. *Norma Jean Jumping Bean.* Illustrated by Lynn Munsinger. New York: Random House, 1987.

Kent, Jack. *Joey.* Englewood Cliffs, NJ: Prentice-Hall, 1984.

Leonard, Marcia. *Counting Kangaroos, A Book About Numbers.* Pictures by Diane Palmisciano. Mahwah, NJ: Troll Associates, 1990.

Moncure, Jane Belk. *Pocketful of Pets.* Illustrated by Linda Hohag. Elgin, IL: Children's Press, 1988.

Ungerer, Tomi. *Adelaide.* New York: Harper and Row, 1959.

LOLLIPOP LION'S FAVORITE CHILDREN'S BOOKS ABOUT LIONS AND OTHER BIG CATS:

LaFontaine, Jean. *Lion and the Rat, A Fable.* Illustrated by Brian Wildsmith. New York: Franklin Watts, 1963.

Overbeck, Cynthia. *Lions*. Photography by Tokumitsu Iwago. Minneapolis: Lerner Publications Co., 1981.

Patterson, Geoffrey. *The Lion and the Gypsy*. New York: Doubleday, 1988.

Peet, Bill. *Randy's Dandy Lion*. Boston: Houghton Mifflin, 1980.

Shannon, George. *More Stories to Solve, Fifteen Folk Tales from Around the World*. Illustrated by Peter Sis. New York: Greenwillow, 1991.

MIKE MacMOOSE'S FAVORITE CHILDREN'S BOOKS ABOUT MOOSE:

Alexander, Martha G. *Even That Moose Won't Listen to Me*. New York: Dial Books, 1988.

Hirschi, Ron. *Headgear*. Photography by Galen Burrell. New York: Dodd, Mead and Co., 1986.

Latimer, James. *Going the Moose Way Home*. Pictures by Donald Carrick. New York: Scribner's, 1988.

Pinkwater, Manus. *Blue Moose*. New York: Dodd, Mead and Co., 1975.

Wiseman, Bernard. *Christmas with Morris and Boris*. Boston: Little, Brown and Co., 1983.

NOODLES NUTHATCH'S FAVORITE CHILDREN'S BOOKS ABOUT BIRD FRIENDS:

Ehlert, Lois. *Feathers for Lunch*. San Diego: Harcourt Brace Jovanovich, 1990.

McLerran, Alice. *The Mountain That Loved a Bird*. Illustrated by Eric Carle. Natick, MA: Picture Book Studio, 1985.

Polacco, Patricia. *Rechenka's Eggs*. New York: Philomel Books, 1988.

Pomerantz, Charlotte. *Flap Your Wings and Try*. Pictures by Nancy Tafuri. New York: Greenwillow Books, 1989.

Weber, William J. *Attracting Birds and Other Wildlife to Your Yard*. New York: Holt, Rinehart and Winston, 1982.

OLLIE OCTOPUS'S FAVORITE CHILDREN'S BOOKS ABOUT SEA CREATURES:

Brandenberg, Franz. *Otto Is Different*. Pictures by James Stevenson. New York: Greenwillow Books, 1985.

Carle, Eric. *Eric Carle's Animals Animals*. New York: Philomel, 1989.

Kraus, Robert. *Herman the Helper*. Pictures by Jose Aruego and Adrienne Dewey. New York: Windmill Books/E. P. Dutton, 1974.

Lionni, Leo. *Frederick's Fables—A Leo Lionni Treasury*. New York: Knopf, 1985.

Ungerer, Tomi. *Emile*. New York: Harper and Row, 1960.

PERCY PENGUIN'S FAVORITE CHILDREN'S BOOKS ABOUT PENGUINS AND OTHER SEA CREATURES:

Bonners, Susan. *A Penguin Year.* New York: Dell Young Yearling Books, 1989.

Leonard, Marcia. *Paintbox Penguins, A Book About Colors.* Pictures by Diane Palmisciano. Mahwah, NJ: Troll Associates, 1990.

Michel, Gay. *Bibi Takes Flight.* New York: Morrow Junior Books, 1984.

Wilhelm, Hans. *Don't Give Up, Josephine.* New York: Random House, 1985.

Wood, Audrey. *Little Penguin's Tale.* San Diego, Harcourt Brace Jovanovich, 1989.

QUEENIE QUAIL'S FAVORITE CHILDREN'S BOOKS ABOUT BIRDS:

Agard, John. *Lend Me Your Wings.* Pictures by Adrienne Kennaway. Boston: Little, Brown and Co., 1987.

Edwards, Michelle. *Chicken Man.* New York: Lothrop, Lee and Shepard, 1991.

Heller, Ruth. *Chickens Aren't the Only Ones.* New York: Putnam's 1981.

Parsons, Alexandra. *Amazing Birds.* New York: McKay, 1990.

Tafuri, Nancy. *Spots, Feathers and Curly Tails.* New York: Greenwillow Books, 1988.

RUDI RABBIT'S FAVORITE CHILDREN'S BOOKS ABOUT RABBITS:

Maris, Ron. *Runaway Rabbit.* New York: Delacorte Press, 1989.

Murrow, Liza Ketchum. *Good-Bye, Sammy.* Illustrated by Gail Owens. New York: Holiday House, 1989.

Rafe, Martin. *Foolish Rabbit's Big Mistake.* New York: Putnam's 1985.

Shannon, George. *Dance Away.* Illustrated by Jose Aruego and Adrienne Dewey. New York: Mulberry Books, 1991.

Tafuri, Nancy. *Rabbit's Morning.* New York: Greenwillow Press, 1985.

STACY SQUIRREL'S FAVORITE CHILDREN'S BOOKS ABOUT SQUIRRELS:

Poskanzer, Susan Cornell. *Superduper Collector.* Illustrated by Paul Harvey. Mahwah, NJ: Troll Associates, 1986.

Potter, Beatrix. *The Tale of Squirrel Nutkin.* New York: Viking Penguin, 1987.

Schumacher, Claire. *Nutty's Birthday.* New York: William Morrow, 1986.

Sharmat, Marjorie Weinman. *Attila the Angry.* Illustrated by Lillian Hoban. New York: Holiday House, 1985.

Wildsmith, Brian. *Squirrels.* New York: Franklin Watts, 1974.

TRACY TURTLE'S FAVORITE CHILDREN'S BOOKS ABOUT TURTLES:

Buckley, Richard. *Foolish Tortoise and the Greedy Python.* Natick, MA: Picture Book Studio, 1985.

Kessler, Leonard. *Old Turtle's 90 Knock-Knocks, Jokes, and Riddles.* New York: Greenwillow Books, 1991.

Koch, Michelle. *By the Sea.* New York: Greenwillow Books, 1991.

Plante, Patricia, and David Bergman. *The Turtle and the Two Ducks* (animal fables retold from Jean LaFontaine). Illustrated by Anne Rockwell. New York: Thomas Y. Crowell, 1981.

Taylor, Kim. *Hidden Under Water.* New York: Delacorte Press, 1990.

UNI UNICORN'S FAVORITE CHILDREN'S BOOKS ABOUT UNICORNS:

Birrer, Cynthia and William. *Lady and the Unicorn.* New York: Lothrop, Lee, and Shepard Books, 1987.

Coville, Bruce and Katherine. *Sarah's Unicorn.* New York: Lippincott, 1979.

Luenn, Nancy. *Unicorn Crossing.* Illustrated by Peter E. Hanson. New York: Atheneum, 1987.

Mayer, Mariana. *Unicorn Alphabet.* Illustrated by Michael Hague. New York: Dial Books, 1988.

Preussler, Otfried. *Tale of the Unicorn.* New York: Dial Books, 1989.

VALDAR VULTURE'S FAVORITE CHILDREN'S BOOKS ABOUT BIRDS:

Baker, Keith. *The Dove's Letter.* San Diego: Harcourt Brace Jovanovich, 1988.

Brown, Ken. *Why Can't I Fly?* New York: Doubleday, 1990.

Prescott, Ernest. *What Comes Out of an Egg?* Illustrated by Don Forrest. New York: Franklin Watts, 1976.

Turner, Ana Warren. *Vultures.* Illustrated by Marian Gray Warren. New York: McKay, 1973.

WALDORF WHALE'S FAVORITE CHILDREN'S BOOKS ABOUT WHALES AND FISH:

Ehlert, Lois. *Fish Eyes, A Book You Count On.* San Diego: Harcourt Brace Jovanovich, 1990.

Johnston, Tony. *Whale Song.* Illustrated by Ed Young. New York: Putnam's, 1987.

Lionni, Leo. *Swimmy.* New York: Pantheon, 1963.

Steig, William. *Amos and Boris.* New York: Farrar, Straus and Giroux, 1971.

Ziefert, Harriet. *Henry's Wrong Turn.* Illustrated by Andrea Baruffi. Boston: Little, Brown and Co., 1989.

FOXY FOX'S FAVORITE CHILDREN'S BOOKS ABOUT THE FOX:

Abolafia, Yossi. *Fox Tale.* New York: Greenwillow Books, 1991.

Galdone, Paul. *What's in Fox's Sack?* New York: Clarion Books, 1982.

McKissack, Patricia C. *Flossie and the Fox.* Pictures by Rachel Isadora. New York: Dial Books, 1986.

Spier, Peter. *The Fox Went Out on a Chilly Night, An Old Song.* Garden City, NY: Doubleday, 1961.

Wildsmith, Brian. *Animal Tricks.* New York: Oxford University Press, 1980.

YANCY YAK'S FAVORITE CHILDREN'S BOOKS ABOUT ANIMALS:

Jonas, Ann. *Aardvarks, Disembark!* New York: Greenwillow, 1990.

Lewis, J. Patrick. *The Czar and the Amazing Cow.* New York: Dial books, 1987.

Marshall, Janet Perry. *My Camera at the Zoo.* Boston: Little, Brown and Co., 1989.

Mason, Margo. *Winter Coats.* Illustrated by Laura Rader. New York: Bantam Books, 1989.

McPhail, David. *Animals A to Z.* New York: Scholastic, 1990.

ZELDA ZEBRA'S FAVORITE CHILDREN'S BOOKS ABOUT ZOOS AND ANIMALS:

Bottner, Barbara. *Zoo Song.* Illustrated by Lynn Munsinger. New York: Scholastic Books, 1987.

Campbell, Rod. *Dear Zoo.* New York: Four Winds Press, 1982.

Carle, Eric. *1, 2, 3 to the Zoo.* New York: Philomel, 1968.

Hoffman, Mary. *Animal Hide and Seek.* Illustrated by Leon Baxter. Morristown, NJ: Silver Burdett, 1986.

Prelutsky, Jack. *Zoo Doings.* Pictures by Paul O. Zelinsky. New York: The Trumpet Club, 1990.

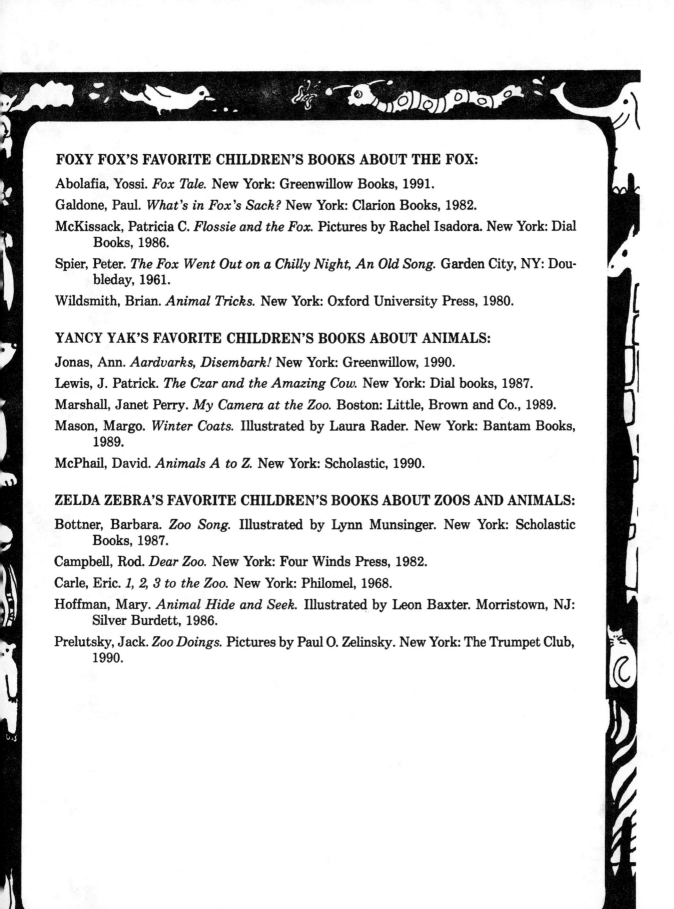